Lecture Notes in Computer Science 12970

More information about this subseries at http://www.springer.com/series/7412

Huazhu Fu · Mona K. Garvin ·
Tom MacGillivray · Yanwu Xu ·
Yalin Zheng (Eds.)

Ophthalmic Medical Image Analysis

8th International Workshop, OMIA 2021
Held in Conjunction with MICCAI 2021
Strasbourg, France, September 27, 2021
Proceedings

Springer

Editors
Huazhu Fu (iD)
Inception Institute of Artificial Intelligence
Abu Dhabi, United Arab Emirates

Mona K. Garvin (iD)
University of Iowa
Iowa City, IA, USA

Tom MacGillivray (iD)
University of Edinburgh
Edinburgh, UK

Yanwu Xu (iD)
Baidu Inc.
Beijing, China

Yalin Zheng (iD)
University of Liverpool
Liverpool, UK

ISSN 0302-9743   ISSN 1611-3349 (electronic)
Lecture Notes in Computer Science
ISBN 978-3-030-86999-1   ISBN 978-3-030-87000-3 (eBook)
https://doi.org/10.1007/978-3-030-87000-3

LNCS Sublibrary: SL6 – Image Processing, Computer Vision, Pattern Recognition, and Graphics

This Springer imprint is published by the registered company Springer Nature Switzerland AG
The registered company address is: Gewerbestrasse 11, 6330 Cham, Switzerland

Preface

The 8th International Workshop on Ophthalmic Medical Image Analysis (OMIA 2021) was held on September 27th, 2021, in conjunction with the 24th International Conference on Medical Image Computing and Computer Assisted Intervention (MICCAI 2021). Due to the breakout of COVID-19, this year was once again a fully virtual conference.

Age-related macular degeneration, diabetic retinopathy, and glaucoma are the main causes of blindness in both developed and developing countries. The cost of blindness to society and individuals is huge, and many cases can be avoided by early intervention. Early and reliable diagnosis strategies and effective treatments are therefore a world priority. At the same time, there is mounting research on the retinal vasculature and neuro-retinal architecture as a source of biomarkers for several high-prevalence conditions like dementia, cardiovascular disease, and of course complications of diabetes. Automatic and semi-automatic software tools for retinal image analysis are being used widely in retinal biomarkers research, and increasingly percolating into clinical practice. Significant challenges remain in terms of reliability and validation, number and type of conditions considered, multi-modal analysis (e.g., fundus, optical coherence tomography, scanning laser ophthalmoscopy), novel imaging technologies, and the effective transfer of advanced computer vision and machine learning technologies, to mention a few. The workshop addressed all these aspects and more, in the ideal interdisciplinary context of MICCAI.

This workshop aimed to bring together scientists, clinicians, and students from multiple disciplines in the growing ophthalmic image analysis community, such as electronic engineering, computer science, mathematics, and medicine, to discuss the latest advancements in the field. A total of 31 full-length papers were submitted to the workshop in response to the call for papers. All submissions were double-blind peer-reviewed by at least three members of the Program Committee. Paper selection was based on methodological innovation, technical merit, results, validation, and application potential. Finally, 20 papers were accepted to the workshop and chosen to be included in this Springer LNCS volume.

We are grateful to the Program Committee for reviewing the submitted papers and giving constructive comments and critiques, to the authors for submitting high-quality papers, to the presenters for excellent presentations, and to all the OMIA 2021 attendees from all around the world.

August 2021

Huazhu Fu
Mona K. Garvin
Tom MacGillivray
Yanwu Xu
Yalin Zheng

Organization

Workshop Organizers

Huazhu Fu	Inception Institute of Artificial Intelligence, UAE
Mona K. Garvin	University of Iowa, USA
Tom MacGillivray	University of Edinburgh, UK
Yanwu Xu	Baidu Inc., China
Yalin Zheng	University of Liverpool, UK

Program Committee

Min Chen	University of Pennsylvania, USA
Geng Chen	Inception Institute of Artificial Intelligence, UAE
Deng-Ping Fan	Inception Institute of Artificial Intelligence, UAE
Dongxu Gao	University of Liverpool, UK
Zaiwang Gu	Southern University of Science and Technology, China
Meijing Guo	ShanghaiTech University, China
Stephen Hogg	University of Dundee, UK
Yan Hu	Southern University of Science and Technology, China
Baiying Lei	Shenzhen University, China
Xiaomeng Li	The Chinese University of Hong Kong, Hong Kong
Huiying Liu	Institute for Infocomm Research, Singapore
Dwarikanath Mahapatra	Inception Institute of Artificial Intelligence, UAE
Muthu Rama Krishnan Mookiah	University of Dundee, UK
Emma Pead	University of Edinburgh, UK
Mingkui Tan	South China University of Technology, China
Jui-Kai Wang	University of Iowa, USA
Jiong Zhang	University of Southern California, USA
Shihao Zhang	South China University of Technology, China
Tianyang Zhang	University of Birmingham, UK
Yitian Zhao	Cixi Institute of Biomedical Engineering, Chinese Academy of Sciences, China
Tao Zhou	Inception Institute of Artificial Intelligence, UAE
Yi Zhou	Inception Institute of Artificial Intelligence, UAE

Contents

Adjacent Scale Fusion and Corneal Position Embedding for Corneal Ulcer Segmentation

Zhonghua Wang, Junyan Lyu, Wenhao Luo, and Xiaoying Tang[✉]

Southern University of Science and Technology, Shenzhen, China
tangxy@sustech.edu.cn

Abstract. Corneal ulcer segmentation from fluorescein staining images is vital for objective and quantitative assessments of ocular surface damages. How to utilize prior information from the fluorescein staining images is a challenge. In this work, we propose and validate a novel method for corneal ulcer segmentation. Leveraging Adjacent Scale Fusion and Corneal Position Embedding, our method can effectively capture fine patterns of the corneal ulcer as well as explicitly characterize the discriminating relative position information within the cornea. We evaluate the corneal ulcer segmentation performance of our method on a publicly-accessible SUSTech-SYSU dataset for automatically segmenting and classifying corneal ulcers, with a mean Dice similarity coefficient of 80.73% and a mean Jaccard Index of 71.63% having been obtained. Quantitative results identify the superiority of the proposed method over representative state-of-the-art deep learning frameworks. In addition, the importance of each key component in the proposed method is analyzed both quantitatively and qualitatively.

Keywords: Corneal ulcer segmentation · Adjacent Scale Fusion · Corneal Position Embedding · Fluorescein staining image

1 Introduction

Cornea functions to focus light in the human visual system. Damages and infections of the cornea may result in loss of vision and blindness [1,2]. One of the most common corneal manifestations is corneal ulcer. It can occur as consequences of various types of keratitis, disorders of the ocular surface, excessive contact lens wear, or topical steroid use [3]. Corneal fluorescein staining is an important tool that can be used for characterizing the pattern of a corneal ulcer which typically stains green because of the necrosis of epithelium cells [4]. It has become a common clinical practice to utilize fluorescein staining for assessing ulcer-related ocular surface damages and monitoring clinical responses to various therapies [5].

Precisely and accurately evaluating the severity of a corneal ulcer is the premise and basis for personalized medical and surgical intervention.

Z. Wang and J. Lyu contributed equally to this work.

© Springer Nature Switzerland AG 2021
H. Fu et al. (Eds.): OMIA 2021, LNCS 12970, pp. 1–10, 2021.
https://doi.org/10.1007/978-3-030-87000-3_1

Researchers have been working on establishing objective criteria for diagnosing corneal ulcers. Currently, the severity of a corneal ulcer is graded mainly utilizing semi-quantitative systems such as the van Bijsterveld, Oxford and National Eye Institute (NEI) scales [6–8]. These grading systems nevertheless largely rely on ophthalmologists' visual examinations, which may lead to inefficiency and subjectivity. A few computer-aided methods have been attempted to provide objective and quantitative evaluations. For example, Peterson et al. employed a digital image processing technique by applying edge-detection and relative-coloration to predict an objective grade, which has been reported to be more sensitive and reliable than subjective grading [9]. Chun et al. developed an automated algorithm by jointly utilizing the difference of Gaussians (DoG) edge detection for morphometry characterization and RGB/HSV color models for color discrimination based on enhanced fluorescein staining images, the results of which showed strong correlations with clinical grading in terms of both Oxford and NEI scales [10]. Deng et al. achieved an accuracy of 98.4% and a Pearson correlation coefficient of 92.1% in automatically segmenting flaky corneal ulcers utilizing a superpixel method [11].

For corneal ulcer segmentation, preocular tear film, reflective areas, as well as fluorescein pooling are difficult to be differentiated from true ulcers since they have very similar pixel intensities and relative locations within the cornea (Fig. 1). Existing corneal ulcer segmentation methods mainly relied on thresholding and traditional machine learning techniques. They generally cannot differentiate the aforementioned ambiguities, especially for low-quality images. In addition, those thresholding and traditional machine learning methodologies relied on pre-selected and typically fixed thresholds and hyperparameters, which had limited performance on images with large individual variability. Deep learning (DL) has seen an impressive number of medical applications in the last few years. Compared to feature-based machine learning, DL has the advantages of end-to-end predictions and better feature distinction abilities, exhibiting state-of-the-art (SOTA) performance in many realms. Recent DL studies on ophthalmologic diseases include diabetic retinopathy, glaucoma and age-related macular degeneration, making use of fundus images and optical coherence tomography images [12–14]. However, studies applying DL to quantitative analyses of corneal ulcers based on fluorescein staining images are relatively rare, because of a lack of large-scale publicly-available datasets which are usually a prerequisite of DL. Recently, a well-constructed and large-scale fluorescein staining image dataset, namely the SUSTech-SYSU dataset, has been released for segmenting and classifying corneal ulcers, which accommodates well the urgent need of developing DL pipelines for corneal ulcer segmentation [15].

In such context, we propose a novel DL pipeline for fluorescein staining image based corneal ulcer segmentation. On the basis of a backbone model for medical image segmentation, U-Net, we introduce Corneal Position Embedding to explicitly characterize the relative position within the cornea of the aforementioned disturbing effects (e.g., fluorescein pooling). Adjacent Scale Fusion is further proposed to capture subtle differences between corneal ulcers and

Occlusion   Fluorescein Pooling   Reflection

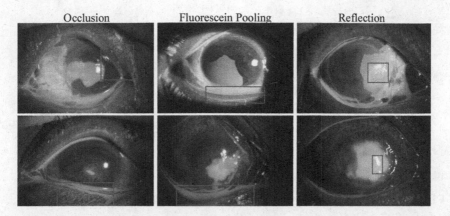

Fig. 1. Several representative factors, including occlusion, fluorescein pooling, and reflection, that make corneal ulcer segmentation challenging.

misleading ambiguities. The proposed method is quantitatively and qualitatively evaluated on 354 samples from the SUSTech-SYSU dataset and compared with several representative SOTA DL frameworks. The source code is available at https://github.com/CRazorback/The-SUSTech-SYSU-dataset-for-automatically-segmenting-and-classifying-corneal-ulcers.

2 Methodology

The proposed method builds upon the classical U-Net and makes use of prior information from the fluorescein staining images to enhance our corneal ulcer segmentation performance. In subsequent subsections, we will describe two novel modules in our pipeline, namely Adjacent Scale Fusion (ASF) and Corneal Position Embedding (CPE). The overall framework is illustrated in Fig. 2.

2.1 Adjacent Scale Fusion

A semantic segmentation result is highly dependent on the input image's scale. Scaled-up images provide more detailed features on edge, texture, color and fine structures, while scaled-down images provide more global context [16]. For corneal ulcer segmentation, we aim at exploiting the texture and color patterns of the ulcer region, which may provide unique and differentiating characteristics. In such context, training a network with high-resolution inputs may greatly benefit our corneal ulcer segmentation. However, it is highly computationally expensive to take the original high-resolution fluorescein staining images as the input, especially at the training stage.

As such, we propose ASF to address the above issue. At the training stage, a given input image is downsampled by factors of 2 and 4 and the downsampled images are then sent into U-Nets with shared weights, producing feature

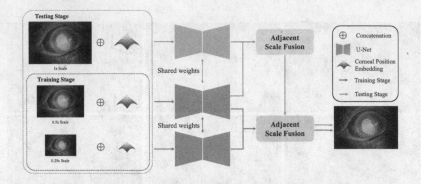

Fig. 2. The overall pipeline of our proposed corneal ulcer segmentation method.

maps $\{\mathbf{M}_{0.25}, \mathbf{M}_{0.5}\}$ and soft segmentation predictions $\{\mathbf{p}_{0.25}, \mathbf{p}_{0.5}\}$. ASF provides spatial attention maps for adjacent-scale predictions $\{\mathbf{p}_{0.25}, \mathbf{p}_{0.5}\}$ via a relation function, which can be formulated as

$$w_{0.25} = f([g(\mathbf{M}_{0.25}), \mathbf{M}_{0.5}]). \tag{1}$$

In this equation, $f(\cdot)$ represents the normalized relation function, implemented as 3×3 Convolution $\rightarrow$ Batch Normalization $\rightarrow$ Rectified Linear Unit (ReLU) $\rightarrow$ 1×1 Convolution $\rightarrow$ Sigmoid, and $g(\cdot)$ denotes a bilinear upsampling operation. Details of ASF are illustrated in Fig. 3.

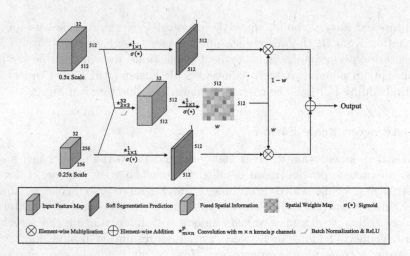

Fig. 3. Details of our Adjacent Scale Fusion module.

Once we obtain pixel-wisely varying weights from ASF, we can fuse the soft segmentation predictions from adjacent scales as below

$$\bar{p}_{0.5} = w_{0.25} * g(p_{0.25}) + (1 - w_{0.25}) * p_{0.5}, \tag{2}$$

where $+$ and $*$ respectively refer to pixel-wise addition and multiplication.

By learning how to compute relative attention maps from adjacent-scale feature maps, ASF can be easily extended to multi-scale scenarios and fuse predictions hierarchically. This can effectively reduce the computation overhead during training but still make use of high-resolution images as the testing input.

2.2 Corneal Position Embedding

Explicit position embedding offers strong spatial inductive bias when training a network. There are several explicit position embedding strategies that have been widely adopted in computer vision and natural language processing, such as Cartesian Spatial Grid (CSG) and Sinusodial Positional Encoding (SPE). These embedding strategies typically consider explicit priors on the image space. CSG normalizes image coordinates by height and width, bringing absolute position information into a network. SPE employs the sinusoidal function, maintaining consistent transformation between neighboring positions and providing relative position information [17].

In a fluorescein staining image, the absolute position information within the cornea is very important; the presence of reflective areas, fluorescein pooling and occlusion which are hard to be differentiated from the true ulcer region is tightly relevant to their distances to the cornea center. The relative position information is also essential; regions outside the cornea may confuse the network, but they still provide more complementary information than zero or reflection padding. Therefore, we propose a novel explicit position embedding function for corneal ulcer segmentation, namely CPE. CPE measures the shortest distance from each pixel of interest to the cornea edge and stays zero outside the cornea. We use $I \to \{0, 1\}$ to represent a binary cornea mask, wherein a pixel value of 0 indicates background and a pixel value of 1 indicates foreground. CPE is defined as

$$P_{CPE}(\mathbf{p}) = \begin{cases} \min\{d(I(\mathbf{p}), I(\mathbf{q})) \mid I(\mathbf{q}) = 0, \mathbf{q} \in O\}, & I(\mathbf{p}) = 1 \\ 0, & I(\mathbf{p}) = 0, \end{cases} \tag{3}$$

where $\mathbf{p}$ represents a spatial location (namely pixel) in the input image space and $\mathbf{q}$ can be any spatial location in the corresponding cornea mask O. $d(\cdot)$ is a normalized distance function, which is implemented as the Euclidean distance normalized by the semi-major axis length of the cornea.

3 Experiment

3.1 Dataset

We evaluate our method on the SUSTech-SYSU dataset for segmenting and classifying corneal ulcers (SUSTech-SYSU). SUSTech-SYSU contains 354 ocular staining images with corneal and corneal ulcer labels, collected at the Zhong-shan Ophthalmic Centre, Sun Yat-sen University. The patients went through fluorescein instillation and got imaged using a Haag-Streit BM 900 slit-lamp microscope (Haag Streit AG, Bern, Switzerland) in combination with a Canon EOS 20D digital camera (Canon, Tokyo, Japan), with the cornea centered in the field of view. All images have resolutions of 2592 × 1728. We perform 5-fold cross-validation on this dataset, with 60% for training, 20% for validation and 20% for testing. Specifically, we split the dataset into 213, 70 and 71 for training, validation and testing in each fold.

3.2   Implementation

Network Parameters. We adopt a modified U-Net as our baseline network. Each of the five resolution levels consists of two 3 × 3 convolutions with batch normalization and ReLU activation and a bilinear resampling module. The feature depths are respective 32, 64, 128, 256 and 512 at the corresponding five levels. The input scales for ASF at the training stage are 0.25 and 0.5, and the input scales at the testing stage are 0.25, 0.5 and 1.0.

Data Augmentation and Preprocessing. To enlarge the training set, randomly resized cropping, horizontal flipping and color distortion including brightness and contrast are applied during training. We first crop the images with respect to the corresponding cornea masks. Images are then bicubicly interpolated to 1024 × 1024 and normalized to have an intensity range of −1 to 1.

Optimization Parameters. Adam optimizer is used to optimize the generalized Dice loss, which performs better on predicting small objects. The initial learning rate is 3×10^{-4} and cosine decayed to be 1.5×10^{-4} within 100 epochs. The network is trained for 100 epochs, with the best model saved based on the validation loss.

3.3   Quantitative Results

In this section, we report quantitative evaluation results using two metrics, namely Dice similarity coefficient (DSC) and Jaccard Index (JI). We analyze the impact of ASF and CPE on the segmentation performance. We also compare our proposed method with representative SOTA DL frameworks.

Ablation Studies: Position Embedding. As shown in Table 1, CPE outperforms the baseline by 1.12% on DSC and 1.84% on JI. This indicates that CPE provides appropriate inductive bias for U-Net and exploits discriminating information from the relative position within the cornea. CPE is observed to significantly outperform another popular position embedding strategy SPE by a large margin. SPE decouples locations and scales, thus being unaware of variations in the cornea size.

Ablation Studies: Multi-scale Fusion. To show the superiority of our proposed ASF, we compare ASF with Explicit Multi-scale Fusion (EMF) in terms of segmentation performance and computation time. EMF averages predictions from multiple inputs of different scales only at the testing stage, and thus does not induce any computation cost during training. Theoretically, the training cost of ASF is 25% higher than EMF but the testing costs are the same. The results shown in Table 1 clearly verify our conjecture; ASF boosts the segmentation performance of U-Net at the cost of a slight increase in the computation during training.

Comparison with SOTA. We compare the proposed method with representative SOTA approaches in Table 2. Experimental results identify the effectiveness of jointly utilizing ASF and CPE, the performance gains obtained from which are huge. The proposed method exhibits superior performance with the highest mean and lowest standard deviation in terms of both DSC and JI. It is also worth mentioning that our proposed modules can be easily extended to stronger baselines since ASF and CPE are decoupled from network structures.

Table 1. Ablation studies on position embedding and multi-scale fusion, wherein T_{train} indicates consumption of the training time (hours). The best results are highlighted in **bold**. '−' means T_{train} is not considered in the corresponding ablation study.

Method	Metrics		
	DSC	JI	T_{train}
U-Net (baseline)	77.31 ± 21.39	67.19 ± 24.30	−
Ablation studies: multi-scale fusion			
U-Net+ASF	78.47 ± 22.14	68.94 ± 24.68	4.05
U-Net+EMF [16]	77.61 ± 21.47	67.61 ± 24.33	**3.31**
Ablation studies: position embedding			
U-Net+CPE	78.43 ± 22.17	69.03 ± 24.21	−
U-Net+SPE [17]	77.18 ± 21.58	67.03 ± 24.17	−
Ablation studies: joint utilization			
U-Net+ASF+CPE	**80.73 ± 20.60**	**71.63 ± 23.31**	−

3.4 Qualitative Results

As demonstrated in Fig. 4, jointly utilizing CPE and ASF can detect and differentiate the true ulcer region from ambiguities such as fluorescein staining pooling and reflective areas. Generally, corneal ulcer with different patterns and sizes can be well-segmented by our proposed method.

Table 2. Performance comparisons with SOTA approaches. The best results in terms of each metric are highlighted in **bold**.

Method	DSC	JI
U-Net [18]	77.31 ± 21.39	67.19 ± 24.30
U-Net++ [19]	78.15 ± 24.96	69.39 ± 26.16
FPN [20]	75.77 ± 24.25	67.32 ± 25.97
PSPNet [21]	74.45 ± 24.60	64.36 ± 26.30
Deeplab-v3 [22]	78.03 ± 22.85	68.59 ± 25.11
Proposed	**80.73 ± 20.60**	**71.63 ± 23.31**

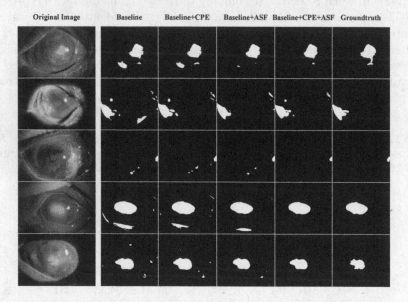

Fig. 4. Randomly selected examples from SUSTech-SYSU. The corneal ulcer regions have been zoomed in for a better visualization purpose.

4   Conclusion

In this paper, we proposed an automated pipeline for corneal ulcer segmentation. Two novel modules, ASF and CPE, have been proposed to utilize prior information. ASF can effectively exploit fine patterns of the corneal ulcer from high-resolution fluorescein staining images with little computation overhead during training. CPE explicitly encodes relative positions within the cornea and makes use of the discriminating power from such position information. We successfully demonstrated that with the two proposed modules, our pipeline outperformed SOTA both quantitatively and qualitatively. Future work involves applying the proposed pipeline to subsequent severity grading and large-scale clinical trials on corneal diseases.

References

1. Whitcher, J.P., Srinivasan, M., Upadhyay, M.P.: Corneal blindness: a global perspective. Bull. World Health Organ. **79**, 214–221 (2001)
2. Bron, A.J., et al.: Methodologies to diagnose and monitor dry eye disease: report of the Diagnostic Methodology Subcommittee of the International Dry Eye Work-Shop. Ocular Surface **5**(2), 108–152 (2007)
3. Diamond, J., et al.: Corneal biopsy with tissue micro homogenisation for isolation of organisms in bacterial keratitis. Eye **13**(4), 545 (1999)
4. Joyce, P.D.: Corneal vital staining. Ir. J. Med. Sci. (1926-1967) **42**(8), 359–367 (1967). https://doi.org/10.1007/BF02954080
5. Passmore, J.W., King, J.H.: Vital staining of conjunctiva and cornea: review of literature and critical study of certain dyes. A.M.A. Arch. Ophthalmol. **53**(4), 568–574 (1955)
6. Van Bijsterveld, O.P.: Diagnostic tests in the sicca syndrome. Arch. Ophthalmol. **82**(1), 10–14 (1969)
7. Olsson, C., Thelin, S., Stahle, E.: Thoracic aortic aneurysm and dissection: increasing prevalence and improved outcomes reported in a nationwide population-based study of more than 14,000 cases from 1987 to 2002. J. Vasc. Surg. **46**(3), 609 (2007)
8. Bron, A.J., Evans, V.E., Smith, J.A.: Grading of corneal and conjunctival staining in the context of other dry eye tests. Cornea **22**(7), 640–650 (2003)
9. Peterson, R.C., Wolffsohn, J.S.: Objective grading of the anterior eye. Optom. Vis. Sci. **86**(3), 273–278 (2009)
10. Chun, Y.S., Yoon, W.B., Kim, K.G., Park, I.K.: Objective assessment of corneal staining using digital image analysis. Investig. Ophthalmol. Vis. Sci. **55**(12), 7896–7903 (2014)
11. Deng, L., Huang, H., Yuan, J., Tang, X.: Superpixel based automatic segmentation of corneal ulcers from ocular staining images. In: IEEE 23rd International Conference on Digital Signal Processing, pp. 1–5 (2018)
12. Fu, H., et al.: Joint optic disc and cup segmentation based on multi-label deep network and polar transformation. IEEE Trans. Med. Imaging **37**(7), 1597–1605 (2018)
13. Gu, Z., et al.: CE-Net: context encoder network for 2d medical image segmentation. IEEE Trans. Med. Imaging **38**(10), 2281–2292 (2019)
14. Huang, Y., et al.: Automated hemorrhage detection from coarsely annotated fundus images in diabetic retinopathy. In: IEEE 17th International Symposium on Biomedical Imaging, pp. 1369–1372 (2020)
15. Deng, L., et al.: The SUSTech-SYSU dataset for automatically segmenting and classifying corneal ulcers. Sci. Data **7**(1), 1–7 (2020)
16. Tao, A., Sapra, K., Catanzaro, B.: Hierarchical multi-scale attention for semantic segmentation. arXiv preprint arXiv:2005.10821 (2020)
17. Xu, R., Wang, X., Chen, K., Zhou, B., Loy, CC.: Positional encoding as spatial inductive bias in GANs. arXiv preprint arXiv:2012.05217 (2020)
18. Ronneberger, O., Fischer, P., Brox, T.: U-Net: convolutional networks for biomedical image segmentation. In: Navab, N., Hornegger, J., Wells, W.M., Frangi, A.F. (eds.) MICCAI 2015. LNCS, vol. 9351, pp. 234–241. Springer, Cham (2015). https://doi.org/10.1007/978-3-319-24574-4_28
19. Zhou, Z., Rahman Siddiquee, M.M., Tajbakhsh, N., Liang, J.: UNet++: a nested U-Net architecture for medical image segmentation. In: Stoyanov, D., et al. (eds.) DLMIA/ML-CDS 2018. LNCS, vol. 11045, pp. 3–11. Springer, Cham (2018). https://doi.org/10.1007/978-3-030-00889-5_1

20. Lin, T.Y., et al.: Feature pyramid networks for object detection. In: Proceedings of the IEEE Conference on Computer Vision and Pattern Recognition, pp. 2117–2125 (2017)
21. Zhao, H., Shi, J., Qi, X., Wang, X., Jia, J.: Pyramid scene parsing network. In: Proceedings of the IEEE Conference on Computer Vision and Pattern Recognition, pp. 2881–2890 (2017)
22. Chen, LC., Papandreou, G., Schroff, F., Adam, H.: Rethinking atrous convolution for semantic image segmentation. arXiv preprint arXiv:1706.05587 (2017)

Longitudinal Detection of Diabetic Retinopathy Early Severity Grade Changes Using Deep Learning

Yutong Yan[1,2,3], Pierre-Henri Conze[2,3(✉)], Gwenolé Quellec[2], Pascale Massin[4], Mathieu Lamard[1,2], Gouenou Coatrieux[2,3], and Béatrice Cochener[1,2,5]

[1] University of Western Brittany, Brest, France
[2] Inserm, LaTIM UMR 1101, Brest, France
[3] IMT Atlantique, Brest, France
pierre-henri.conze@imt-atlantique.fr
[4] Lariboisière Hospital, AP-HP, Paris, France
[5] University Hospital of Brest, Brest, France

Abstract. Longitudinal medical image analysis is crucial for identifying the unobvious emergence and evolution of early lesions, towards earlier and better patient-specific pathology management. However, traditional computer-aided diagnosis (CAD) systems for diabetic retinopathy (DR) rarely make use of longitudinal information to improve DR analysis. In this work, we present a deep information fusion framework that exploits two consecutive longitudinal studies for the assessment of early DR severity changes. In particular, three fusion schemes are investigated: (1) early fusion of inputs, (2) intermediate fusion of feature vectors incorporating Spatial Transformer Networks (STN) and (3) late fusion of feature vectors. Exhaustive experiments compared with respect to no-fusion baselines validate that incorporating prior DR studies can improve the referable DR severity classification performance through the late fusion scheme whose AUC reaches 0.9296. Advantages and limitations of the different fusion methods are discussed in depth. We also propose different pre-training strategies which are employed to bring considerable performance gains for DR severity grade change detection purposes.

Keywords: Diabetic retinopathy · Deep learning · Information fusion · Longitudinal analysis · Computer-aided diagnosis

1 Introduction

As a common and high-risk complication of diabetes, diabetic retinopathy (DR) is a leading cause of visual impairment and blindness worldwide [9]. The overall prevalence of DR is up to 27.0%, comprising non-proliferative DR (NPDR) for 25.2% and proliferative DR (PDR) for 1.4% [22]. A regular annual DR screening is recommended to diabetic patients. General retinal screening uses the color

© Springer Nature Switzerland AG 2021
H. Fu et al. (Eds.): OMIA 2021, LNCS 12970, pp. 11–20, 2021.
https://doi.org/10.1007/978-3-030-87000-3_2

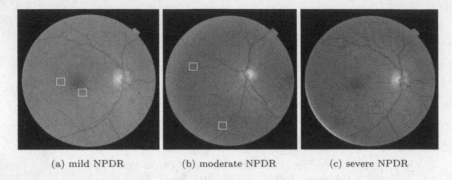

(a) mild NPDR   (b) moderate NPDR   (c) severe NPDR

Fig. 1. Evolution from mild to severe NPDR. Yellow, red and magenta boxes resp. represent microaneurysms, hemorrhages and exudates. Images from OPHDIAT [7] dataset. (Color figure online)

fundus photography (CFP) for DR diagnosis by examining the presence of retinal lesions such as microaneurysms, hemorrhages, soft or hard exudates (Fig. 1). The international clinical DR severity scale includes: no apparent DR, mild NPDR, moderate NPDR, severe NPDR and PDR [23], labeled as grades 0, 1, 2, 3, and 4. NPDR (grades 1, 2, 3) corresponds to the early-to-middle stage of DR and deals with a progressive microvascular disease characterized by small vessel damages and occlusions. PDR (grade = 4) corresponds to the period of potential visual loss due to massive hemorrhage. Early detection and adapted treatment, especially in the mild to moderate stage of NPDR, could help to slow down the DR progression, thereby preventing the occurrence of diabetesrelated visual impairment and blindness.

DR analysis has been an active research area over the last few decades. Recently, deep learning (DL) has been widely adopted in various tasks of retinal image processing. Many studies [4,6,12,13,18,19] have focused on the image-level DR grading classification, as severity labels can be easily extracted from clinical reports. [12] proposed a multiple-instance learning framework which only exploits image-level labels for both automatic DR scale prediction and pixel-wise pathological area detection. They further developed an instant automatic DR diagnosis system [13] which incorporates multiple convolutional neural networks (CNN) and targets three classification tasks: laterality identification, referable DR detection and severity assessment. More recently, [18] applied a synergic DL model incorporating histogram-based region-of-interest segmentation for DR classification. [19] dealt with DR classification from retinal images using extreme gradient boosting (XGBoost) based on intensity and texture features extracted from CFP.

Previous studies have demonstrated the potential of fusion methods in medical imaging, such as multi-view [3,10,24,25] or bilateral [3] fusion. Several studies attempted the automatic analysis of longitudinal medical images. [17] analyzed the evolution of longitudinal chest X-rays using long short-term memory (LSTM) networks. [11] compared four DL longitudinal fusion methods of mammogram series: early fusion, feature fusion based on gradient boosting or LSTM, late fusion. [8] targeted a unified analysis of both vascular and non-vascular changes that are observed in longitudinal CFP time-series. [2] used a microaneurysm-tracker to evaluate DR progression in a follow-up study whereas [1] presented a flexible multistage approach for tracking retinal changes in longitudinal images. However, the number of existing DL methods that analyze longitudinal screenings to assist in DR classification is still exceedingly limited.

In this regard, we aim to integrate longitudinal information of CFP images to help in predicting referable DR (moderate to severe) severity changes (Fig. 1). Specifically, we target the change detection between no DR/mild NPDR (grade = 0 or 1) and more severe DR (grade $\geq$ 2) through two consecutive follow-ups. To this end, we explore three fusion methods that incorporate current and prior studies: (1) early fusion of input images, (2) intermediate fusion of feature vectors incorporating Spatial Transformer Networks (STN) and (3) late fusion of feature vectors. We conduct a comprehensive evaluation by comparing these pipelines on the OPHDIAT dataset [7]. To our knowledge, this work is the first to automatically assess the early DR severity changes between consecutive images.

2   Methods

In this work, we study the severity grade change from normal/mild NPDR to more severe DR between a pair of follow-up CFP images $\{I_{t-1}, I_t\}$. Two backbone networks are used: VGG16 [20] and InceptionV4 [21], which are proven to be effective in many image recognition tasks. Figure 2 uses a simplified architecture for the sake of clarity. Image pair selection and pre-processing are detailed in Sect. 3.

2.1   Longitudinal Fusion Schemes

Early Fusion. We firstly perform image registration from I_{t-1} to I_t using affine transformation to get I'_{t-1} (Fig. 2(a)). Afterwards, I'_{t-1} and I_t are concatenated as input tensor (6 channels). We then employ a convolutional layer at the beginning of the architecture to adjust the model channels (3) to standard VGG16 or InceptionV4 networks, for the purpose of fine-tuning from pre-trained models. Other layers remain unchanged. The output of such one-stream network is the confidence score of whether there is a grade change between $t - 1$ and t.

Intermediate Fusion. The intermediate fusion implements fusion at the feature-level, i.e. at an intermediate level within the model. As shown in Fig. 2(b), we employ a Siamese network combined with specific fusion modules, Spatial Transformer Networks (STN), that actively transform feature maps without any extra supervision. The STN module was first proposed by [5] to be inserted into existing convolutional architectures, resulting in better model invariance to spatial translation, rotation and scaling. An STN module consists of three steps: (1) a localization network to compute parameters θ of the spatial transformation to be applied to the feature map U, (2) a grid generator to create a parameterized

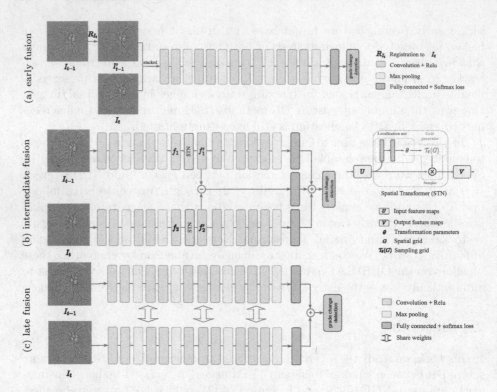

Fig. 2. Early, intermediate and late fusion for DR severity grade change assessment.

sampling grid $\tau_\theta(G)$ and (3) a differentiable image sampler to produce the output feature map V based on the estimated spatial transformation (Fig. 2(b)). Ordinarily, STNs are used to modify the feature volumes of one-stream networks. In our case, we adaptively modified the use of STN in order to adjust the feature maps arising from the two branches of the Siamese network.

A Siamese network normally includes two identical branches with shared weights, such that features from two different input images are jointly extracted and learned. Instead, in the proposed intermediate fusion scheme, both branches are trained without weight sharing because the fusion operation is desired to be performed in the STN modules. The two branches are not supposed to be commutative. As seen in Fig. 2(b), we provide the Siamese network with non-registered image pairs $\{I_{t-1}, I_t\}$. Each image is processed independently up to a given convolutional layer L_{break} (before dense layers), outputting two sets of features f_1 and f_2. Then, we add two independent STN modules after the given convolutional layer L_{break} to obtain two sets of transformed feature volumes f_1' and f_2'. Specifically, the STN modules are inserted before the 8th convolutional layer of VGG16 and before the first Inception-C module of InceptionV4. Thereafter, a fusion operation is applied to the two sets of feature maps, which allows the back-propagation of the loss which minimizes the difference between feature

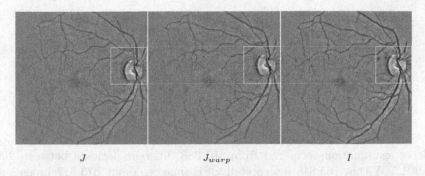

$$J \qquad\qquad J_{warp} \qquad\qquad I$$

Fig. 3. Example of image registration between image at time t−1 (J) and image at time t (I). An affine transformation is applied to align J to I to obtain J_{warp}.

maps. Hence, a mean square error (MSE) loss is employed as fusion operator. Finally, the transformed feature maps f_1' and f_2' are processed with the remaining layers of the network. In practice, we use cross-entropy loss to optimize both branches of the Siamese network. The final loss function is designed as: $L_{interfusion} = L_{bce} + \lambda \cdot L_{MSE}$ where $\lambda = 100$ balances the loss terms.

Late Fusion. Similar to intermediate fusion, the late fusion scheme also incorporates a Siamese network (Fig. 2(c)). Non-registered image pairs $\{I_{t-1}, I_t\}$ are provided as inputs since the fusion operation is performed at the feature vector level and is invariant to spatial transformations of inputs. Two identical branches with shared weights are trained simultaneously, so that the training parameters can be largely reduced. We concatenated the extracted feature vectors of size $1 \times$ dim into a $2 \times$ dim vector (dim = 512 for VGG16, 1536 for InceptionV4), which is used for the final classification of severity grade change between I_{t-1} and I_t.

2.2 Pre-training

Among the 101,383 patients from the OPHDIAT database [7], about 70% have no follow-up and the proportion of normal cases exceeds 79%. This means that most of the data cannot be employed for the longitudinal study. Nevertheless, it can be used for pre-training purposes. In practice, we compare three pre-training strategies: (1) using pre-trained weights from ImageNet [15], (2) based on (1), training a K-label classification model using cross-entropy loss. The output of the softmax layer is K scores with $K = 5$ representing the five following classes: grade = 0, 1, 2, 3 and 4, (3) based on (1), training a K-logistic multi-classifier model with BCEWithLogits loss. In this setting, $K = 4$ represents four binary classifiers: grade ≥ 1, grade ≥ 2, grade ≥ 3 and grade ≥ 4.

3   Dataset

The proposed models are trained and evaluated on OPHDIAT [7], a massive CFP database collected from the Ophthalmology Diabetes Telemedicine network and

Table 1. Distribution of pairs with change/non-change in each subset.

Subset	Change	Non-change	Total pairs
Train (60%)	4839	10666	15505
Validation (20%)	1613	3556	5169
Test (20%)	1626	3543	5169

made of examinations acquired from 101,383 different patients between 2004 and 2017. Within 763,848 interpreted CFP images, about 673,017 images are assigned with a DR severity grade. Image sizes vary from 1440 × 960 to 3504 × 2336 pixels. Each examination contains at least 2 images for each eye.

Image Pair Selection. From the entire OPHDIAT database, we first select patients with up to two-year follow-up screenings and whose severity grade changes from grade $= 0$ or 1 to grade ≥ 2. To train our longitudinal fusion frameworks, the input image pairs $\{I_{t-1}, I_t\}$ should meet the following conditions: (1) arising from the same patient, (2) captured from the same viewpoint of the ipsilateral eye, (3) coming from two different screening times $\{t - 1, t\}$. Image pairing and registration are fundamental pre-processing steps for longitudinal analysis [16]. To avoid the influence of position shifts, scales or other factors related to the heterogeneity of OPHDIAT, we first select image pairs captured from almost the same viewpoint from two consecutive image series $\{E_{t-1}, E_t\}$ according to the following steps. For each image I from E_t and each image J from E_{t-1}, we use an affine transformation to align J to I and obtain J_{warp} (Fig. 3). This transformation could not be done inversely (i.e. from I to J) since lesions may appear between time $t-1$ (image J) and time t (image I). Then, we calculate MSE between $\{I, J_{warp}\}$. The image J that minimizes MSE(I, J_{warp}) is considered as a correspondence of image I. The image pairing is necessary for all proposed fusion schemes, whereas only the pre-fusion scheme requires the registered image J_{warp} as input. Following the above process, we finally obtained 25,843 pairs of images from 2668 patients as data for longitudinal fusion. This dataset is further randomly divided into training (60%), validation (20%) and test (20%) sets. The number of pairs with/without grade change is shown for each subset in Table 1.

Data for Pre-training. By excluding ungradable images based on the attached diagnosis report and the patients used for the longitudinal study, we finally use 649,365 images for pre-training. We randomly choose 80% as the training set and 20% for validation.

Data Pre-processing. Given the diversity of image resolutions, colors, contrast and illuminations in the OPHDIAT database, several preprocessing steps are performed, as specified by [12]. Firstly, images are adaptively cropped to the

Table 2. Hyper-parameters used for each deep network

Network	Imsize	Learning rate	Batch size	Iteration
VGG16	224	0.005	32	20k
InceptionV4	299	0.005	16	20k

Table 3. Quantitative results using VGG16 [20] and InceptionV4 [21] backbones.

Fusion	Pre-training			VGG16		InceptionV4	
	ImageNet	K-label	K-logistic	acc	AUC	acc	AUC
No fusion (only I_t)	✓			0.8594	0.9143	0.8510	0.9087
		✓		0.8603	0.9261	0.8692	0.9206
			✓	0.8555	0.9209	0.8632	0.9148
Early fusion	✓			0.7684	0.8034	0.8187	0.8742
		✓		0.8140	0.8618	0.8392	0.8995
			✓	0.8179	0.8771	0.8383	0.8965
Intermediate fusion	✓			0.7855	0.8513	0.7934	0.8451
		✓		0.8483	0.9032	0.8623	0.9091
			✓	0.8551	0.9151	0.8619	0.9088
Late fusion	✓			0.8580	0.9216	0.8392	0.8993
		✓		**0.8696**	0.9289	**0.8756**	**0.9293**
			✓	0.8684	**0.9296**	0.8696	0.9168

width of the field of view (i.e. the eye area in the CPF image) and are adjusted to various sizes depending on the model used. The InceptionV4 (resp. VGG16) network receives as input images with size $299 \times 299 \times 3$ (resp. $224 \times 224 \times 3$). Secondly, in order to attenuate the strong intensity variations among the dataset, the background is estimated by a Gaussian filter in each color channel then subtracted from the image. Finally, the field of view is eroded by 5% to eliminate illumination artifacts around edges. Random resized crops ([0.96, 1.0] as scale range and [0.95, 1.05] as aspect ratio range) are applied for data augmentation.

4   Experiments and Results

The various proposed longitudinal fusion models are implemented using `pytorch`. Experiments are performed on an Nvidia GeForce GTX 1080Ti and trained using the SGD optimizer. We list in Table 2 the hyper-parameters used for VGG16 and InceptionV4 networks. The performance of each method is measured using the classification accuracy (`acc`) and the area under the receiver operating characteristics curve (AUC). The statistical significance was estimated using DeLong's t-test [14] to analyze and compare ROC curves. We perform comparative experiments between the different fusion schemes on two CNN architectures: VGG16 and InceptionV4. Three pre-training strategies are investigated for each model and each fusion scheme. To fairly compare these methods, we list in Table 3 their classification `acc` and AUC. The baseline of each longitudinal fusion scheme is to train a CNN classifier using a single image I_t, without involving prior images.

Fusion Results Comparison. According to our experimental results (Table 3), the late-fusion achieved the best performance for both models ($acc = 0.8696$, $AUC = 0.9296$, $p = 0.007$ for VGG16, $acc = 0.8756$, $AUC = 0.9293$, $p = 0.006$ for InceptionV4). Surprisingly, for both models, incorporating the fusion of longitudinal studies in prior to the network (early fusion) or in the middle of the network (intermediate fusion) showed a considerable decrease compared to the no-fusion baseline. Nevertheless, it is noteworthy that the late fusion scheme remains a relevant strategy for both models, with better performance than other fusion schemes. In particular, the late fusion brings 0.2%–0.9% AUC improvements to the baseline, with statistical significance ($p < 0.05$).

Pre-train Comparison. Regardless of the fusion scheme, pre-training on OPHDIAT dataset largely boosts the classification performance, from 0.6% AUC (no fusion) to 7.37% (intermediate fusion with VGG16). The K-label pre-training brings average AUC improvements of 2.86% (3.94%) for VGG16 (InceptionV4) while the K-logistic pre-training leads to 3.36% (3.58%) gains. The K-label model is slightly better than the K-logistic one, in most cases.

5   Discussion

In this study, we addressed the early-grade DR severity change detection by analyzing the fusion of two consecutive follow-up images. Deep learning based DR classification that incorporates prior screening has not been exploited in existing studies whereas the comparison with prior screening is an important step for clinicians towards better decision-making. Specifically, we studied the impact of the position of the fusion operations on network performance. Extensive experiments have demonstrated that both early and intermediate fusions can not bring further performance improvement with respect to the no-fusion baseline. Conversely, a simple late fusion has shown stable performance gain (Table 3). Our explanations are as follows. The experimental results of the no-fusion baseline have revealed that the network can classify I_t with fairly good performance ($AUC > 90\%$), indicating that the network has the ability to extract effective features from single-image DR severity classification. However, to make early or intermediate fusions robustly work, the network should be able to focus on the lesion evolution at image or feature-map levels. This requires high-quality registration of consecutive images to make sure that the lesion areas are well aligned. Moreover, due to the diversity of DR lesions and the subtlety of early lesions, it is more difficult for the network to target the lesion evolution. Regarding the late fusion scheme, the network firstly extracts effective features from $I_t - 1$ and I_t, followed by a global average pooling layer. Then, the fusion operation is performed based on the subsequent feature vectors that no longer contain spatial information. Accordingly, the mis-alignment does not affect the fusion results.

The main limitation of this work deals with image registration between longitudinal follow-up images. As a pre-processing step, it requires higher registration quality. As a feature-level step, it is difficult to achieve automatic alignment at an intermediate level of the network. From the current point of view, the late fusion strategy remains the simplest and most efficient method of image fusion. Experimental results validate that incorporating prior DR studies can improve the early-grade DR severity classification performance with respect to single-image scenarios. This conclusion could be extended to other retinal image classification tasks. In the future, our method will be further investigated using multiple previous studies or for other longitudinal pathology analysis, towards more accurate CAD systems. We also claim that more in-depth works are required to explore the interpretability of fusion networks applied to longitudinal image series.

References

1. Adal, K.M., Van Etten, P.G., Martinez, J.P., Rouwen, K.W., Vermeer, K.A., van Vliet, L.J.: An automated system for the detection and classification of retinal changes due to red lesions in longitudinal fundus images. IEEE Trans. Biomed. Eng. **65**(6), 1382–1390 (2017)
2. Bernardes, R., et al.: Computer-assisted microaneurysm turnover in the early stages of diabetic retinopathy. Ophthalmologica **223**(5), 284–291 (2009)
3. Geras, K.J., et al.: High-resolution breast cancer screening with multi-view deep convolutional neural networks. arXiv preprint arXiv:1703.07047 (2017)
4. Gulshan, V., et al.: Development and validation of a deep learning algorithm for detection of diabetic retinopathy in retinal fundus photographs. JAMA **316**(22), 2402–2410 (2016)
5. Jaderberg, M., Simonyan, K., Zisserman, A., Kavukcuoglu, K.: Spatial transformer networks. arXiv preprint arXiv:1506.02025 (2015)
6. Liu, H., Yue, K., Cheng, S., Pan, C., Sun, J., Li, W.: Hybrid model structure for diabetic retinopathy classification. J. Healthcare Eng. **2020**, Article id: 8840174 (2020)
7. Massin, P., et al.: OPHDIAT: a telemedical network screening system for diabetic retinopathy in the île-de-france. Diab. Meta. **34**(3), 227–234 (2008)
8. Narasimha-Iyer, H., Can, A., Roysam, B., Tanenbaum, H.L., Majerovics, A.: Integrated analysis of vascular and nonvascular changes from color retinal fundus image sequences. IEEE Trans. Biomed. Eng. **54**(8), 1436–1445 (2007)
9. Ogurtsova, K., et al.: IDF diabetes atlas: global estimates for the prevalence of diabetes for 2015 and 2040. Diab. Res. Clin. Pract. **128**, 40–50 (2017)
10. Perek, S., Hazan, A., Barkan, E., Akselrod-Ballin, A.: Siamese network for dual-view mammography mass matching. In: Image Analysis for Moving Organ, Breast, and Thoracic Images, pp. 55–63 (2018)
11. Perek, S., Ness, L., Amit, M., Barkan, E., Amit, G.: Learning from longitudinal mammography studies. In: International Conference on Medical Image Computing and Computer-Assisted Intervention, pp. 712–720 (2019)
12. Quellec, G., Charrière, K., Boudi, Y., Cochener, B., Lamard, M.: Deep image mining for diabetic retinopathy screening. Med. Image Anal. **39**, 178–193 (2017)
13. Quellec, G., et al.: Instant automatic diagnosis of diabetic retinopathy. arXiv preprint arXiv:1906.11875 (2019)
14. Robin, X., et al.: pROC: an open-source package for R and S+ to analyze and compare ROC curves. BMC Bioinf. **12**(1), 1–8 (2011)
15. Russakovsky, O., et al.: Imagenet large scale visual recognition challenge. Int. J. Comput. Vis. **115**(3), 211–252 (2015)

16. Saha, S.K., Xiao, D., Bhuiyan, A., Wong, T.Y., Kanagasingam, Y.: Color fundus image registration techniques and applications for automated analysis of diabetic retinopathy progression: a review. Biomed. Signal Process. Control **47**, 288–302 (2019)
17. Santeramo, R., Withey, S., Montana, G.: Longitudinal detection of radiological abnormalities with time-modulated LSTM. In: Deep Learning in Medical Image Analysis and Multimodal Learning for Clinical Decision Support, pp. 326–333 (2018)
18. Shankar, K., Sait, A.R.W., Gupta, D., Lakshmanaprabu, S., Khanna, A., Pandey, H.M.: Automated detection and classification of fundus diabetic retinopathy images using synergic deep learning model. Pattern Recogn. Lett. **133**, 210–216 (2020)
19. Sikder, N., Masud, M., Bairagi, A.K., Arif, A.S.M., Nahid, A.A., Alhumyani, H.A.: Severity classification of diabetic retinopathy using an ensemble learning algorithm through analyzing retinal images. Symmetry **13**(4), 670 (2021)
20. Simonyan, K., Zisserman, A.: Very deep convolutional networks for large-scale image recognition. arXiv preprint arXiv:1409.1556 (2014)
21. Szegedy, C., Ioffe, S., Vanhoucke, V., Alemi, A.: Inception-v4, Inception-ResNet and the impact of residual connections on learning. In: AAAI Conference on Artificial Intelligence, vol. 31 (2017)
22. Thomas, R., Halim, S., Gurudas, S., Sivaprasad, S., Owens, D.: IDF diabetes atlas: a review of studies utilising retinal photography on the global prevalence of diabetes related retinopathy between 2015 and 2018. Diab. Res. Clin. Pract. **157**, 107840 (2019)
23. Wilkinson, C., et al.: Proposed international clinical diabetic retinopathy and diabetic macular edema disease severity scales. Ophthalmology **110**(9), 1677–1682 (2003)
24. Yan, Y., Conze, P.H., Lamard, M., Quellec, G., Cochener, B., Coatrieux, G.: Multitasking siamese networks for breast mass detection using dual-view mammogram matching. In: International Workshop on Machine Learning in Medical Imaging, pp. 312–321 (2020)
25. Yan, Y., Conze, P.H., Lamard, M., Quellec, G., Cochener, B., Coatrieux, G.: Towards improved breast mass detection using dual-view mammogram matching. Med. Image Anal. **71**, 102083 (2021)

Intra-operative OCT (iOCT) Image Quality Enhancement: A Super-Resolution Approach Using High Quality iOCT 3D Scans

Charalampos Komninos[1]([✉])[iD], Theodoros Pissas[1,2][iD], Blanca Flores[3][iD], Edward Bloch[2,3][iD], Tom Vercauteren[1][iD], Sébastien Ourselin[3][iD], Lyndon Da Cruz[3,4][iD], and Christos Bergeles[1][iD]

[1] School of Biomedical Engineering and Imaging Sciences, King's College London, London SE1 7EU, UK
charalampos.komninos@kcl.ac.uk
[2] Wellcome/EPSRC Centre for Interventional and Surgical Sciences, University College London, London W1W 7TS, UK
[3] Moorfields Eye Hospital, London EC1V 2PD, UK
[4] Institute of Ophthalmology, University College London, London EC1V 9EL, UK

Abstract. Effective treatment of degenerative retinal diseases will require robot-assisted intraretinal therapy delivery supported by excellent retinal layer visualisation capabilities. Intra-operative Optical Coherence Tomography (iOCT) is an imaging modality which provides real-time, cross-sectional retinal images partially allowing visualisation of the layers where the sight restoring treatments should be delivered. Unfortunately, iOCT systems sacrifice image quality for high frame rates, making the identification of pertinent layers challenging. This paper proposes a Super-Resolution pipeline to enhance the quality of iOCT images leveraging information from iOCT 3D cube scans. We first explore whether 3D iOCT cube scans can indeed be used as high-resolution images by performing Image Quality Assessment. Then, we apply non-rigid image registration to generate partially aligned pairs, and we carry out data augmentation to increase the available training data. Finally, we use CycleGAN to transfer the quality between low-resolution (LR) and high-resolution (HR) domain. Quantitative analysis demonstrates that iOCT quality increases with statistical significance, but a qualitative study with expert clinicians is inconclusive with regards to their preferences.

Keywords: iOCT · Super-resolution · Image quality assessment

L. Da Cruz and C. Bergeles—Supported by King's Centre for Doctoral Studies - Centre for Doctoral Training in Surgical & Interventional Engineering, and an ERC Starting Grant [714562]. L. Da Cruz and C. Bergeles are equally contributing senior authors.

H. Fu et al. (Eds.): OMIA 2021, LNCS 12970, pp. 21–31, 2021.
https://doi.org/10.1007/978-3-030-87000-3_3

1   Introduction

Regenerative therapies are considered as promising treatments for retinal diseases such as Age-Related Macular Degeneration (AMD) [2] that cause blindness. These novel therapies, however, must be precisely delivered subretinally or intraretinally over prolonged periods of time. Retinal layers cannot be visualised under conventional vitreoretinal surgical protocols, i.e. with en face binocular biomicroscopy, which calls for the use of Intra-operative Optical Coherence Tomography (iOCT) to capture cross-sectional retinal images (Fig. 1a).

OCT is a non-invasive imaging modality, which uses light in the near-infrared spectral range to visualise tissue layer information. Pre-operatively acquired OCT images are of excellent quality taking advantage of spatiotemporal signal averaging albeit requiring a prohibitively long acquisition time for real-time visualisation of interventions. iOCT, on the other hand, allows real-time scanning but at the cost of inferior image quality making iOCT interpretation and layer discrimination challenging. Therefore, the interventional utility of iOCT images generated from current commercial systems is debatable.

In parallel with development of advanced iOCT hardware carried out internationally, we are pursuing computational enhancement of iOCT image quality to support the microprecise delivery of sight-restoring therapies within the retina. Previous studies on iOCT mainly focused on needle localisation [23], tool tracking [16] and anterior segment anatomies detection [17] but the enhancement of posterior eye segment visualisation in iOCT is still unaddressed.

Several classical software-based techniques have been proposed to reduce speckle noise in OCT images [1] and thus improve image quality. Averaging multiple registered B-scans of uncorrelated speckle noise, acquired at the same position on the retina [9,19] and single B-scan filtering [1,14] have positive denoising results. However, the need for prolonged scans and perfect alignment lessen the effectiveness of solutions for intra-operative applications and iOCT.

Deep learning approaches have been developed for image quality enhancement and super-resolution in natural images [7,8,11,24]. In the medical imaging domain [4] proposed autoencoders built using convolutional layers for denoising, while in [22] a generative adversarial network (GAN) accompanied by Wasserstein distance and perceptual similarity was used to successfully denoise CT images. In [15,21], the authors focused on unsupervised Super-Resolution (SR) techniques while several works developed SR models for OCT image denoising [3,10].

This paper reports underpinning work towards real-time iOCT Super Resolution. First, we perform No-Reference Image Quality Assessment (IQA) to investigate whether the available 3D iOCT scans are of better quality than low resolution (LR) 2D iOCT frames and thus if they can be used as high resolution (HR) images. Second, in order to provide weak supervision to the network, we apply non-rigid registration to create partially aligned pairs of LR and HR images. Then, we augment our initial paired dataset by exploiting the temporal continuity in 2D iOCT frames and use CycleGAN for quality transfer between LR and HR domain. We evaluate our pipeline through quantitative analysis

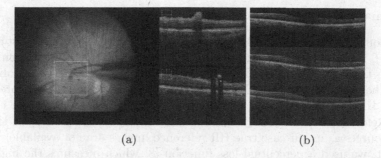

Fig. 1. (a): Left: Surgical microscope view. Right: iOCT B-scans. (b) From top to bottom:**V-iOCT**, **C-iOCT** and **C-pOCT**.

using four different IQA metrics calculated on the super-resolved iOCT image. We also report qualitative data by capturing the individual preferences of 11 vitreoretinal surgeons with regards to original versus SR iOCT images.

2 Methods

In this section we present the Image Quality Assessment between the two iOCT image types, the partial alignment between LR and HR images and the generation of Super-resolved images using adversarial training with cycle consistency.

2.1 Datasets

The data used in this study originate from an internal dataset of intra-operative retinal surgery videos and OCT/iOCT scans from 66 patients acquired at Moorfields Eye Hospital, London, UK. The data was acquired in accordance with the Declaration of Helsinki (1983 Revision) and its ethical principles. To qualify for inclusion in our dataset, a "patient" should have all of the following three types of OCT data acquired by ZEISS devices (Carl Zeiss Meditec Inc., Dublin, CA):

1. Intra-operative OCT video frames (**V-iOCT**), recorded from RESCAN 700 integrated into the OPMI LUMERA 700 acquired during surgery.
2. Intra-operative OCT cube frames (**C-iOCT**), extracted from $512 \times 1024 \times 128$ OCT cubes, acquired at the onset of surgery using RESCAN 700.
3. Preoperative OCT cube frames (**C-pOCT**), extracted from $512 \times 1024 \times 128$ OCT cubes, acquired prior to the intervention using Cirrus 5000.

This led to a subset 18 data tuples/patients to be considered in this paper.

As a preprocessing step, we manually identified the frames of the three OCT sources that contain corresponding underlying anatomy given that the videos and the scans of the same patient visualise alike retinal structures. We ended up having 983 images per type (**V-iOCT**, **C-iOCT**,**C-pOCT**).

2.2   Image Quality Assessment

Even though arguably **C-pOCT** scans are the OCT images with the best quality (Fig. 1b), we investigated whether **C-iOCT** can be used as the HR domain to enhance the **V-iOCT** (LR). As both **C-iOCT** and **V-iOCT** were obtained under the same conditions (device, date, patient position), they represent a smaller HR/LR domain gap. Therefore, we explored methods in the context of No-Reference Image Quality Assessment to compare the quality of the two iOCT sources as in our case true HR reference images are not available.

First, we used a perceptual loss function [8] which measures the high level perceptual difference between input and target images through their distance in the feature space of Imagenet-pretrained Deep Convolutional Network [18]. Specifically, for each patient and for each OCT type, e.g., **V-iOCT**, we extracted the VGG-16 [20] **conv**$_{43}$ feature representations for every input **V-iOCT** image and we averaged them generating one averaged feature map for the **V-iOCT** images. We applied the same process for **C-iOCT** and **C-pOCT** images obtaining two more averaged feature maps per patient. Then, we calculated pairwise Euclidean distances between the averaged feature maps (Φ) of **V-iOCT** and **C-pOCT** as well as between **C-iOCT** and **C-pOCT**:

$$\ell_{feat} = \|\Phi_i - \Phi_p\|_2 \tag{1}$$

The per patient ℓ_{feat} values indicate the perceptual similarity of **V-iOCT** and **C-iOCT** relative to **C-pOCT**.

Furthermore, we used Frechet Inception Distance (FID)[6], a metric used to evaluate the performance of GANs [5]. For image generation tasks using GANs, FID can capture how similar two sets of images are by comparing the statistics of the distributions of feature representations extracted from the ImageNet-pretrained Inception-v3. In this context, we use FID to calculate the similarity of **V-iOCT-C-pOCT** and **C-iOCT-C-pOCT** datasets across the 18 patients:

$$FID = \|\mu_i - \mu_p\|^2 + Tr(\Sigma_i + \Sigma_p - 2(\Sigma_i \Sigma_p)^{1/2}) \tag{2}$$

where $X_i \sim N(\mu_i, \Sigma_i)$ and $X_p \sim N(\mu_p, \Sigma_p)$ are the activations of the first max pooling layer for intra-operative (**V-iOCT**, **C-iOCT**) and preoperative (**C-pOCT**) samples respectively. We chose the first max pooling layer 64-dimensional features of Inception-v3 as every patient contains at least 64 images per OCT type which are sufficient to calculate the statistics.

Finally, we considered Natural Image Quality Evaluator (NIQE) [13], one of the state-of-the-art No-Reference IQA metrics. We trained a custom NIQE model from the database of **C-pOCT** images, and we calculated the NIQE score for each **V-iOCT** and **C-iOCT** image.

Lower NIQE scores indicate better perceptual quality of the examined iOCT image with respect to **C-pOCT**.

The intuition behind the above methods is that if the values of ℓ_{feat}, FID and NIQE for **C-iOCT** images across the 18 patients are lower than the corresponding values of **V-iOCT**, then **C-iOCT** would be perceptually more similar to the

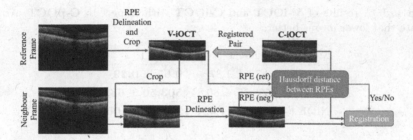

Fig. 2. Overview of the proposed augmentation approach.

C-pOCT which are the highest quality images of our dataset. Therefore, considering **C-iOCT**'s as the HR domain would be meaningful. IQA results, reported in Sect. 3.1, demonstrate that **C-iOCT** are perceptually closer to the **C-pOCT** and thus they will be used as HR domain throughout the next sections.

2.3 Registration

Despite the fact that **V-iOCT** and **C-iOCT** frames were both acquired intra-operatively and under the same conditions, there were misalignments between underlying structures due to patient motion. CycleGAN which is the SR model of our pipeline, has been used mainly for unpaired datasets. However, in our first experiments we noticed that unpaired **V-iOCT** and **C-iOCT** data led to incosistent SR results, so we decided to partially register them aiming to provide weak supervision to the network. In order to create a valid set of paired **V-iOCT-C-iOCT** images, we applied an affine transformation as initialization and performed multi-resolution non-rigid registration using B-splines as parameterisation between the **V-iOCT** (fixed) and **C-iOCT** frames (moving).

Following registration, we applied Retinal Pigment Epithelium (RPE) layer delineation using a heuristic method in the resulting moved image. The method considers the RPE as the most hyper-reflective retinal layer and estimates RPE points by calculating the brightest pixels across the A-scans (columns) of the iOCT image. Then, based on the calculated RPE points, we defined the horizontal and vertical cropping points considering as useful part of the moved image the region between RPE and ILM. The cropping points defined the crop region for both moved (**C-iOCT**) and fixed (**V-iOCT**) frames leading to images of size 380×150.

2.4 Data Augmentation

We exploited the temporal continuity in **V-iOCT** frames to augment the training pairs (so far 537). Knowing the position of one of the already paired **V-iOCT** (reference), we examined which of the ± 5 neighbour frames capture relevant retinal tissue. We delineated the RPE layers in neighbour frames and calculated their Hausdorff Distance with respect to the reference's RPE. Registration with

Table 1. IQA results of **V-iOCT** and **C-iOCT** with respect to **C-pOCT**. Arrows indicate that lower means better.

Metric	V-iOCT	C-iOCT
FID ($\downarrow$)	3.77 ± 1.87	$\mathbf{0.65 \pm 0.22}$
$\ell_{feat}(\downarrow)$	597.57 ± 80.84	$\mathbf{503.50 \pm 66.72}$
NIQE ($\downarrow$)	26.29 ± 1.52	$\mathbf{16.32 \pm 2.06}$

the reference's **C-iOCT** image was performed only for the neighbour frames where Hausdorff Distance was less than 15 (pixels). We then rigidly registered the selected frames to the reference's **C-iOCT**. This data augmentation methodology (Fig. 2) led to a total of 1022 paired images. The source code of our methods will be available online at https://github.com/RViMLab/OMIA2021-iOCT-Super-Resolution.

2.5   Super Resolution with Cycle Consistency

To perform Super Resolution (SR), we adopted CycleGAN's architecture [24], which is widely used in image-to-image translation tasks. Given two datasets of LR (**V-iOCT**) and HR (**C-iOCT**) images, CycleGAN can learn a mapping $G : LR \rightarrow HR$ such that the distribution of the generated images $G(LR)$ is indistinguishable from the distribution of HR images. Unlike to typical GANs, it also learns an inverse mapping from output to input $G : HR \rightarrow LR$ and uses cycle consistency to enforce mappings in both directions.

3   Results

In this section, we present the results obtained from IQA between **C-iOCT** and **V-iOCT** as well as the quantitative and the qualitative analysis that we conducted to validate our Super-Resolution pipeline.

3.1   Image Quality Assessment

Table 1 summarises IQA results. The reported values are the averaged results across 18 patients. The values of the three metrics ($FID, \ell_{feat}, NIQE$) are lower for **C-iOCT** which indicates better perceptual quality with respect to **C-pOCT**. Therefore, **C-iOCT** are closer to the preoperative data (**C-pOCT**), which implies that they contain more information than **V-iOCT** and thus they can be used as HR images. The statistical significances of the pairwise comparisons were assessed using paired t-test and all the p-values were $p < 0.001$.

| V-iOCT | X1.5 | SR-iOCT(CGAN) | X1.5 |

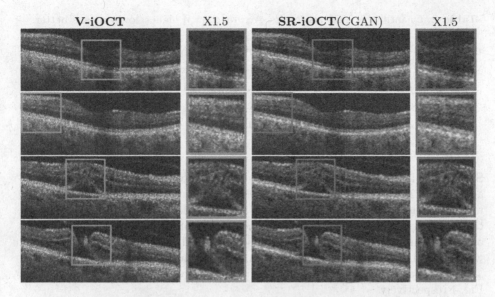

Fig. 3. LR **V-iOCT** images and their Super-resolved **SR-iOCT**.

| V-iOCT | SR-iOCT(CGAN) | SR-iOCT(Pix) | C-iOCT |

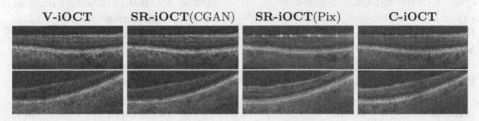

Fig. 4. From left to right: **V-iOCT**(LR), SR by CycleGAN, SR by Pix2Pix, **C-iOCT**(HR).

3.2 Quantitative Analysis

We performed quantitative analysis to validate the quality enhancement of the SR images (Fig. 3) with respect to **C-iOCT**. The analysis was based on the: **V-iOCT** (LR), **SR-iOCT**(CGAN) (SR) and **C-iOCT** (HR) test sets (204 images each). Three already analysed in Sec. 2.2 metrics ($FID, \ell_{feat}, NIQE$) and the no-reference Global Contrast Factor (GCF) [12] metric were used.

First, we divided the test set to 3 subsets of 64 images each and we calculated the FID between **SR-iOCT** and **C-iOCT** as well as the FID between **V-iOCT** and **C-iOCT** and we averaged the results across the 3 subsets. ℓ_{feat} was computed between each **V-iOCT**, **SR-iOCT** and its corresponding **C-iOCT** frame while NIQE score was obtained per **V-iOCT**, **SR-iOCT** image after training a model on **C-iOCT** images. GCF, a reference-free metric which calculates the image contrast, was also computed per **V-iOCT**, **SR-iOCT**. The reported values (Table 2) are the averaged results across the 204 **V-iOCT** and

Table 2. Quantitative analysis results. Arrows show if higher/lower means better.

Metric	V-iOCT	SR-iOCT(CGAN)	SR-iOCT(Pix)
FID ($\downarrow$)	**3.18 $\pm$ 0.93**	3.22 $\pm$ 0.39	3.26 $\pm$ 0.64
$\ell_{feat}(\downarrow)$	632.31 $\pm$ 74.29	**602.55 $\pm$ 77.24**	621.94 $\pm$ 72.99
NIQE ($\downarrow$)	32.01 $\pm$ 5.81	**28.22 $\pm$ 4.74**	39.07 $\pm$ 3.60
GCF ($\uparrow$)	7.85 $\pm$ 0.60	**8.21 $\pm$ 0.58**	6.49 $\pm$ 0.46

SR-iOCT images. To further validate our work, we compared our approach against Pix2Pix, **SR-iOCT**(Pix), which which is one of the state-of-the-art methodologies for image-to-image translation tasks. Pix2Pix is an implementation of the Conditional GAN where the generation of an image is conditional on a given image. It needs aligned pairs of LR and HR images, a requirement which is fulfilled to a great extent in our case because of the registration step. The quantitative and visual results of the method are presented in Table 2 and Fig. 4 respectively.

Our analysis aimed at investigating whether our pipeline can improve the quality of the LR OCT frames. From these results, **SR-iOCT**(CGAN) images, super-resolved images using CycleGAN, are perceptually more similar to the HR than the corresponding LR according to ℓ_{feat}. Furthermore, lower NIQE score and higher GCF values show that **SR-iOCT**(CGAN) has better perceptual quality and higher contrast respectively compared to **V-iOCT**. However, FID demonstrates that **V-iOCT** statistics are more similar to **C-iOCT**, which is probably because the metric uses lower layer features trying to address the problem of having limited samples for statistics calculation. On the other hand, **SR-iOCT**(Pix) images are worse than the LR images according to three out of four metrics (Table 2). Pix2Pix's architecture does not include a Cycle Consistency Loss term and as a result structures from original sample may not appear in the reconstructed sample. We assessed the statistical significance of the results using paired t-test and the p-values for all the metrics except FID were $p < 0.001$. It is also worth mentioning that CycleGAN needs 0.029 (s) time to generate one super-resolved image of size 350×350 which is acceptable for the real-time requirement of our application.

3.3   Qualitative Analysis

Our survey included 30 pairs of **V-iOCT** and **SR-iOCT**(CGAN) frames (Fig. 3), randomly arranged to avoid order bias during the evaluation. We asked 11 retinal doctors/surgeons to select the image that they would prefer to observe in a clinical setting. The results indicate that clinicians marginally prefer the Super-resolved OCT obtained by our methodology, as 51% of the total experts' answers are in favour of **SR-iOCT** instead of **V-iOCT**. Furthermore, it is worth noting that 2 out of the 11 clinicians strongly preferred the **SR-iOCT** (in 83.33% and 73.33% of the occasions), 3 were against **SR-iOCT** (less than 35%

cases) and the rest fluctuated between 46% and 63%. In addition, in 5 out of 30 pairs, more than 73% of the experts tend to prefer **SR-iOCT** than the original **V-iOCT**.

Therefore, despite the fact that our quantitative metrics demonstrate that our pipeline can produce images of higher quality than the original **V-iOCT** frames, the qualitative analysis shows that most participants, in the majority of the cases were unable to choose between **V-iOCT** and **SR-iOCT**, showcasing the need for further work to deliver qualitatively superior iOCT images.

4   Discussion and Conclusions

This paper presents initial work on the Super-resolution of intra-operative Optical Coherence Tomography images obtained in real-time during various vitreo-retinal surgical procedures.

First, we assessed the quality of **C-iOCT** and **V-iOCT** using three different No Reference Image Quality Assessment methods demonstrating that **C-iOCT** can be used as HR domain. Furthermore, we performed Non-rigid Registration between LR and HR images and we deployed an automatic way to augment the available training dataset. Finally, we used CycleGAN to apply Super-Resolution by quality transfer between LR and HR domains.

We evaluated our pipeline by performing both quantitative and qualitative analysis. In the former case, the obtained results showed that the proposed method can generate enhanced iOCT images, while the later analysis demonstrated that there is not a clear preference between original and Super-resolved images in the majority of the occasions.

To the best of our knowledge, this paper is the first which addresses the problem of Super-Resolution in intra-operative OCT images leveraging the available HR iOCT 3D scans. Further research into temporal alignment of iOCT frames must be carried out to maximise the potential of creating iOCT frames of truly superior image quality than what currently available.

References

1. Adler, D.C., Ko, T.H., Fujimoto, J.G.: Speckle reduction in optical coherence tomography images by use of a spatially adaptive wavelet filter. Opt. Lett. **29**(24), 2878–2880 (2004)
2. da Cruz, L., et al.: Phase 1 clinical study of an embryonic stem cell-derived retinal pigment epithelium patch in age-related macular degeneration. Nat. Biotechnol. **36**(4), 328 (2018)
3. Devalla, S.K., et al.: A deep learning approach to denoise optical coherence tomography images of the optic nerve head. Sci. Rep. **9**(1), 1–13 (2019)
4. Gondara, L.: Medical image denoising using convolutional denoising autoencoders. In: 2016 IEEE 16th International Conference on Data Mining Workshops (ICDMW), pp. 241–246. IEEE (2016)
5. Goodfellow, I., et al.: Generative adversarial nets. In: Advances in Neural Information Processing Systems, p. 27 (2014)

6. Heusel, M., Ramsauer, H., Unterthiner, T., Nessler, B., Hochreiter, S.: GANs trained by a two time-scale update rule converge to a local nash equilibrium. arXiv preprint arXiv:1706.08500 (2017)
7. Isola, P., Zhu, J.Y., Zhou, T., Efros, A.A.: Image-to-image translation with conditional adversarial networks. In: Proceedings of the IEEE Conference on Computer Vision and Pattern Recognition, pp. 1125–1134 (2017)
8. Johnson, J., Alahi, A., Fei-Fei, L.: Perceptual losses for real-time style transfer and super-resolution. In: Leibe, B., Matas, J., Sebe, N., Welling, M. (eds.) ECCV 2016. LNCS, vol. 9906, pp. 694–711. Springer, Cham (2016). https://doi.org/10.1007/978-3-319-46475-6_43
9. Jørgensen, T.M., Thomadsen, J., Christensen, U., Soliman, W., Sander, B.A.: Enhancing the signal-to-noise ratio in ophthalmic optical coherence tomography by image registration-method and clinical examples. J. Biomed. Opt. 12(4), 041208 (2007)
10. Lazaridis, G., Lorenzi, M., Ourselin, S., Garway-Heath, D.: Improving statistical power of glaucoma clinical trials using an ensemble of cyclical generative adversarial networks. Med. Image Anal. 68, 101906 (2021)
11. Ledig, C., et al.: Photo-realistic single image super-resolution using a generative adversarial network. In: Proceedings of the IEEE Conference on Computer Vision and Pattern Recognition, pp. 4681–4690 (2017)
12. Matkovic, K., Neumann, L., Neumann, A., Psik, T., Purgathofer, W.: Global contrast factor-a new approach to image contrast. Comput. Aesthet. 2005(159–168), 1 (2005)
13. Mittal, A., Soundararajan, R., Bovik, A.C.: Making a "completely blind" image quality analyzer. IEEE Signal Process. Lett. 20(3), 209–212 (2012)
14. Ozcan, A., Bilenca, A., Desjardins, A.E., Bouma, B.E., Tearney, G.J.: Speckle reduction in optical coherence tomography images using digital filtering. JOSA A 24(7), 1901–1910 (2007)
15. Ravì, D., Szczotka, A.B., Pereira, S.P., Vercauteren, T.: Adversarial training with cycle consistency for unsupervised super-resolution in endomicroscopy. Med. Image Anal. 53, 123–131 (2019)
16. Rieke, N., et al.: Surgical tool tracking and pose estimation in retinal microsurgery. In: Navab, N., Hornegger, J., Wells, W.M., Frangi, A.F. (eds.) MICCAI 2015. LNCS, vol. 9349, pp. 266–273. Springer, Cham (2015). https://doi.org/10.1007/978-3-319-24553-9_33
17. Roodaki, H., Grimm, M., Navab, N., Eslami, A.: Real-time scene understanding in ophthalmic anterior segment OCT images. Investig. Ophthalmol. Vis. Sci. 60(11), PB095–PB095 (2019)
18. Russakovsky, O., et al.: Imagenet large scale visual recognition challenge. Int. J. Comput. Vis. 115(3), 211–252 (2015)
19. Sander, B., Larsen, M., Thrane, L., Hougaard, J.L., Jørgensen, T.M.: Enhanced optical coherence tomography imaging by multiple scan averaging. Br. J. Ophthalmol. 89(2), 207–212 (2005)
20. Simonyan, K., Zisserman, A.: Very deep convolutional networks for large-scale image recognition. arXiv preprint arXiv:1409.1556 (2014)
21. Wolterink, J.M., Dinkla, A.M., Savenije, M.H.F., Seevinck, P.R., van den Berg, C.A.T., Išgum, I.: Deep MR to CT synthesis using unpaired data. In: Tsaftaris, S.A., Gooya, A., Frangi, A.F., Prince, J.L. (eds.) SASHIMI 2017. LNCS, vol. 10557, pp. 14–23. Springer, Cham (2017). https://doi.org/10.1007/978-3-319-68127-6_2

22. Yang, Q., et al.: Low-dose CT image denoising using a generative adversarial network with Wasserstein distance and perceptual loss. IEEE Trans. Med. Imaging **37**(6), 1348–1357 (2018)
23. Zhou, M., et al.: Precision needle tip localization using optical coherence tomography images for subretinal injection. In: 2018 IEEE International Conference on Robotics and Automation (ICRA), pp. 4033–4040. IEEE (2018)
24. Zhu, J.Y., Park, T., Isola, P., Efros, A.A.: Unpaired image-to-image translation using cycle-consistent adversarial networks. In: Proceedings of the IEEE International Conference on Computer Vision, pp. 2223–2232 (2017)

Diabetic Retinopathy Detection Based on Weakly Supervised Object Localization and Knowledge Driven Attribute Mining

Xinliang Wang[1], Yunchao Gu[1(✉)], Junjun Pan[1,2], and Liyun Jia[3]

[1] State Key Laboratory of Virtual Reality Technology and Systems, Beihang University, Beijing 100191, China
{wangxinliang,guyunchao,pan_junjun}@buaa.edu.cn
[2] Peng Cheng Laboratory, Shenzhen 518000, China
[3] Beijing Tongren Eye Center, Beijing Tongren Hospital, Capital Medical University, Beijing 100730, China

Abstract. Disease grading and lesion identification are two important tasks for diabetic retinopathy detection. Disease grading uses image-level annotation but lesion identification often needs the fine-grained annotations, which requires a lot of time and effort of professional doctors. Therefore, it is a great challenge to complete disease grading and lesion identification simultaneously with the limited labeled data. We propose a method based on weakly supervised object localization and knowledge driven attribute mining to conduct disease grading and lesion identification using only image-level annotation. We first propose an Attention-Drop-Highlight Layer (ADHL), which enables the CNN to accurately and comprehensively focus on the various lesion features. Then, we design a search space and employ neural architecture search (NAS) to select the best settings of the ADHL, to maximize the performance of the model. Finally, we regard the lesion attributes corresponding to different disease grades as weakly supervised classification labels representing prior knowledge, and propose an Attribute Mining (AM) method to further improve the effect of disease grading and complete lesion identification. Extensive experiments and a user study have proved that our method can capture more lesion features, improve the performance of disease grading, and obtain state-of-the-art results compared to the methods only using image-level annotation.

Keywords: Diabetic retinopathy detection · Disease grading · Lesion identification

1 Introduction

The technology of disease grading and lesion identification provides great help for diabetic retinopathy (DR) detection [11–13]. Disease grading predicts grading of DR and assists doctors to complete early diagnosis. Lesion identification can

Electronic supplementary material The online version of this chapter (https://doi.org/10.1007/978-3-030-87000-3_4) contains supplementary material, which is available to authorized users.

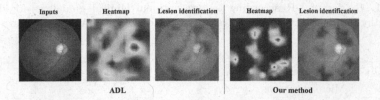

Fig. 1. Compared with the ADL [3] method, our method can locate the lesions more accurately and provide the category of lesions. Blue and cyan represents microaneurysm and hemorrhages, black represents no category prediction, just highlighted. (Color figure online)

directly locate the focus and provide an interpretable diagnostic basis for doctors and patients. Disease grading is usually regarded as classification task. Several methods based on convolutional neural network have been designed to classify DR [5,6,12]. Most lesion identification methods are based on object detection and semantic segmentation [12,15]. The task of disease grading needs to use the data with image-level annotation; but lesion identification needs to use the fine-grained bounding box or pixel-level annotation, which is time-consuming and laborious for professional doctors. Therefore, it is a challenge to complete disease grading and lesion identification with limited labeled data.

In this paper, we propose a weakly supervised object localization [14] and attribute mining method, which only uses image-level annotation and lesion attribute annotation derived from prior knowledge to complete disease grading and lesion identification of DR. As shown in Fig. 1, we propose a weakly supervised object localization method, Attention-Drop-Highlight Layer (ADHL), which enables the network to pay attention to more lesion features and provides comprehensive and accurate information for disease grading and lesion identification. However, the insertion location and parameter settings of ADHL will greatly affect the training effect of CNN. Therefore, we design a search space, using neural architecture search (NAS) [17] to search suitable setting of these parameters, to maximize the performance of the ADHL. Finally, we take the basis of lesion classification in Table 1 as the prior knowledge attribute tag, and propose an attribute mining (AM) method to enable the model to learn more specific information about attributes, to further improve the disease grading performance. Additionally, the specific attribute information obtained in the process of AM is used as the results of lesion identification. Quantitative and qualitative experiments on three public datasets and a user survey prove the effectiveness of our proposed method.

2   Method

2.1   Attention-Drop-Highlight Layer (ADHL)

CNN tends to employ the most discriminative features to conduct image classification, resulting in ignorance of other potentially useful information [3].

Table 1. Grades of DR according to international clinical guidelines for diabetic retinopathy [2]. IRMA stands for Intra Retinal Microvascular Abnormalities.

Grade	Criterion
0 - No DR	No Abnormalities
1 - Mild	Microaneurysms
2 - Moderate	More than just microaneurysms but less than Grade 3
3 - Severe	Intraretinal hemorrhages or Definite venous beading or Prominent IRMA
4 - PDR	Neovascularization or Preretinal hemorrhage

However, it is often necessary to make disease grading by comprehensive evaluation of multiple lesions in medical images. We propose an ADHL to solve this problem. Figure 2 (b) shows the structure of the ADHL. The Attention branch implements self-attention on the input feature map, to enhance the representation of important features. The function of the Drop branch is to drop the most discriminative features and force the network to notice and capture other lesion features that are helpful to classify the current disease. The Highlight branch, the complement of the Drop branch, avoids the overfitting caused by the network paying too much attention to extensive lesion features.

The input of the ADHL is a feature map F ($F \in R^{H \times W \times D}$, where H, W, D are height, width and depth of F). After channel-wise average pooling, the attention map A ($A \in R^{H \times W}$) is obtained. The value of A is mapped to [0,1] after sigmoid to reflect the discriminant of the feature. The part of A whose value is greater than the parameter Drop threshold t_D will be set to 0, which means that the most discriminative feature in this spatial dimension is discarded. The part of A whose value is less than the parameter Highlight threshold t_H will be set to 0, indicating that the features in this part of spatial dimension that may be useless for classification are discarded. Then, the network enters the branch selection stage with the probabilities of the three branches P_A, P_D and P_H ($P_A + P_D + P_H = 1$). The new feature map F' is obtained by multiplying the selected branch feature with the input feature map F:

$$F' = \begin{cases} A \times F, & r \in [0, P_A) \\ D \times F, & r \in [P_A, P_A + P_D) \\ H \times F, & r \in [P_A + P_D, 1] \end{cases} \tag{1}$$

where $r \in [0, 1]$ is a random number generated during training, $\times$ is point-wise multiply, A, D and H are the outputs of Attention, Drop and Highlight branch.

2.2   NAS-ADHL

In our proposed ADHL, there are some parameters and settings directly related to the performance of disease grading and lesion identification, including the insertion position of ADHL, the selection probability of three branches (P_A, P_D, P_H), and

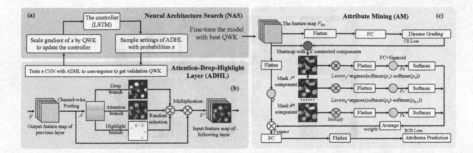

Fig. 2. Pipeline of our method. NAS controls the parameters in the ADHL. After iterative optimization by reinforcement learning, the model with the best performance on the validation set is selected, and the AM is applied to complete the attribute prediction and disease grading. The white regions on the heatmaps are dropped features. Note that the QWK is the quadratic weighted kappa metric.

the threshold of Drop and Highlight (t_D, t_H). Therefore, in order to avoid adjusting parameters manually and maximize the role of the ADHL, we use the NAS method to search for these parameters. The NAS module we designed is responsible for determining whether to insert ADHL after a convolutional layer, and selecting the probability of three branches, Drop threshold and Highlight threshold. Additionally, we use the strategy similar to NASNet [17], to update the parameters with proximal policy optimization (PPO) [8].

2.3   Attribute Mining (AM)

We take the criterion of each DR grade in Table 1 as prior knowledge, and get six attributes: microaneurysm (MA), hemorrhage (HE), definite venous beading, prominent IRMA, neovascularization (NV) and preretinal hemorrhage. We use these attributes to train a multi-label classification task. However, the prior knowledge attribute tags we obtain are not completely correct, because the lesion features represented by the fundus images of the same category are not exactly the same. For example, one sample with grading 4 may have preretinal hemorrhage and microaneurysms, and another sample with the same grading may have neovascularization and hemorrhage.

The first effectiveness of AM is to solve the problem above and further improve disease grading performance. As shown in Fig. 2 (c), F_{NA} is the output of the last convolutional layer of CNN trained with NAS-ADHL. The disease grading task is finished first using Cross Entropy Loss conducted with the predictions of the model and DR grading labels. The calculation of attributes prediction goes ahead by a function f with a fully connected layer and a sigmoid layer. p ($p \in R^6$) represents the prediction probabilities of the six lesion attributes.

Then, we use Grad-CAM [9] to get the heatmap of F_{NA} and use a threshold t to obtain the K activated regions on the heatmap to form K connected components, with each connected component as a lesion area. The AM iteratively

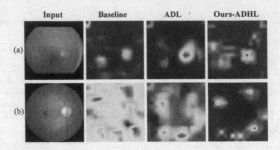

Fig. 3. Qualitative evaluation of the ADHL and others. The locations highlighted in heatmap are the potential lesions found by models.

calculates the heatmap for K times, each time drops one connected area on the feature map and multiplies with F_{NA}, and shares the weight of f to obtain the new attribute estimation p_k ($p_k \in R^6$). We can obtain the lesion attribute weight of this iteration through the softmax layer, and finally take the average value as the lesion attribute weight, which can be defined as:

$$weight = \frac{1}{K+1} \sum_{k=0}^{K} softmax(p_k) \tag{2}$$

where $softmax(\cdot)$ is the function of softmax layer, and $k = 0$ means the calculation on original heatmap. Then, the adjusted attribute prediction, $p_{weighted}$, is conducted by multiplying the $weight$ with p. Finally, $P_{weighted}$ passes through a fully connected layer and a sigmoid layer to calculate Binary Cross Entropy Loss (BCE) loss with the attribute tags.

The second effectiveness of AM is to identify lesions. In the k-th calculation of iterative lesion attribute mining, each drop position is a lesion area. The proposed AM conducts k-th lesion identification using the formula as follow:

$$Lesion_k = \arg\max_{k \in \{1,2,\cdots,K\}} (softmax(p_k) - softmax(p_{k-1})), \tag{3}$$

where $Lesion_k$ is the category of the k-th lesion area.

3   Experimental Results

3.1   Settings

Datasets and Evaluation Metrics EyePACS [1] contains 35,126 training and 53,576 testing images with the same five classes as Table 1, but with a class imbalance problem. **Messidor** [4] contains 1,200 fundus images with four classes (0 to 3). This dataset is usually used for two binary tasks: referral/non-referral and normal/abnormal. For the former task, tags 0 and 1 are used as non-referrals, 2 and 3 are used as referrals. For the latter task, tag 0 is regarded

Table 2. Contrastive experiments on the EyePACS dataset.

Method	A_p	D_p	H_p	QWK	Acc.
ADL	0.8	0.2	-	0.845	0.838
	0.2	0.8	-	0.842	0.831
	0.6	0.4	-	0.845	0.841
	0.4	0.6	-	0.843	0.836
Baseline	-	-	-	0.844	0.836
ADHL	0.8	0.1	0.1	0.848	**0.844**
	0.1	0.8	0.1	0.847	0.839
	0.1	0.1	0.8	0.845	0.841
	0.6	0.2	0.2	**0.850**	0.839
	0.2	0.6	0.2	0.847	0.836
	0.2	0.2	0.6	0.848	0.842

Table 3. Quantitative evaluation results of the NAS-ADHL. L denotes the insertion of ADHL and x-y means the y-th convolutional layer in the Stage x of ResNet.

L	A_p	D_p	H_p	t_D	t_H	QWK	Acc
5-3	0.32	0.48	0.20	0.90	0.75	0.851	0.844
5-3	0.27	0.24	0.49	0.75	0.75	**0.853**	0.843
5-2	0.38	0.46	0.16	0.75	0.85	0.852	0.838
5-3	0.22	0.45	0.33	0.95	0.90		
4-3	0.45	0.41	0.14	0.95	0.95	0.848	**0.847**
4-6	0.38	0.34	0.28	0.90	0.75	0.850	0.842
5-3	0.12	0.48	0.40	0.95	0.85		

as normal and the others as abnormal samples. In addition, we use **FGADR** [16] dataset which has 1842 samples with pixel-level annotation for six type of lesions but has the problem of unbalanced labels, to verify the performance of lesion identification. For disease grading, we use accuracy (Acc.), quadratic weighted kappa (QWK) [1] and the area under curve (AUC) as the evaluation metrics. For lesion identification, we use DICE to conduct quantitative evaluation and design a user study for qualitative evaluation.

Implementation Details. We resize the fundus images to 512×512, use ResNet50 as the baseline, and employ basic augmentations. We first train 30 epochs using NAS-ADHL. Then the ADHL with the optimal parameters is used to train an additional 30 epochs. Finally, we add AM and finetune 20 epochs to enable the model to complete lesion identification. More information about implementation details can be found in the supplementary material.

3.2   Ablation Studies

Effect of ADHL. We conduct a comparative experiment among our proposed ADHL, baseline (ResNet50) and a weakly supervised object location method (ADL [3]) Figure 3 shows the lesion areas considered useful for classification by the model. We can see that baseline is not comprehensive enough for lesion capture; ADL can capture a wider range of lesion features than the baseline, but it is still not accurate enough. Our ADHL shows the best effect, as it can capture more lesion features. In Fig. 3 (b), the ADL and baseline focus on too many features, and our ADHL can capture lesion features in details. The quantitative results are shown in Table 2. The performance of ADHL is better than that of the ADL and the baseline. Specifically, with the same attention selection probability, QWK and Acc. are improved after a part of the selection probability is allocated

Table 4. Performance comparison of DR grading on the Eye-PACS dataset.

Methods	QWK
CLSC [15]	0.872
AFN [6]	0.859
Min-Pooling	0.849
o_O	0.845
RG	0.839
Zoom-in-Net [12]	0.849
CABNet(ResNet50) [5]	0.851
Ours	**0.856**

Table 5. Quantitative evaluation results on the Messidor dataset.

Task	Referral		Normal	
Methods	AUC	Acc.	AUC	Acc.
CLSC [15]	0.976	0.939	0.943	0.922
AFN [6]	0.968	-	0.935	-
VNXK [10]	0.887	0.893	0.870	0.871
CKML [10]	0.891	0.897	0.862	0.858
Expert [7]	0.940	-	0.922	-
Zoom-in-Net [12]	0.957	0.911	0.921	**0.905**
Ours	**0.960**	**0.911**	**0.937**	0.900

from the Drop branch to the Highlight branch. This result illustrates that our method can improve the effect of disease classification after a comprehensive capturing of the key lesion information in the image.

Effect of NAS-ADHL. We select the NAS-ADHL structure ranked top 5 on the QWK metric on the validation set, train models with the method in the section of implementation, and obtain the results shown in Table 3. We can see that in ResNet50, only convolutional layers in Stage4 and Stage5 are selected, indicating that ADHL can achieve better disease classification effect when it is applied to the deep layer of CNN. Compared to other models, our model ranked second in the validation set has higher value of highlight probability, and achieves better results in the final test set. This shows that the Highlight branch can assist the model in comprehensively capturing lesion features and highlighting the features utility for disease grading. Additionally, the experimental results show that too high threshold of Drop or Highlight will damage the feature representation ability of the model and reduce the QWK score on the validation set.

Effect of AM. The quantitative results of DR grading are shown in Table 4. Compared with the best QWK in Table 3, the disease grading performance of the model can be further improved after using the AM. We conduct a cross-validation segmentation experiment on FGADR dataset to verify the performance of lesion recognition, and get: MA 0.0543, HE 0.1664, IRMA 0.0022, and NV 0.0028. The results of fully supervised segmentation are MA 0.1774, HE 0.3877, IRMA 0.0119, and NV 0.0339. It can be seen that our AM has good localization ability for MA and HE. However, it is a difficult problem to locate IRMA and NV, and even the fully supervised segmentation method can not locate them well. In addition, the result without using AM is None, because the network has no ability to complete recognition through image-level annotation. Note that the other two lesions, hard exudates and soft exudates are not in Table 1, so we don't

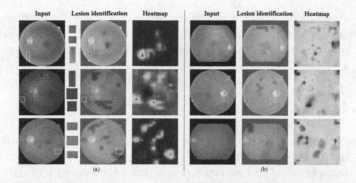

Fig. 4. Qualitative results of lesion identification. Blue, cyan, green and yellow represent microaneurysms, hemorrhages, definite venous beading and prominent IRMA. In part (a), we manually display three representative regions of lesion in each sample, crop and enlarge them from the input images. Failure cases are shown in part (b), which are caused by the recognition of too much information with our method. (Color figure online)

evaluate them. Figure 4 shows the effectiveness of AM on lesion identification. In part (a), it can be seen that our method can complete the lesion identification only using image-level labels. In each sample, three lesions are selected for magnification, and their location and category predictions are correct. Part (b) is the demonstration of failure cases. Although the disease grading results of these samples are correct, limited by the serious class imbalance problem of EyePACS, some rare lesions make the model difficult to accurately predict their location.

3.3   Comparison with SOTA Methods on Disease Grading

Table 4 shows the results of quantitative comparison with the SOTA methods on EyePACS. The methods in the upper part of the table use additional fine-grained annotations. CLSC [15] used pixel-level annotation and AFN [6] utilized bounding box annotation. Methods in the lower part of the table only used the image-level annotation. Our methods outperform them in terms of QWK score. Table 5 shows the results of comparison of different methods on Messidor. It shows that our method can achieve good performance in both referral/non-referral and normal/abnormal tasks, especially in the AUC metric, which shows that our model can effectively process the fundus Images with diseases.

3.4   User Study on Lesion Identification

We randomly select 50 samples in test set, and use the visualization method similar to Fig. 4 to display the heatmap of ADHL and ADL. Five doctors are asked to compare the two lesion capture effects of each sample. According to statistics, on average, doctors think that the results of the ADHL are better, accounting for 90.4% of the total sample. Then we ask doctors to compare the results of ADHL with category prediction (lesion identification results of AM) with those of ADL without category. As a result, they all think that the prediction with category is better. To sum up, our method can identify lesions more comprehensively and accurately, and has certain significance for clinical auxiliary diagnosis.

4   Conclusion

We propose a method to complete disease grading and lesion identification of DR with only image-level annotation. The proposed ADHL enables CNN to focus on comprehensive and accurate lesion information, and we use NAS to maximize the performance of ADHL. The designed AM method can use the prior knowledge tags to identify the lesions. Experiments and a user survey show that our proposed method is better than the previous methods which only use image-level annotation, and lesion identification with our method can have a positive role in clinical diagnosis.

Acknowledgments. This research is supported by National Key R&D Program of China (No. 2018YFC0115102), National Natural Science Foundation of China (Nos. 61872020, U20A20195), Beijing Natural Science Foundation Haidian Primitive Innovation Joint Fund (L182016), Beijing Advanced Innovation Center for Biomedical Engineering (ZF138G1714), Research Unit of Virtual Human and Virtual Surgery, Chinese Academy of Medical Sciences (2019RU004), Shenzhen Research Institute of Big Data, Shenzhen, 518000, and Global Visiting Fellowship of Bournemouth University.

References

1. Kaggle diabetic retinopathy detection competition. https://www.kaggle.com/c/diabetic-retinopathy-detection
2. Bajwa, M.N., Taniguchi, Y., Malik, M.I., Neumeier, W., Dengel, A., Ahmed, S.: Combining fine- and coarse-grained classifiers for diabetic retinopathy detection. In: Zheng, Y., Williams, B.M., Chen, K. (eds.) MIUA 2019. CCIS, vol. 1065, pp. 242–253. Springer, Cham (2020). https://doi.org/10.1007/978-3-030-39343-4_21
3. Choe, J., Shim, H.: Attention-based dropout layer for weakly supervised object localization. In: CVPR, pp. 2219–2228 (2019)
4. Decencière, E., et al.: Feedback on a publicly distributed image database: the Messidor database. Image Anal. Stereol. **33**(3), 231–234 (2014)
5. He, A., Li, T., Li, N., Wang, K., Fu, H.: Cabnet: category attention block for imbalanced diabetic retinopathy grading. IEEE Trans. Med. Imaging **40**, 143–153 (2020)
6. Lin, Z., et al.: A framework for identifying diabetic retinopathy based on anti-noise detection and attention-based fusion. In: Frangi, A.F., Schnabel, J.A., Davatzikos, C., Alberola-López, C., Fichtinger, G. (eds.) MICCAI 2018. LNCS, vol. 11071, pp. 74–82. Springer, Cham (2018). https://doi.org/10.1007/978-3-030-00934-2_9
7. Sánchez, C.I., Niemeijer, M., Dumitrescu, A.V., Suttorp-Schulten, M.S., Abramoff, M.D., van Ginneken, B.: Evaluation of a computer-aided diagnosis system for diabetic retinopathy screening on public data. Invest. Ophthalmol. Vis. Sci. **52**(7), 4866–4871 (2011)

8. Schulman, J., Wolski, F., Dhariwal, P., Radford, A., Klimov, O.: Proximal policy optimization algorithms. arXiv preprint arXiv:1707.06347 (2017)
9. Selvaraju, R.R., Cogswell, M., Das, A., Vedantam, R., Parikh, D., Batra, D.: Grad-CAM: visual explanations from deep networks via gradient-based localization. In: ICCV, pp. 618–626 (2017)
10. Vo, H.H., Verma, A.: New deep neural nets for fine-grained diabetic retinopathy recognition on hybrid color space. In: 2016 IEEE International Symposium on Multimedia (ISM), pp. 209–215. IEEE (2016)
11. Wang, X., et al.: Unifying structure analysis and surrogate-driven function regression for glaucoma OCT image screening. In: Shen, D., et al. (eds.) MICCAI 2019. LNCS, vol. 11764, pp. 39–47. Springer, Cham (2019). https://doi.org/10.1007/978-3-030-32239-7_5
12. Wang, Z., Yin, Y., Shi, J., Fang, W., Li, H., Wang, X.: Zoom-in-net: deep mining lesions for diabetic retinopathy detection. In: Descoteaux, M., Maier-Hein, L., Franz, A., Jannin, P., Collins, D.L., Duchesne, S. (eds.) MICCAI 2017. LNCS, vol. 10435, pp. 267–275. Springer, Cham (2017). https://doi.org/10.1007/978-3-319-66179-7_31
13. Xing, X., et al.: Dynamic spectral graph convolution networks with assistant task training for early MCI diagnosis. In: Shen, D., et al. (eds.) MICCAI 2019. LNCS, vol. 11767, pp. 639–646. Springer, Cham (2019). https://doi.org/10.1007/978-3-030-32251-9_70
14. Zhang, C.L., Cao, Y.H., Wu, J.: Rethinking the route towards weakly supervised object localization. In: CVPR, pp. 13460–13469 (2020)
15. Zhou, Y., et al.: Collaborative learning of semi-supervised segmentation and classification for medical images. In: CVPR, pp. 2079–2088 (2019)
16. Zhou, Y., Wang, B., Huang, L., Cui, S., Shao, L.: A benchmark for studying diabetic retinopathy: segmentation, grading, and transferability. IEEE Trans. Med. Imaging 40(3), 818–828 (2020)
17. Zoph, B., Vasudevan, V., Shlens, J., Le, Q.V.: Learning transferable architectures for scalable image recognition. In: CVPR, pp. 8697–8710 (2018)

FARGO: A Joint Framework for FAZ and RV Segmentation from OCTA Images

Linkai Peng[1], Li Lin[1,2], Pujin Cheng[1], Zhonghua Wang[1],
and Xiaoying Tang[1(✉)]

[1] Department of Electrical and Electronic Engineering, Southern University of
Science and Technology, Shenzhen, China
tangxy@sustech.edu.cn
[2] Department of Electrical and Electronic Engineering, The University of Hong
Kong, Hong Kong SAR, China

Abstract. Optical coherence tomography angiography (OCTA) is a
recent advance in ophthalmic imaging, which provides detailed visualization of two important anatomical landmarks, namely foveal avascular zone
(FAZ) and retinal vessels (RV). Studies have shown that both FAZ and
RV play significant roles in the diagnoses of various eye-related diseases.
Therefore, accurate segmentation of FAZ and RV from OCTA images is
highly in need. However, due to complicated microstructures and inhomogeneous image quality, there is still room for improvement in existing methods. In this paper, we propose a novel and efficient deep learning framework containing two subnetworks for simultaneously segmenting
FAZ and RV from *en-face* OCTA images, named FARGO. For FAZ, we use
RV segmentation as an auxiliary task, which may provide supplementary
information especially for low-contrast and low-quality OCTA images. A
ResNeSt based encoder with split attention and ImageNet pretraining is
employed for FAZ segmentation. For RV, we introduce a coarse-to-fine
cascaded network composed of a main segmentation model and several
small ones for progressive refining. Spatial attention and channel attention
modules are utilized for adaptively integrating local features with global
dependencies. Through extensive experiments, FARGO is found to yield
outstanding segmentation results for both FAZ and RV on the OCTA-500
dataset, performing even better than methods that utilize 3D OCTA volume as an extra input.

Keywords: Foveal avascular zone · Retinal vessels · Joint
segmentation · Coarse-to-fine · OCTA · ResNeSt.

1 Introduction

Optical coherence tomography angiography (OCTA) is a recent advance in ophthalmic imaging. It is a non-invasive imaging modality that does not require intra-
venously administering fluorescent dyes [2], which is much safer than prevenient

---

L. Peng and L. Lin contributed equally to this work.

© Springer Nature Switzerland AG 2021
H. Fu et al. (Eds.): OMIA 2021, LNCS 12970, pp. 42–51, 2021.
https://doi.org/10.1007/978-3-030-87000-3_5

forms of imaging. It provides details of vascular structures within the retina as well as images of blood flow in the retina and choroid [21]. Due to the high resolution of OCTA images, detailed microvascular structures can be displayed, which is beneficial for accurate extractions of foveal avascular zone (FAZ) and retinal vessels (RV) in the retina. These two anatomical landmarks play significant roles in the diagnoses of various eye diseases and eye-related systemic diseases [1]. For instance, the morphology and contour irregularity of FAZ is related to the condition of age-related macular degeneration [11,15] and the severity of glaucoma [4,22] and morphological changes in the RV tortuosity and caliber can reflect the progression of diabetic retinopathy [10,19]. Therefore, an efficient and accurate method for simultaneous FAZ and RV segmentation utilizing OCTA images is in need.

In the research direction of FAZ and RV segmentation from OCTA images, there exist a small number of related works [8,24,26]. For example, Díaz et al. [6] created a FAZ segmentation pipeline based on morphological processing and transformation methods. Eladawi et al. [7] proposed a joint Markov-Gibbs random field model to segment RV and used a Generalized Gauss-Markov random field model for denoising. In addition to traditional methods, a variety of deep learning based methods have been developed to tackle the medical image segmentation task in recent years. Ronneberger et al. [20] proposed the classical U-Net, concatenating the outputs of the encoders and the inputs of the decoders. Several U-Net variants such as U-Net++ [27] have also been proposed. For FAZ and RV segmentation, there have also been ongoing research efforts in this direction. For example, Ma et al. [16] introduced a split-based coarse-to-fine vessel segmentation network containing a coarse segmentation module and a refined segmentation module. Deng et al. [5] developed a U-Net based approach to segment and classify avascular, hypovascular, and capillary-dense areas. Li et al. [13] designed a 3D-to-2D image projection network which utilizes 3D OCTA and OCT volumes as the input to mitigate erroneous retina layer segmentation and to better segment FAZ and RV.

However, these methods still have limitations. For example, [16] and [13] require multi-stage training or a large quantity of model parameters. Also, most of them suffer from inhomogeneous OCTA image quality and complicated structures of FAZ and RV. For example, inferior image quality and erroneous layer projection may cause a network of interest to confuse FAZ with interfering structures, leading to imprecise boundaries and inevitable outliers. Retinal vessels are multi-scaled and it is difficult for fine vessels or terminal branches in noisy images to be segmented accurately. It will be even more complicated if there exist lesions, e.g., microaneurysms and non-perfusion. Such lesions may result in mis-segmentation of vessels and make this task even more challenging. Furthermore, existing works for simultaneously and fully-automatically segmenting FAZ and RV from OCTA images are relatively rare.

In such context, we propose a novel joint FAZ and RV segmentation framework, which mitigates the aforementioned issues and exhibits superior performance. This framework contains two subnetworks. For FAZ, we build a ResNeSt based U-Net with split attention and ImageNet pretraining for better segmentation performance. More importantly, we employ RV segmentation as an auxiliary task to provide complementary edge and position information, which further improves the FAZ segmentation accuracy, especially for images wherein the contrast between FAZ and its neighborhood is low or the FAZ contours are blurry. For RV, we design a coarse-to-fine cascaded network flow to refine the output of each subnetwork step by step. Spatial attention and channel attention modules are also applied to promote inter-class discrimination and intra-class aggregation [9,17,18]. The final predictions are obtained by merging the outputs of the FAZ subnetwork and the RV subnetwork.

The main contributions of this paper are four-fold: (1) We propose an innovative joint framework for simultaneous FAZ and RV segmentation from OCTA images, achieving superior performance over representative state-of-the-art (SOTA) methods on the publicly-available OCTA-500 dataset [14]. (2) For FAZ segmentation, we make use of RV segmentation as an auxiliary task and a ResNeSt based U-Net structure with split attention and pretrained parameters for initialization. (3) For RV segmentation, we employ a spatial-and-channel dual-attention mechanism in a cascaded coarse-to-fine fashion to gradually refine the outputs. (4) Extensive comparison experiments are conducted, both quantitatively and qualitatively. The source code is available at https://github.com/lkpengcs/FARGO.

2 Methodology

2.1 The Proposed Architecture

The proposed framework is shown in Fig. 1, which consists of a joint FAZ segmentation subnetwork and a coarse-to-fine RV segmentation subnetwork.

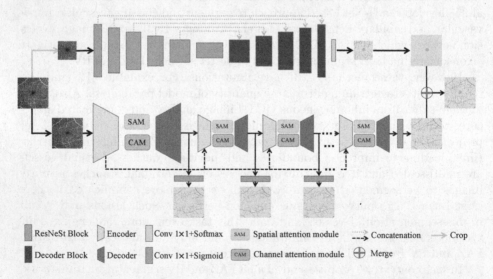

Fig. 1. Schematic demonstration of the architecture of our proposed framework FARGO. The upper part represents the FAZ subnetwork with region of interest extraction and ResNeSt blocks. The lower part represents the RV subnetwork including a main segmentation model and $\mathcal{N}$ small refining models. Spatial attention and channel attention modules are applied in the RV subnetwork.

FAZ Segmentation. Disturbing structures often interfere with the segmentation of FAZ, resulting in outlier predictions and inaccurate contours. Clinically, FAZ is defined as the area without any retinal vessel in the fovea, and thus it is natural to use retinal vessels as prior knowledge to constrain the position of FAZ and assist in distinguishing FAZ boundaries from interfering surroundings. Therefore, we build a joint segmentation model with an encoder-decoder structure to segment FAZ. Instead of treating it as a single-class segmentation task, we train our network to segment FAZ and RV together. It is desirable for such a joint segmentation model to learn the relationship between the distribution of RV and the location and shape of FAZ. Here, we define a weighted loss for FAZ segmentation, with $\lambda_1, \lambda_2, \lambda_3$ being trade-off parameters

$$L_{weighted} = \lambda_1 \mathcal{L}_{faz} + \lambda_2 \mathcal{L}_{rv} + \lambda_3 \mathcal{L}_{bg}, \tag{1}$$

where $\mathcal{L}_{faz}, \mathcal{L}_{rv}, \mathcal{L}_{bg}$ respectively denote the Dice loss for FAZ, RV and the background. We use ResNeSt50 [23] backbone with split attention and ImageNet pre-training initialization as the encoder to speed up network training and converging, resulting in better segmentation performance. Besides, appropriate region of interest (ROI) extraction is performed to focus on regions where FAZ is most likely to appear and reduce the influence of background noise.

RV Segmentation. Given retinal vessels are multi-scaled and are likely to be interfered by similar structures, resulting in disconnected vessels or outliers, we design a coarse-to-fine framework with an iterative correction mechanism. The refining framework consists of a main segmentation model and $\mathcal{N}$ small refining models. Compared to FAZ, retinal vessels are typically slender, and thus we employ shallower networks with fewer downsampling operations. Refining is simpler than segmentation, so we utilize four encoder blocks in the main model and three in the refining models. Each encoder block comprises two layers of 3 × 3 filters, batch normalization (BN), ReLU and maxpooling. RV segmentation from the input OCTA image is accomplished by the main model and the refining models mainly focus on removing potential errors and generating refined results. The input to the first refining model is the feature maps from the penultimate layer of the main model, and other refining models follow similarly [12]. Features obtained from the first layer of the main model are also concatenated with features from the first layer of each refining model. This allows each refining model to receive different inputs and to encounter differences and changes produced by preceding models. In this way, the main model can generate coarse vessel predictions from OCTA images and the refining models can polish those predictions by identifying potentially-missed vessels, eliminating outliers and recovering continuous details.

Furthermore, spatial and channel attention modules are employed in both the main model and each refining model. The features from the encoder are fed into two parallel attention blocks - a channel attention module (CAM) and a spatial attention module (SAM) as shown in Fig. 2. CAM utilizes features from each channel of the feature maps and improves feature representation by adaptively assigning weights to channels. SAM obtains spatial information and selectively aggregates contexts by generating a spatial attention map [18]. For training the RV subnetwork, cross entropy is used for outputs from each model and then they are summed up with certain weights, defined as:

$$\mathcal{L}_i = -y_i \log (p_i) - (1 - y_i) \log (1 - p_i) \tag{2}$$

$$\mathcal{L}_{rv} = \sum_i w_i L_i \tag{3}$$

where y_i and p_i respectively represent the groundtruth and prediction of pixel i, and all w_i are set to be 1 since we do not treat any output specially.

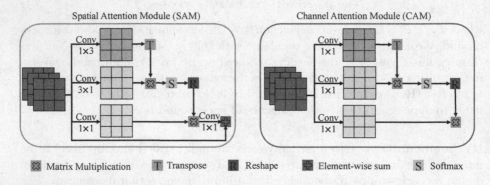

Fig. 2. Illustration of Spatial Attention Module (SAM) and Channel Attention Module (CAM).

3   Experiments

3.1   Dataset and Image Preprocessing

The OCTA-500 dataset are divided into two subsets according to the field of view (FOV) type. One subset contains 300 samples with 6 mm × 6 mm FOV, named OCTA_6M. The other subset contains 200 samples with 3 mm × 3 mm FOV, named OCTA_3M [14]. Please refer to the original paper for relevant biostatistic information [14]. We utilize *en-face* OCTA images generated by maximum-projection between internal limiting membrane layer and outer plexiform layer. Manual annotations for both FAZ and RV are provided. To generalize the entire pipeline, we employ the following data enhancement methods: random horizontal & vertical flipping and random rotation. In addition, for the two different subsets of OCTA-500, namely OCTA_6M and OCTA_3M, we respectively pad the images from 400 × 400 and 304 × 304 to 416 × 416 and 320 × 320 with reflect padding to meet the downsampling requirement that the input resolution of the network should be a power of 2.

3.2   Experimental Setting

We train and evaluate our pipeline on both OCTA_6M and OCTA_3M. For fair comparison, the training set, validation set and test set are divided according to [14]. All compared methods and the proposed one are implemented with Pytorch using NVIDIA TITAN RTX GPUs. We use the Adam optimizer with a learning rate of 1×10^{-4} with no learning rate policy and train the network for a total of 1000 epochs. The coefficients $\lambda_1, \lambda_2, \lambda_3$ in the weighted loss for FAZ segmentation are respectively set to be 0.6, 0.2, 0.2. Empirically, we choose $\mathcal{N} = 3$, i.e., three refining models for the RV segmentation task.

3.3   Results

All methods are evaluated using four metrics, i.e., Dice[%], Jaccard[%], 95% Hausdorff Distance (HD[px]) and Average Symmetric Surface Distance (ASSD[px]), the results of which are tabulated in Table 1. We compare our proposed framework with several SOTA segmentation models such as Deeplabv3+ [3] and PSPNet [25] for natural image segmentation as well as U-Net and U-Net++ for medical image segmentation. Apparently, our proposed framework FARGO achieves the best performance on both FAZ and RV segmentation on OCTA-500 among all methods that only use *en face* OCTA as the input. Compared with the most advanced IPN V2+ [14], our framework achieves overwhelming FAZ segmentation performance and competitive RV segmentation performance (slightly inferior), with much less computational complexity and memory consumption. To be noted, it is reasonable for IPN V2+ to achieve comparable or even better performance on some subsets or tasks due to its utilizations of 3D volume information and more complicated network structures.

Table 1. Quantitative evaluations of different methods for FAZ and RV segmentation. ‡ indicates the value is directly obtained from the cited paper.

FAZ	OCTA_6M				OCTA_3M			
Method	Dice↑	Jaccard↑	HD↓	ASSD↓	Dice↑	Jaccard↑	HD↓	ASSD↓
Deeplabv3+ [3]	87.75± 12.36	79.71 ± 14.44	8.05 ± 12.49	1.92 ± 3.07	95.43 ± 3.17	91.42 ± 5.51	**3.51 ± 2.56**	0.71 ± 0.27
Pspnet [25]	84.93 ± 13.09	75.56 ± 15.79	10.77 ± 21.84	2.01 ± 2.97	94.04 ± 3.87	88.99 ± 6.41	5.32 ± 7.20	0.95 ± 0.57
U-Net [20]	89.27 ± 12.51	82.27 ± 15.05	**6.40 ± 8.91**	**1.31 ± 1.94**	95.41 ± 4.27	91.51 ± 7.06	4.85 ± 4.39	0.75 ± 0.46
U-Net++ [27]	88.55 ± 15.90	81.90 ± 17.67	10.13 ± 24.54	2.15 ± 5.00	96.91 ± 1.59	94.06 ± 2.93	4.24 ± 3.26	**0.63 ± 0.35**
IPN V2+‡ [14]	90.54 ± 10.05	84.00 ± 14.16	–	–	97.42 ± 2.16	95.04 ± 3.88	–	–
Ours	**92.72 ± 6.74**	**87.01 ± 10.60**	7.76 ± 12.17	1.58 ± 3.07	**98.39 ± 0.92**	**96.84 ± 1.76**	3.11 ± 2.29	0.40 ± 0.27
RV	OCTA_6M				OCTA_3M			
Method	Dice↑	Jaccard↑	HD↓	ASSD↓	Dice↑	Jaccard↑	HD↓	ASSD↓
Deeplabv3+ [3]	78.82 ± 2.99	65.14 ± 3.93	5.51 ± 4.06	0.90 ± 0.31	78.74 ± 2.84	65.02 ± 3.79	11.94 ± 8.00	1.37 ± 0.71
Pspnet [25]	67.35 ± 2.84	50.84 ± 3.23	12.13 ± 2.48	1.88 ± 0.32	58.02 ± 2.99	40.93 ± 3.02	9.57 ± 4.79	1.93 ± 0.37
U-Net [20]	88.40 ± 2.69	79.32 ± 4.10	4.98 ± 4.29	0.64 ± 0.34	90.40 ± 2.04	82.54 ± 3.27	**3.20 ± 2.61**	**0.54 ± 0.25**
U-Net++ [27]	88.49 ± 2.55	79.44 ± 3.94	4.44 ± 3.34	**0.62 ± 0.26**	90.66 ± 2.01	82.97 ± 3.26	3.26 ± 2.40	0.56 ± 0.29
IPN V2+‡ [14]	**89.41 ± 2.74**	**80.95 ± 4.32**	–	–	**92.74 ± 3.95**	**86.67 ± 5.88**	–	–
Ours	89.15 ± 2.39	80.50 ± 3.75	4.47 ± 3.73	0.61 ± 0.28	91.68 ± 2.05	84.70 ± 3.34	2.78 ± 2.67	0.44 ± 0.25

Representative visualization results from FARGO on OCTA_6M and OCTA_3M are shown in Fig. 3. Clearly, the segmentation results of both FAZ and RV produced by FARGO are more precise and more accurate than those produced by other compared methods. Representative segmentation results for both high-quality images (row 2 and row 4) and low-quality images (row 1 and row 3) are presented in that figure. Our proposed framework has the highest Dice scores in all cases.

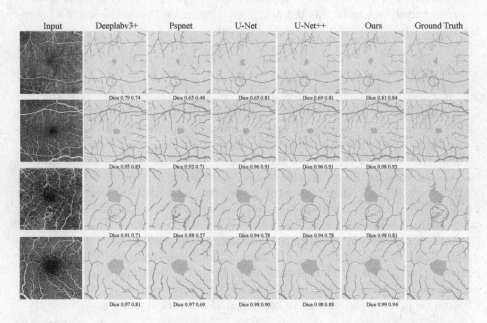

Fig. 3. Representative visualization results from OCTA_6M and OCTA_3M. The first two rows are results from OCTA_6M and the last two rows are results from OCTA_3M. Purple areas represent FAZ and the purple numbers represent their corresponding Dice scores. Red areas represent RV and the red numbers represent their corresponding Dice scores. Areas highlighted by blue circles reflect the ability of our framework to segment fine retinal vessels, even when the input image is of relatively low quality. (Color figure online)

In order to evaluate the effectiveness of several key components in FARGO, we also conduct several ablation studies. For FAZ segmentation, we compare with the proposed FAZ subnetwork without segmenting RV as an auxiliary task, without center ROI extraction, without ResNeSt as the encoder (using the original encoder of U-Net with BN), without pretrained parameters from ImageNet. As shown in Table 2, the Dice score of the original FAZ subnetwork is higher than that of the same network w/o the RV auxiliary task, that w/o center ROI extraction, that w/o ResNeSt as the encoder and that w/o pretrained parameters by 0.60%, 0.69%, 0.84% and 3.31% on OCTA_6M and by 0.17% and 0.27%, 0.54% and 1.25% on OCTA_3M, demonstrating the effectiveness of each component in the FAZ segmentation subnetwork.

Table 2. Ablation analysis results for FAZ segmentation.

RV	ROI	ResNeSt	Pretrain	OCTA_6M				OCTA_3M			
				Dice	Jaccard	HD	ASSD	Dice	Jaccard	HD	ASSD
	✓	✓	✓	92.12	86.69	9.53	1.76	98.22	96.35	4.41	0.49
✓		✓	✓	92.03	86.21	8.12	2.03	98.12	96.35	3.72	0.54
✓	✓		✓	91.88	86.14	10.26	1.80	97.85	95.82	3.87	0.58
✓	✓	✓		89.41	82.57	12.03	2.64	97.14	94.49	5.92	0.82
✓	✓	✓	✓	**92.72**	**87.01**	**7.76**	**1.58**	**98.39**	**96.84**	**3.11**	**0.40**

For RV segmentation, we demonstrate the significance of the two attention modules via ablation studies as well, the results of which are tabulated in Table 3. It is evident that the performance degrades when removing either SAM or CAM. Specifically, the Dice score decreases by 0.24% and 0.15% on OCTA_6M and decreases by 0.12% and 0.33% on OCTA_3M when removing CAM and SAM.

Table 3. The importance of the two attention modules for RV segmentation.

Method	OCTA_6M				OCTA_3M			
	Dice	Jaccard	HD	ASSD	Dice	Jaccard	HD	ASSD
w/o SAM&CAM	89.09 ± 2.57	80.43 ± 3.98	5.25 ± 3.94	0.68 ±0.30	87.65 ± 3.99	78.21 ± 5.75	8.58 ± 7.99	0.81 ± 0.50
w/o CAM	88.91 ± 2.59	80.13 ± 3.98	5.54 ± 4.08	0.70 ± 0.34	91.56 ± 2.25	84.50 ± 3.63	2.91 ± 2.76	0.47 ± 0.28
w/o SAM	89.00 ± 2.67	80.29 ± 4.10	5.42 ± 4.62	0.70 ± 0.35	91.35 ± 2.21	84.15 ± 3.56	3.44 ± 4.25	0.52 ± 0.33
Ours (w SAM&CAM)	**89.15 ± 2.39**	**80.50 ± 3.75**	**4.47 ± 3.73**	**0.61 ± 0.28**	**91.68 ± 2.05**	**84.70 ± 3.34**	**2.78 ± 2.67**	**0.44 ± 0.25**

The influence of the number of the refining models is also explored. The corresponding result is shown in Table 4. We observe that the one with 3 refining models achieves relatively good performance and has reasonable model complexity. The one with 2 refining models has lots of false positives or false negatives to be corrected and that with 4 refining models has a serious overfitting issue by misclassifying many interference structures as RV.

Table 4. The effect of the number of refining models for RV segmentation.

RV	OCTA_6M				OCTA_3M			
Method	Dice	Jaccard	HD	ASSD	Dice	Jaccard	HD	ASSD
2 refining models	88.96 ± 2.60	80.21 ± 4.02	5.37 ± 3.84	0.69 ± 0.30	91.26 ± 2.20	83.99 ± 3.55	3.49 ± 3.61	0.49 ± 0.29
3 refining models	**89.15 ± 2.39**	**80.50 ± 3.75**	**4.47 ± 3.73**	**0.61 ± 0.28**	**91.68 ± 2.05**	**84.70 ± 3.34**	2.78 ± 2.67	**0.44 ± 0.25**
4 refining models	88.99 ± 2.72	80.26 ± 4.16	5.72 ± 4.55	0.71 ± 0.37	91.53 ± 2.21	84.46 ± 3.56	**2.76 ± 2.98**	0.45 ± 0.30

4   Conclusion

In this work, we proposed and validated a novel framework for simultaneously segmenting FAZ and RV from OCTA images. For FAZ, we proposed a joint segmentation network with RV segmentation as an auxiliary task and ResNeSt with split attention as the encoder. Center ROI extraction and ImageNet pretraining were also employed for further improvements. For RV, we designed a coarse-to-fine flow with two attention modules to refine the RV segmentation results step by step. Based on extensive quantitative and qualitative experiments, the proposed method was found to be competitive or even better than representative SOTA segmentation methods, including the methods from the authors of the OCTA-500 dataset utilizing both 3D OCTA volumes and 2D OCTA images, particularly for the FAZ segmentation.

References

1. Abràmoff, M.D., Garvin, M.K., Sonka, M.: Retinal imaging and image analysis. IEEE Rev. Biomed. Eng. **3**, 169–208 (2010)
2. Ang, M., et al.: Optical coherence tomography angiography: a review of current and future clinical applications. Graefes Arch. Clin. Exp. Ophthalmol. **256**(2), 237–245 (2018). https://doi.org/10.1007/s00417-017-3896-2
3. Chen, L.-C., Zhu, Y., Papandreou, G., Schroff, F., Adam, H.: Encoder-decoder with atrous separable convolution for semantic image segmentation. In: Ferrari, V., Hebert, M., Sminchisescu, C., Weiss, Y. (eds.) ECCV 2018. LNCS, vol. 11211, pp. 833–851. Springer, Cham (2018). https://doi.org/10.1007/978-3-030-01234-2_49
4. Cheng, K.K., et al.: Macular vessel density, branching complexity and foveal avascular zone size in normal tension glaucoma. Sci. Rep. **11**(1), 1–9 (2021)
5. Deng, W., Tamplin, M.R., Grumbach, I.M., Kardon, R.H., Garvin, M.K.: Region-based segmentation of capillary density in optical coherence tomography angiography. In: Fu, H., Garvin, M.K., MacGillivray, T., Xu, Y., Zheng, Y. (eds.) OMIA 2019. LNCS, vol. 11855, pp. 18–25. Springer, Cham (2019). https://doi.org/10.1007/978-3-030-32956-3_3
6. Díaz, M., Novo, J., Cutrín, P., Gómez-Ulla, F., Penedo, M.G., Ortega, M.: Automatic segmentation of the foveal avascular zone in ophthalmological OCT-A images. PLoS ONE **14**(2), e0212364 (2019)
7. Eladawi, N., et al.: Automatic blood vessels segmentation based on different retinal maps from OCTA scans. Comput. Biol. Med. **89**, 150–161 (2017)
8. Fu, H., Xu, Y., Lin, S., Kee Wong, D.W., Liu, J.: DeepVessel: retinal vessel segmentation via deep learning and conditional random field. In: Ourselin, S., Joskowicz, L., Sabuncu, M.R., Unal, G., Wells, W. (eds.) MICCAI 2016. LNCS, vol. 9901, pp. 132–139. Springer, Cham (2016). https://doi.org/10.1007/978-3-319-46723-8_16
9. Fu, J., et al.: Dual attention network for scene segmentation. In: Proceedings of the IEEE/CVF Conference on Computer Vision and Pattern Recognition, pp. 3146–3154 (2019)
10. Klein, R., Myers, C.E., Lee, K.E., Gangnon, R., Klein, B.E.: Changes in retinal vessel diameter and incidence and progression of diabetic retinopathy. Arch. Ophthalmol. **130**(6), 749–755 (2012)

11. Koskosas, A., Muldrew, K., Patton, W., Topouzis, F., Chakravarthy, U.: Foveal avascular zone (FAZ) area in aging and age related macular degeneration (AMD). Investig. Ophthalmol. Vis. Sci. **50**(13), 948 (2009)

12. Li, L., Verma, M., Nakashima, Y., Nagahara, H., Kawasaki, R.: IterNet: retinal image segmentation utilizing structural redundancy in vessel networks. In: The IEEE Winter Conference on Applications of Computer Vision (WACV), March 2020

13. Li, M., et al.: Image projection network: 3d to 2d image segmentation in OCTA images. IEEE Trans. Med. Imaging **39**(11), 3343–3354 (2020)

14. Li, M., et al.: IPN-V2 and OCTA-500: methodology and dataset for retinal image segmentation. arXiv preprint arXiv:2012.07261 (2020)

15. Liu, H., Wong, D.W.K., Fu, H., Xu, Y., Liu, J.: DeepAMD: detect early age-related macular degeneration by applying deep learning in a multiple instance learning framework. In: Jawahar, C.V., Li, H., Mori, G., Schindler, K. (eds.) ACCV 2018. LNCS, vol. 11365, pp. 625–640. Springer, Cham (2019). https://doi.org/10.1007/978-3-030-20873-8_40

16. Ma, Y., et al.: ROSE: a retinal OCT-angiography vessel segmentation dataset and new model. IEEE Trans. Med. Imaging **40**(3), 928–939 (2020)

17. Mou, L., et al.: CS-Net: channel and spatial attention network for curvilinear structure segmentation. In: Shen, D., et al. (eds.) MICCAI 2019. LNCS, vol. 11764, pp. 721–730. Springer, Cham (2019). https://doi.org/10.1007/978-3-030-32239-7_80

18. Mou, L., et al.: CS2-Net: deep learning segmentation of curvilinear structures in medical imaging. Med. Image Anal. **67**, 101874 (2021)

19. Pratt, H., Coenen, F., Broadbent, D.M., Harding, S.P., Zheng, Y.: Convolutional neural networks for diabetic retinopathy. Proc. Comput. Sci. **90**, 200–205 (2016)

20. Ronneberger, O., Fischer, P., Brox, T.: U-Net: convolutional networks for biomedical image segmentation. In: Navab, N., Hornegger, J., Wells, W.M., Frangi, A.F. (eds.) MICCAI 2015. LNCS, vol. 9351, pp. 234–241. Springer, Cham (2015). https://doi.org/10.1007/978-3-319-24574-4_28

21. Spaide, R.F., Fujimoto, J.G., Waheed, N.K., Sadda, S.R., Staurenghi, G.: Optical coherence tomography angiography. Prog. Retin. Eye Res. **64**, 1–55 (2018)

22. Yip, V.C., et al.: Optical coherence tomography angiography of optic disc and macula vessel density in glaucoma and healthy eyes. J. Glaucoma **28**(1), 80–87 (2019)

23. Zhang, H., et al.: RESNest: split-attention networks. arXiv preprint arXiv:2004.08955 (2020)

24. Zhang, S., et al.: Attention guided network for retinal image segmentation. In: Shen, D., et al. (eds.) MICCAI 2019. LNCS, vol. 11764, pp. 797–805. Springer, Cham (2019). https://doi.org/10.1007/978-3-030-32239-7_88

25. Zhao, H., Shi, J., Qi, X., Wang, X., Jia, J.: Pyramid scene parsing network. In: Proceedings of the IEEE Conference on Computer Vision and Pattern Recognition, pp. 2881–2890 (2017)

26. Zheng, Y., Gandhi, J.S., Stangos, A.N., Campa, C., Broadbent, D.M., Harding, S.P.: Automated segmentation of foveal avascular zone in fundus fluorescein angiography. Invest. Ophthalmol. Vis. Sci. **51**(7), 3653–3659 (2010)

27. Zhou, Z., Rahman Siddiquee, M.M., Tajbakhsh, N., Liang, J.: UNet++: a nested U-Net architecture for medical image segmentation. In: Stoyanov, D., et al. (eds.) DLMIA/ML-CDS 2018. LNCS, vol. 11045, pp. 3–11. Springer, Cham (2018). https://doi.org/10.1007/978-3-030-00889-5_1

CDLRS: Collaborative Deep Learning Model with Joint Regression and Segmentation for Automatic Fovea Localization

Ziyang Chen[1], Yongsheng Pan[1,2(✉)], and Yong Xia[1(✉)]

[1] National Engineering Laboratory for Integrated Aero-Space-Ground-Ocean Big Data Application Technology, School of Computer Science and Engineering, Northwestern Polytechnical University, Xi'an 710072, China
yspan@mail.nwpu.edu.cn, yxia@nwpu.edu.cn
[2] School of Biomedical and Engineering, ShanghaiTech University, Shanghai 201210, China

Abstract. With the development of information technology, eyes are easily overworked for modern people, which increases the burden of ophthalmologists. This leads to the urgent need of the computer-aided early screening system for vision examination, where the color fundus photography (CFP) is the most economical and noninvasive fundus examination of ophthalmology. The macula, whose center (i.e., fovea) is the most sensitive part of vision, is an important area in fundus images since lesions on it often lead to decreased vision. As macula is usually difficult to identify in a fundus image, automated methods for fovea localization can help a doctor or a screening system quickly determine whether there are macular lesions. However, most localization methods usually can not give realistic locations for fovea with acceptable biases in a large-scale fundus image. To address this issue, we proposed a two-stage framework for accurate fovea localization, where the first stage resorts traditional image processing to roughly find a candidate region of the macula in each fundus image while the second stage resorts a collaborative neural network to obtain a finer location on the candidate region. Experimental results on the dataset of REFUGE2 Challenge suggest that our algorithms can localize fovea accurately and achieve advanced performance, which is potentially useful in practice.

Keywords: Macula · Fovea · Fundus image · Object localization · Collaborative learning · REFUGE2

1 Introduction

Age-related macular degeneration is one of the most common diseases, which can cause vision loss and has become a growing public health concern in the United States [1]. Under normal circumstances, checking the visual ability of the macular area is an important part of human vision examination. The fovea

© Springer Nature Switzerland AG 2021
H. Fu et al. (Eds.): OMIA 2021, LNCS 12970, pp. 52–61, 2021.
https://doi.org/10.1007/978-3-030-87000-3_6

is the most sensitive part of vision and is an important indicator of macular area [6]. So, it is important to find where the fovea is.

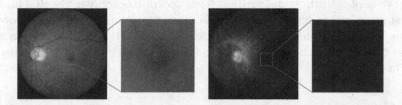

Fig. 1. Illustration of fundus images. The image on the left is easy to find where macula is, but the right one is difficult because of bad illumination.

Currently, color fundus photography (CFP) is the most economical and non-invasive fundus examination of ophthalmology [15]. However, due to the influence of illumination, instruments and fundus lesions, the macular area is sometimes difficult to distinguish (as examples shown in Fig. 1). The detection of fovea on colored fundus images is a time-consuming and subjective process. An automated fovea localization method can help doctors quickly determine whether there are macular lesions [18].

Recently, some efforts on computer-aided fovea localization have been devoted based on machine learning and traditional image processing techniques [2,4,9,11,14,20–22]. Previous work for fovea detection can be divided into three groups. The first group extract the vessels and localize fovea by the density and shape of vessels [2,4,14,22]. The vascular density around the fovea is usually the minimum in the fundus image and only some small vessels can penetrate fovea's perimeter. This fact is used to detect fovea's position in these methods. The second group do not extract the vessels but extract the image features with traditional methods [9,20], such as texture features and intensity features. These methods regard the fovea area as a circular and dark area relative to its surrounding area and use this as a prior condition to resist the interference of unbalanced illumination. But designing features manually is cumbersome, not robust and also easily affected by image quality. With the development of deep learning, the third group [11,21] attempt to use the neural network to localize the fovea. However, most of these methods can only find a rough location, which may be because they abandon the traditional image pre-processing. For example, it is unrealistic to input the whole image into a neural network as the fundus images usually have large sizes (e.g., $1,940 \times 1,940$) which may not only cost more computation resources but also withstand a fine location regression. In such situation, a more realistic strategy is to first (1) roughly but fast extract a small ROI around the object location and then (2) input the ROI to a neural network to obtain a fine location.

In this paper, we proposed a two-stage framework for accurate fovea localization with above considerations. Specifically, in the first stage, we resort traditional image processing, to roughly find an ROI of the macula in each fundus image. This stage is only executed once, thus is simple and efficient. In the second stage, we obtain a finer location by a neural network with collaborative learning of a regression task and a pseudo segmentation task. The neural network intently extracts complex features and predicts fovea coordinates only in the ROI found in the first stage and utilizes a simultaneous segmentation task to help improve the performance. Experimental results on the dataset of REFUGE2 Challenge [15] suggest that our algorithms can localize fovea accurately and achieve advanced performance.

2   Materials

The REFUGE2 [15] Challenge dataset[1] is a public dataset of retinal fundus. This dataset contains $1,600$ fundus images, where $1,200$ images were released in Phase-1 with manual annotations of the fovea locations and 400 were released in Phase-2 with holding the annotations for online validation. The images in Phase-1 are with three different sizes, i.e., $2,124 \times 2,056$, $1,634 \times 1,634$, $1,940 \times 1,940$ while those in Phase-2 are all with size of $1,940 \times 1,940$. The official evaluation metric (Euclidean distance, ED) is calculated as follows:

$$ED\left(X, Y\right) = \frac{1}{n} \sum_{i}^{n} \|X_i - Y_i\|_2 \tag{1}$$

where vectors X_i and Y_i with length of 2 denote the predicted location and the groundtruth of the i-th image, respectively.

3   Method

We proposed a two-stage framework for accurate fovea localization. In the first stage, we resort traditional image processing as flowchart in Fig. 2, to roughly find an ROI of the macula in each fundus image. In the second stage, we train a fine localization model under the collaboration of multiple tasks.

Stage 1–Roughly Macula Detection: This stage has two steps. In the first step, we take a manner to suppress the blood vessel, which may cause interfering information [4], by removing the high frequency part since it contains most blood vessels as shown in Fig. 3. We conducted all the following study in the green channel of each image according to the fact that the macula is more visible in the green channel. We transform the image into frequency domain via fast fourier transform (FFT) [8] and split it into high and low frequency part and then transform the low frequency part (within 0.02 times the height (H) and width (W) of a frequency-domain image) back to image space via inverse FFT. After that, we apply the contrast limited adaptive histogram equalization

---

[1] https://refuge.grand-challenge.org/.

(CLAHE) [19] to each image to weaken the impact of noise and light. In this step, we can remove most of the interference and enhance the part of interest. Compared with other methods of removing blood vessels, our method is faster and more effective, will not eliminate other useful area by mistake.

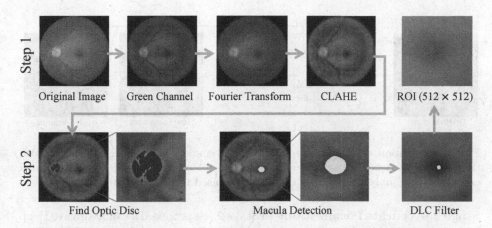

Fig. 2. Pipeline of our proposed image processing. Step 1: suppress the blood vessels. Step 2: locate the macula roughly.

In the second step of Stage 1, we locate the macula in each fundus image roughly according to the clinical knowledge, as the fovea is usually a dark spot in the center of macula and its distance to the optic disc is about 5 times the radius of the optic disc [12]. Therefore, we then find the optic disc which is usually the maximum and brightest connected region in an image, and find the macula with distance to optic disc between 3−8 times the radius of optic disc. We use a sliding window with size of 600×600 to get the rough regions of optic disc and macula. For optic disc, we first segment the original image by a threshold which equals the 0.75 times of the maximum intensity of an image. This thresholding can get a segmentation with most optic disc area and a few other parts (as shown in Fig. 2), where we select the window with the maximum segmentation region and re-segment it by a threshold which is the 0.75 times the maximum intensity of the selected window. Then, we calculate the height and center of the segmentation region as the diameter and center of the optic disc. This step is simple, fast, and effective. We then select the macula from those windows, each of which has eligible distance to the optic disc and average intensity larger than the average intensity of its inner center region (100 × 100). If there are more than one eligible windows, the window with the maximum intensity difference between inner and outer regions is selected. Because the blood vessels are strips and the macula is round, the weight of each window's inner center region is enhanced to distinguish blood vessels and macula. The macula is segmented by using the average value of the average intensity and the minimum intensity as the thresholding value. Finally, the candidate macula region is further screened by directional local contrast (DLC) filter [23], which can shrink the candidate region of fovea (in macula), and remove those unqualified single spots. We regard the qualified spots as the center, and cut out the ROI (512×512). This process is without training and learnable parameters, the final ROI can contain all the macula area. In the testing phase, the detecting rate of our processing algorithm is 100%.

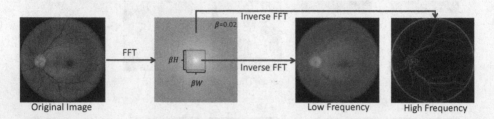

Fig. 3. Illustration of our proposed method to remove blood vessels. It can be seen that the high frequency part contains almost all blood vessels and even some small endings. Hence, only the low frequency image is used to find the optic disc.

Stage 2–Accurate Localization: In Stage 2, we proposed a Collaborative Deep Learning model with joint Regression task and Segmentation task (CDLRS) for accurate fovea localization around the macula center. The model uptakes both the structure of PyConvResNet-50 [7] and U-Net [17], where the former focuses on the coordinate regression task and the latter focuses on the segmentation task.

As illustrated in Fig. 4, our CDLRS have three modules, including a feature extraction module ($\mathbf{F}$) to extract features from each input image, a regression module ($\mathbf{R}$) to regress the fovea location with extracted features, and a segmentation module ($\mathbf{S}$) to segment a pseudo mask of the macula center. The modules $\mathbf{F}$ and $\mathbf{R}$ share the same structure with PyConvResNet-50 [7] while module $\mathbf{S}$ shares same structure with the decoder part (i.e., U-Net [17]). Namely, $\mathbf{F}$ consists of 1 convolutional layer and 4 pyramid convolutional (i.e., pyconv) blocks, the last two blocks are both constructed with dropblock as a kind of regularization to avoid over-fit problem. $\mathbf{R}$ consists of a global average pooling layer and 3 fully connected layers, while $\mathbf{S}$ consists of 5 deconvolutional layers and 6 convolutional layers. To recover the resolution downsampled by the first layer of PyConvResNet-50, an additional convolutional layer is used to provide non-downsampled features to the last layer of module $\mathbf{S}$. We utilize the last feature map of $\mathbf{F}$ to complete such two tasks, so as to let the segmentation branch help ameliorate the regression branch.

After Stage 1, a rough region of the macula center has been detected from each fundus image. Thus, in Stage 2, our CDLRS focuses only on the macula center, i.e., we crop a patch of 128×128 around the macula center with random shift within $[-32, 32]$ in both X-axis and Y-axis. This patch is then is random augmented by horizontal flip, vertical flip, and random-angle rotation. For the regression task, the location of fovea is synchronously computed with the augmentation process. For the segmentation task, the pseudo mask is a span with radius of 30 pixels centered at the location of fovea.

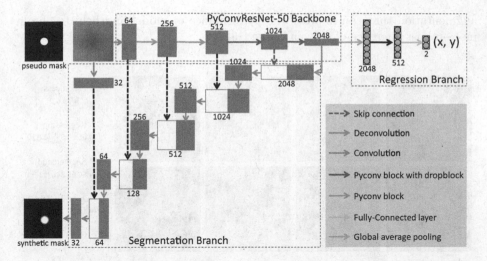

Fig. 4. Architecture of proposed CDLRS model. PyConvResNet-50 [7] is used as our backbone with adding dropblock after the 3rd and 4th pyconv-blocks. The regression branch consists of three fully-connected layers with "tanh" activation in the last layer while the segmentation branch concatenates the feature maps in a U-Net [17] form.

While training the proposed CDLRS, We resort the MAE loss and Euclidean distance loss to guide the regression task and resort the dice loss and cross entropy loss to guide the segmentation task. Namely, the loss function for regression task is

$$L_r = \frac{1}{n} \sum_i^n \left(\|\hat{P}_i - P_i\| + \|\hat{P}_i - P_i\|_2 \right), \qquad (2)$$

where P_* is ground-truth coordinate and $\hat{P}_*$ is the predicted coordinate obtained by the regression module. The loss function for segmentation task (denoted as L_{seg}) is

$$L_s = \frac{1}{n} \sum_i^n \left(1 - \frac{2\left|M_i \cap \hat{M}_i\right| + 1}{|M_i| + \left|\hat{M}_i\right| + 1} + \log\left(1 - \hat{M}_i\right) - M_i \log \frac{\hat{M}_i}{1 - \hat{M}_i} \right). \qquad (3)$$

where M_* is the pseudo span mask and $\hat{M}_*$ is the predicted mask obtained by the module. Therefore, the total loss of our CDLRS is $L - L_r \mid \beta L_s$, where β is an equilibrium coefficient and is set to 0.8 in our experiments according to the validation in the training set.

For the test set, we do the same crop and augmentation for each image (random shift $[-32, 32]$ pixels (50 times), with/without left-right flip, with/without up-down flip, with/without 90° rotation), thus, we have 400 patches for each image. The fovea location of each input patch is calculated as the average of the center of the synthetic mask and the regression result and the overall fovea location of each image is the average of these patches. This is a kind of test-time augmentation that can improve the performance of model and help to obtain more robust inference of a given image [13].

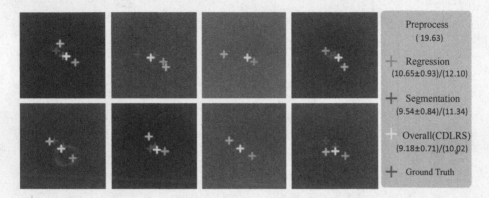

Fig. 5. Effort of these three parts (preprocession, regression, and segmentation) in CDLRS to fovea localization. The left part are the results for eight typical images while the right part is the quantified results on training and test phase.

4   Experiments and Results

We performed two groups of experiments in this work. In the first group, we evaluated the contribution of each major components. In the second group, we compared our CDLRS with some state-of-the-art localization methods as well as some results on the semi-final leaderboard of REFUGE2. On the first and second group of experiments, we randomly split these 1200 images of training phase in five parts and conducted 5-fold cross-validation. Hence, we have five well-trained models in total. While applying to these 400 images of test phase, the predicted locations of these five models on each image are averaged as the final prediction of this image. The average euclidean distance on test phase is obtained by submission the prediction to the REFUGE2 challenge platform. All our experiments are conducted in Python with Pytorch library on a Linux platform with a NVIDIA GTX 1080Ti GPU and an Intel i5-7200U CPU. Our CDLRS is trained 100 epochs via the SGD optimizer with momentum $= 0.9$, initial learning rate $= 0.0003$, batch size $= 64$. We also use cosine annealing to update the learning rate.

Ablation Study: In the first group, we compared the localization ability of the major stages of our algorithm, including the preprocessing step, the segmentation branch, and the regression branch. The results of these three part as well as the overall performance by their joint efforts and the ground truth are illustrated in Fig. 5. The left part visualized some results for eight typical images while the right part provided the quantified results of the 5-fold cross-validation and on the test phase, which are denoted as $(* * \pm * *)$ and $(**)$, respectively.

From Fig. 5, it could be found that the preprocessing step can provide a rough location for the fovea which could be further promoted by our CDLRS. Meanwhile, the segmentation module achieves results slightly better than the regression module, while the overall results is even better than both of them. It suggests that even a pseudo mask can provide the model abundant supervision information and obtain more robust results. Altogether, our CDLRS is an efficient system with strong localization ability, thus is potentially very useful in practice.

Compare with Other Methods: In the second group, we compared the localization ability of our CDLRS with four state-of-the-art methods, including Mask R-CNN [10], Faster R-CNN [16], YOLOv4 [3], and DETR [5]. All these competing methods resort the same preprocessing step and test-time augmentation with our CDLRS to make a fair comparison. Results are list in Table 1, where we reports both the results of the 5-fold cross-validation on train phase and the results on the test phase for all methods. And we also do the statistical test and calculate the p-value to verify that our method is significant on the results of training phase. From Table 1, two observations can be found. (1) Our CDLRS achieves the lowest mean ED on both phase than other methods, which implies the superiority of our CDLRS in fovea localization. And our CDLRS is significantly better than other methods from the result of statistical test. (2) These methods (CDLRS, Mask R-CNN) with two branches consistently outperform those (Faster R-CNN, YOLOv4, DETR) with single branch. It suggests that resorting a segmentation branch can help improve the performance in localization task, even if the referred segmentation mask is pseudo. The potential reason may be that using a region other than a dot can provide more information, thus is more robust to unexpected annotation error and prediction bias. We also reports some results derived from the semi-final leaderboard of REFUGE2[2] in Table 1, where we can see that our result is between the 5th and 6th and only has a small gap (1.61) to the 1st one.

Table 1. The results of comparision with other state-of-the-art methods on object detection. All of these methods are tuned to fit the localization task. In each block of training phase, the first line is mean ± std and the second line is the maximum value.

	Ours	Mask R-CNN [10]	Faster R-CNN [16]	YOLOv4 [3]	DETR [5]
Training phase	9.18 ± 0.71	9.57 ± 0.69	9.87 ± 1.08	10.02 ± 0.72	10.30 ± 1.45
	9.89	10.51	11.65	11.26	11.83
(p-Value)	\	1.94×10^{-5}	6.52×10^{-3}	7.66×10^{-4}	1.74×10^{-3}
Final phase	**10.02**	10.98	11.57	11.45	11.90
Methods on leaderboard	MAI (1st): 8.41 lip_frog (5th): 9.99 cheeron (6th): 10.08				

---

[2] https://refuge.grand-challenge.org/Semi_final_Leaderboards/.

5   Conclusion

In this paper, we proposed a two-stage framework for accurate fovea localization. Specifically, in the first stage, we resort traditional image processing to roughly find a candidate region of the macula in each fundus image. In the second stage, we proposed the CDLRS for accurate fovea localization around the macula center. This framework achieved acceptable euclidean distance on fovea localization task of REFUGE2, which may be useful in practice. In this task, the pseudo mask considers that the fovea in reality is not a single spot but an area. It is reasonable that regarding it as a segmentation task and a coordinate regression task can help model pay more attention to the center of fovea. This is why we use a collaborative deep learning method to solve this problem. Our future work will attempt to build hierarchical cascade framework and uptake domain adaption techniques to result finer and more accurate localization.

Acknowledgments. This work was supported in part by the China Postdoctoral Science Foundation under Grants BX2021333, and in part by the National Natural Science Foundation of China under Grants 61771397.

References

1. Abràmoff, M.D., Garvin, M.K., Sonka, M.: Retinal imaging and image analysis. IEEE Rev. Biomed. Eng. **3**, 169–208 (2010)
2. Asim, K.M., Basit, A., Jalil, A.: Detection and localization of fovea in human retinal fundus images. In: International Conference on Emerging Technologies, pp. 1–5. ICET (2012)
3. Bochkovskiy, A., Wang, C.Y., Liao, H.Y.M.: YOLOv4: optimal speed and accuracy of object detection. arXiv preprint. arXiv:2004.10934 (2020)
4. Budai, A., Mogalle, K., Brost, A., Hornegger, J., Michelson, G.: Automatic fovea localization in fundus images. Bildverarbeitung für die Medizin, pp. 114–119 (2014)
5. Carion, N., Massa, F., Synnaeve, G., Usunier, N., Kirillov, A., Zagoruyko, S.: End-to-end object detection with transformers. In: Vedaldi, A., Bischof, H., Brox, T., Frahm, J.M. (eds.) ECCV 2020. LNCS, vol. 12346, pp. 213–229. Springer, Cham (2020). https://doi.org/10.1007/978-3-030-58452-8_13
6. Chung, S.T.: Reading in the presence of macular disease: a mini-review. Ophthalmic Physiol. Opt. **40**(2), 171–186 (2020)
7. Duta, I.C., Liu, L., Zhu, F., Shao, L.: Pyramidal convolution: rethinking convolutional neural networks for visual recognition. arXiv preprint. arXiv:2006.11538 (2020)
8. Frigo, M., Johnson, S.G.: FFTW: an adaptive software architecture for the FFT. In: IEEE International Conference on Acoustics, Speech and Signal Processing, vol. 3, pp. 1381–1384. IEEE (1998)
9. Guo, X., Wang, H., Lu, X., Hu, X., Che, S., Lu, Y.: Robust fovea localization based on symmetry measure. IEEE J. Biomed. Health Inform. **24**(8), 2315–2326 (2020)
10. He, K., Gkioxari, G., Dollar, P., Girshick, R.: Mask R-CNN. IEEE Trans. Pattern Anal. Mach. Intell. **42**(2), 386–397 (2018)
11. Huang, Y., Zhong, Z., Yuan, J., Tang, X.: Efficient and robust optic disc detection and fovea localization using region proposal network and cascaded network. Biomed. Sig. Process. Control **60**, 101939 (2020)

12. Li, H., Chutatape, O.: Automated feature extraction in color retinal images by a model based approach. IEEE Trans. Bio-Med. Eng. **51**, 246–54 (2004)

13. Moshkov, N., Mathe, B., Kertesz-Farkas, A., Hollandi, R., Horvath, P.: Test-time augmentation for deep learning-based cell segmentation on microscopy images. Sci. Rep. **10**(1), 5068 (2020)

14. Niemeijer, M., Abramoff, M., Van Ginneken, B.: Automated localization of the optic disc and the fovea. In: 30th Annual International Conference of the IEEE Engineering in Medicine and Biology Society, pp. 3538–3541 (2008)

15. Orlando, J.I., et al.: Refuge challenge: a unified framework for evaluating automated methods for glaucoma assessment from fundus photographs. Med. Image Anal. **59**, 101570 (2020)

16. Ren, S., He, K., Girshick, R., Sun, J.: Faster R-CNN: towards real-time object detection with region proposal networks. IEEE Trans. Pattern Anal. Mach. Intell. **39**(6), 1137–1149 (2017)

17. Ronneberger, O., Fischer, P., Brox, T.: U-net: convolutional networks for biomedical image segmentation. In: Navab, N., Hornegger, J., Wells, W., Frangi, A. (eds.) MICCAI 2015. LNCS, vol. 9351, pp. 234–241. Springer, Cham (2015). https://doi.org/10.1007/978-3-319-24574-4_28

18. Sekhar, S., Abd El-Samie, F.E., Yu, P., Al-Nuaimy, W., Nandi, A.K.: Automated localization of retinal features. Appl. Opt. **50**(19), 3064–3075 (2011)

19. Stark, J.A.: Adaptive image contrast enhancement using generalizations of histogram equalization. IEEE Trans. Image Process. **9**(5), 889–896 (2000)

20. Xiao, Z.T., et al.: Automatic localization of macula fovea based on wavelet transformation and gray contours. J. Med. Imaging Health Inform. **5**(8), 1816–1820 (2015)

21. Xie, R., et al.: End-to-end fovea localisation in colour fundus images with a hierarchical deep regression network. IEEE Trans. Med. Imaging **40**(1), 116–128 (2021)

22. Ying, H., Liu, J.C.: Automated localization of macula-fovea area on retina images using blood vessel network topology. In: IEEE International Conference on Acoustics, Speech and Signal Processing, pp. 650–653 (2010)

23. Zhang, M., Liu, J.C.: Directional local contrast based blood vessel detection in retinal images. In: IEEE International Conference on Image Processing, vol. 4, pp. IV-317–320. IEEE (2007)

U-Net with Hierarchical Bottleneck Attention for Landmark Detection in Fundus Images of the Degenerated Retina

Shuyun Tang, Ziming Qi, Jacob Granley, and Michael Beyeler[✉]

University of California, Santa Barbara, CA 93106, USA
{shuyun,zimingqi,jgranley,mbeyeler}@ucsb.edu

Abstract. Fundus photography has routinely been used to document the presence and severity of retinal degenerative diseases such as age-related macular degeneration (AMD), glaucoma, and diabetic retinopathy (DR) in clinical practice, for which the fovea and optic disc (OD) are important retinal landmarks. However, the occurrence of lesions, drusen, and other retinal abnormalities during retinal degeneration severely complicates automatic landmark detection and segmentation. Here we propose HBA-U-Net: a U-Net backbone enriched with hierarchical bottleneck attention. The network consists of a novel bottleneck attention block that combines and refines self-attention, channel attention, and relative-position attention to highlight retinal abnormalities that may be important for fovea and OD segmentation in the degenerated retina. HBA-U-Net achieved state-of-the-art results on fovea detection across datasets and eye conditions (ADAM: Euclidean distance (ED) of 25.4 pixels, REFUGE: 32.5 pixels, IDRiD: 32.1 pixels), on OD segmentation for AMD (ADAM: Dice coefficient (DC) of 0.947), and on OD detection for DR (IDRiD: ED of 20.5 pixels). We further validated the design of our network with an ablation study. Our results suggest that HBA-U-Net may be well suited for landmark detection in the presence of a variety of retinal degenerative diseases.

Keywords: Deep learning · Landmark detection · Segmentation · Self-attention · Fundus · Fovea · Optic disc · Retinal degeneration · Age-related macular degeneration · Diabetic retinopathy · Glaucoma

1 Introduction

Age-related macular degeneration (AMD), glaucoma, and diabetic retinopathy (DR) are three of the most common causes of blindness in the world [2]. Fundus photography has routinely been used to document the presence and severity of these retinal degenerative diseases in clinical practice. Among the landmarks of interest are the fovea, which is a small depression in the macula, and the optic disc (OD), which is where the optic nerve and blood vessels leave the retina.

H. Fu et al. (Eds.): OMIA 2021, LNCS 12970, pp. 62–71, 2021.
https://doi.org/10.1007/978-3-030-87000-3_7

However, detecting retinal abnormalities associated with these diseases (e.g., drusen in AMD, hemorrhage in DR) is a labor-intensive and time-consuming process, thus necessitating the need for automated fundus image analysis.

In recent years, numerous methods have been proposed for retinal structure detection. Jiang et al. [7] proposed an encoder-decoder network with deep residual structure and recursive learning mechanism for robust OD localization, followed by an end-to-end region-based convolutional neural network (R-CNN) for joint optic disc and cup segmentation [8]. Similarly, numerous studies have employed various convolutional neural network (CNN) models for fovea localization (e.g., [1,15]). Although fovea and OD are spatially correlated with each other, only a few studies (e.g., [10,22]) have focused on joint fovea and OD segmentation. Furthermore, models trained on healthy eyes tend not to generalize well to diseased eyes due to retinal abnormalities. A notable exception is Kamble et al. [9] who achieved state-of-the-art (SOTA) performance on landmark detection for AMD and glaucoma using a modified U-Net++ with an EfficientNet encoder. However, there is potential merit in combining convolutional backbone networks with attentional mechanisms [19] to highlight retinal abnormalities that may be important for landmark detection in the degenerated retina.

To develop a segmentation model that is well suited for retinal degeneration, we propose HBA-U-Net: a U-Net backbone enriched with hierarchical bottleneck attention. The main contributions of this work are:

1. We propose a hierarchical bottleneck attention (HBA) block: a novel attention mechanism that combines and refines self-attention [19], channel attention [21], and relative-position attention [13] to highlight retinal abnormalities important for landmark detection in the degenerated retina.
2. We integrate the HBA block into bottleneck skip connections across all layers of a U-Net backbone network to form HBA-U-Net, and test the network's performance on three benchmark datasets for retinal degeneration: ADAM [4] for AMD, REFUGE [11] for glaucoma, and IDRiD [12] for DR.
3. We validate the design of HBA-U-Net with an ablation study.
4. We demonstrate SOTA performance on fovea detection across datasets and eye conditions, on OD segmentation for AMD, and on OD detection for DR.

2   Methods

2.1   Model Architecture

HBA-U-Net. The proposed network architecture is illustrated in Fig. 1. First, ImageNet pretrained ResNet-50 blocks were used as encoders to obtain feature maps at different spatial resolutions. These feature maps, along with the original image, were then fed into a modified U-Net structure [10,14] with HBA blocks added to skip connections. The outputs of the HBA blocks were up-sampled and aggregated to produce the final fovea and OD segmentation mask.

Our goal was to incorporate HBA blocks into the U-Net without drastically increasing the computational complexity. Consistent with [16], we noticed that adding a self-attention mechanism to the bottleneck layers (a shrinking path, the

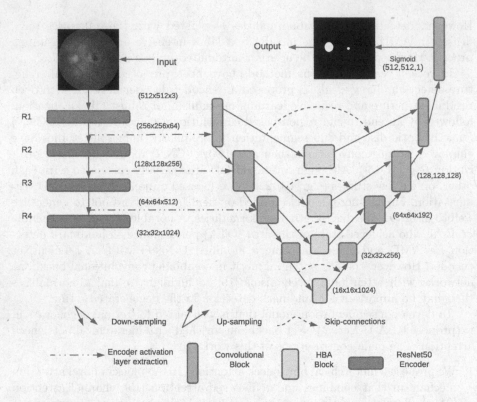

Fig. 1. HBA-U-Net architecture. A U-Net enriched with a novel attention block and re-designed skip-connection paths jointly locates the fovea and segments the optic disc. ResNet-50 was used as encoder. Note that the number of local bottlenecks and the down/up-sampling projection rate depends on the image dimensions.

attention module, and an expanding path) significantly boosted the network's performance. However, the original U-Net contains only a single bottleneck layer (between the last down-sampling block and the first up-sampling block). To incorporate multiple HBA blocks into the network, we therefore re-designed the U-Net by creating local bottleneck structures in each skip-connection pair (see Fig. 1). After each down-convolution block, the features were down-sampled by pooling and passed to the HBA block, followed by up-sampling to the original size. In this way, the pairs of down/up-sampling convolution blocks could be treated as local bottleneck structures operating at different spatial resolutions.

HBA Block. Recently, attention mechanisms have seen widespread adoption in various tasks [19]. Inspired by [16,21], our HBA block (Fig. 2) consisted of channel, content, and relative-position attention modules, each described in detail below. We denote the query, key, value, input feature map, relative height logit, and relative weight logit as q, k, v, F, R_h, R_w, respectively.

In the proposed HBA block, content attention (blue box in Fig. 2) attended to individual pixels in each spatial feature map. For each attention head, dense

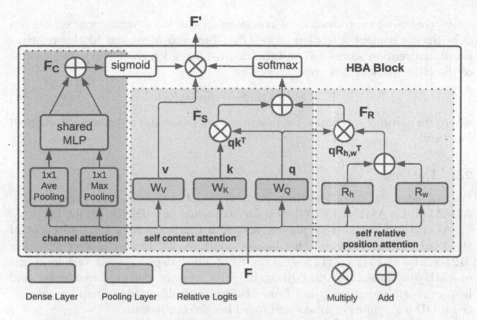

Fig. 2. HBA block architecture, consisting of channel attention (green box outputs F_C), content attention using multi-head self-attention (blue box outputs F_S), and relative position attention (pink box outputs F_R). (Color figure online)

layers (W_Q, W_K, W_V) were used to calculate the query $(q = W_Q(F))$, key $(k = W_K(F))$, and value $(v = W_V(F))$ for each pixel. The output of the content attention was an attention score (F_S) between key (k) and query vectors (q):

$$\mathrm{F_S} = qk^T. \tag{1}$$

Inspired by [13,16], we included relative-position attention (pink box in Fig. 2) to encode the relative position of different retinal landmarks (e.g., to relate the fovea to the OD location). Relative logits were used to store the x and y offsets $(R_h$ and $R_w)$ between each key and query. These were added and the relative positional attention score F_R was computed using the dot product:

$$\mathrm{F_R} = q(R_h + R_w)^T. \tag{2}$$

In a U-Net, spatial information is encoded to different channels through down/up-sampling. We believe channel-wise attention is well suited to utilize this information in the bottleneck layers, which usually have many channels. We therefore used the channel attention module proposed in [21] (green box in Fig. 2). The input feature map F was passed in parallel to average pooling and max pooling layers, compressing each channel to one value. These two feature maps were forwarded through a single, shared multi-layer perceptron (MLP) with one hidden layer and added to compute the final channel attention score (F_C):

$$\mathrm{F_C} = MLP(AvgPool(F)) + MLP(MaxPool(F)). \tag{3}$$

In contrast to a conventional transformer, the value vector was scaled not only by the content attention score (F_S), but also according to the relative-position attention score (F_R) and the channel attention score (F_C). The output of the HBA block (F′) is given as follows:

$$F' = softmax(F_S + F_R)\sigma(F_C)v, \qquad (4)$$

where the softmax was applied across attention heads and σ denotes the sigmoid function.

2.2   Datasets

We evaluated our model on three prominent datasets for retinal degeneration: ADAM [4] for AMD, REFUGE [11] for glaucoma, and IDRiD [12] for DR.

ADAM was released as part of a Grand Challenge at a satellite event of the ISBI 2020 conference. The dataset contains 400 fundus images at either 2124×2056 or 1444×1444 resolution, 87 of which depict eyes at various stages of AMD progression (typical signs include the presence of drusen, exudation, and hemorrhage), and the rest are from healthy controls. ADAM includes ground-truth OD segmentation masks and fovea image coordinates.

REFUGE was released as part of a Grand Challenge of the OMIA5 workshop at MICCAI 2018. The dataset contains 1200 fundus images at either 2124×2056 or 1634×1634 resolution, 120 of which depict eyes with glaucoma, and the rest are from healthy controls. REFUGE includes ground-truth OD segmentation masks and fovea image coordinates.

IDRiD was released as part of a Grand Challenge at ISBI 2018. The dataset contains 516 images at 4288×2848 resolution divided into 413 train images and 103 test images, all of which contain pathological conditions such as DR and diabetic macular edema. IDRiD includes ground-truth image coordinates for the fovea and OD center, but not segmentation masks.

2.3   Implementation Details

Data Preprocessing and Augmentation. First, we resized every image in the dataset to 512×512 pixels. Second, we followed [9] to generate circular segmentation masks from the ground-truth fovea coordinates and combined them with the ground-truth OD segmentation masks. Third, we applied random image rotations (uniformly sampled from $[-0.2, 0.2]$ rad), and horizontal/vertical flips to augment the original dataset on-the-fly. Fourth, we split the data 85-15 into train and test sets and held out 20% of the training images for validation.

Training Procedure. The model was trained using the adam optimizer, the Dice loss [17], and early stopping, with a custom learning rate scheduler (start rate 0.0025, decay rate 0.985 after 150 epochs), and batch size 8 for 500 epochs. Initial weights were pre-trained on ImageNet. The model was implemented using Keras 2.4.3 (Python 3.7) and run on an NVIDIA Tesla K80 (12 GB of RAM). The code is available at github.com/bionicvisionlab/2021-HBA-U-Net.

Evaluation Metrics. We evaluated the performance of the model using Euclidean distance (ED) [10], where only image coordinates were given, and Dice coefficient (DC), where segmentation masks were given. Since none of the three datasets came with fovea segmentation masks, we followed [10] to create a circular disc centered over the ground-truth fovea coordinates, which was then used to train our network. After training, we recovered predicted coordinates by extracting the centroid of the predicted segmentation mask using scikit-image.

3   Experiments and Results

3.1   Joint Fovea and OD Detection in the Degenerated Retina

Table 1 summarizes our results on three prominent datasets for retinal degeneration: ADAM for AMD, REFUGE for glaucoma, and IDRiD for DR.

HBA-U-Net achieved SOTA performance on fovea detection across all datasets (ADAM: ED 25.4 px; REFUGE: ED 32.5 px; IDRiD: 32.1 px) and thus across eye conditions, despite the fact that these datasets were previously used in Grand Challenges that featured convolutional [9], attentional [23], and adversarial [20] approaches, some of which had a considerably larger number of trainable parameters. Because all three datasets are relatively new, the number of published results is still relatively small.

HBA-U-Net also achieved SOTA performance on OD segmentation for AMD (DC of 0.947, on par with [9]) and on OD detection for DR (ED of 20.5). Our OD segmentation was slightly worse than competing models, with the SOTA belonging to [20], a patch-based morphology-aware segmentation network.

However, please note that the test data of these challenges is not made available to the public. To offer a fair comparison across models, we therefore re-implemented a number of commonly used alternative network architectures and compared their performance using our own train/test split. These alternative

Table 1. Landmark detection on ADAM, REFUGE, and IDRiD. Note that Challenge test data is not publicly available. ED: Euclidean Distance. DC: Dice Coefficient.

| | | Fovea | Optic Disc | |
	Model	ED	ED	DC
ADAM	Aira matrix [9] (ISBI 2020 Challenge Winner)	26.2	–	**0.947**
	HBA-U-Net (this paper)	**25.4**	–	**0.947**
REFUGE	Fu *et al.* [5]	–	–	0.936
	Zhang *et al.* [23]	–	–	0.953
	Kamble *et al.* [9]	35.2	–	0.957
	Wang *et al.* [20]	–	–	**0.960**
	HBA-U-Net (this paper)	**32.5**	–	0.947
IDRiD	DeepDR (IDRiD Subchallenge-3 Winner, on-site)	64.5	21.1	–
	ZJU-BII-SGEX (IDRiD Subchallenge-3 Winner, online)	45.9	25.6	–
	HBA-U-Net (this paper)	**32.1**	**20.5**	–

Table 2. Landmark detection for different reimplemented models tested on ADAM, REFUGE, and IDRiD. ED: Euclidean Distance, DC: Dice Coefficient, F: Fovea, OD: Optic Disc.

Model	ADAM		REFUGE		IDRiD	
	ED_F	DC_{OD}	ED_F	DC_{OD}	ED_F	ED_{OD}
U-Net [14]	70.7	0.741	65.2	0.806	87.1	53.7
EfficientNet encoded U-Net++ [9]	26.9	0.867	37.6	0.935	50.4	28.1
HBA-U-Net (this paper)	**25.4**	**0.947**	**32.5**	**0.947**	**32.1**	**20.5**

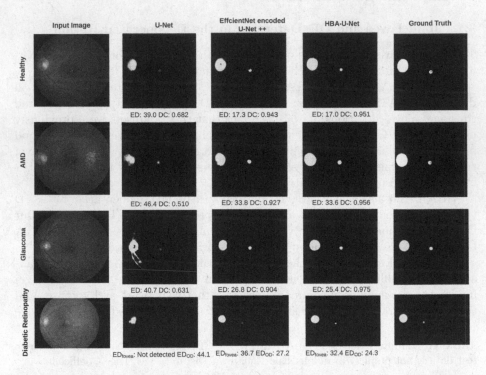

Fig. 3. Representative example predictions for a healthy eye (*top row*), AMD (*second row*), glaucoma (*third row*), and DR (*bottom row*). Predictions are shown for a re-implemented U-Net (*second column*), EfficientNet encoded U-Net++ with scSE blocks (*third column*), and HBA-U-Net (*fourth column*), and compared against ground truth (*rightmost column*). Error rates are given below each prediction panel.

networks included the classical U-Net [14] and an EfficientNet [18] encoded U-Net++ with scSE blocks (similar to [9]). Results are given in Table 2 and example predictions are shown in Fig. 3. HBA-U-Net outperformed the baseline models on all three datasets.

Table 3. Ablation studies on each network component. Starting from a U-Net backbone [10,14], we gradually added a ResNet-50 encoder [6], a standard self-attention block [13] ('Self-Att'), a single HBA block in the bottleneck ('HBA-1'), and HBA blocks across all levels of the hierarchy ('HBA-all').

U-Net	ResNet	Self-Att	HBA-1	HBA-all	Params	Fovea ED	OD DC
✓					8.7M	70.7	0.741
✓	✓				20.8M	34.8	0.902
✓	✓	✓			21.1M	29.8	0.925
✓	✓	✓	✓		21.3M	25.8	0.920
✓	✓	✓	✓	✓	22.2M	**25.4**	**0.947**

3.2 Ablation Study

To measure the impact of the HBA block on different versions of our proposed model architecture, we performed an ablation study on ADAM (see Table 3).

Starting with the original U-Net [10,14] as a baseline, we were able to reduce fovea ED by a factor of two by adding a ResNet-50 encoder [6]. Adding the original self-attention block [13] (without relative position and channel-wise attention; labeled 'Self-Att' in Table 3) at the bottleneck part of the U-Net improved fovea ED by ∼5%, but led to a ∼2% decrease in DC for OD segmentation. Upgrading the self-attention block to our proposed HBA block at the bottleneck part of the U-Net (labeled 'HBA-1') resulted in both the ED and DC improving by ∼4%. Finally, creating local bottlenecks with HBA blocks at each skip connection in the hierarchy (labeled 'HBA-all') led to SOTA performance.

4   Conclusions

We have proposed a re-designed U-Net architecture with hierarchical bottleneck attention and demonstrated its utility for fundus analysis. The proposed network achieved SOTA performance on fovea detection across datasets and eye conditions, on OD segmentation for AMD, and on OD detection for DR.

Although self-attention, channel attention, and relative-position have been deployed separately in other computer vision tasks, here we refined, simplified, and combined their potential in segmenting retinal abnormalities. Furthermore, our ablation study demonstrates the benefit of the local bottleneck structures and HBA blocks for retinal landmark segmentation. Compared to content self-attention alone, HBA does not add much overhead: relative position attention does not have any learnable parameters and channel attention consists of a shared MLP with one hidden layer. Compared to other pure attention networks such as ViT [3], HBA blocks are more resourceful and better suited to work in combination with convolutional modules commonly used in segmentation tasks.

Overall our results suggest that HBA-U-Net may be well suited for landmark detection in the presence of a variety of retinal degenerative diseases.

References

1. Alais, R., Dokládal, P., Erginay, A., Figliuzzi, B., Decencière, E.: Fast macula detection and application to retinal image quality assessment. Biomed. Signal Process. Control **55**, 101567 (2020)
2. Blindness, G., Collaborators, V.I.: Causes of blindness and vision impairment in 2020 and trends over 30 years, and prevalence of avoidable blindness in relation to VISION 2020: the Right to Sight: an analysis for the Global Burden of Disease Study. Lancet Global Health **9**(2), e144–e160 (2021)
3. Dosovitskiy, A., et al.: An image is worth 16x16 words: transformers for image recognition at scale (2021)
4. Fu, H.: ADAM: Automatic detection challenge on age-related macular degeneration, January 2020. Publisher: IEEE type: dataset
5. Fu, H., et al.: Disc-aware ensemble network for glaucoma screening from fundus image. IEEE Trans. Med. Imaging **37**(11), 2493–2501 (2018). Conference Name: IEEE Transactions on Medical Imaging
6. He, K., Zhang, X., Ren, S., Sun, J.: Deep residual learning for image recognition. In: 2016 IEEE Conference on Computer Vision and Pattern Recognition (CVPR), pp. 770–778 (2016). iSSN: 1063–6919
7. Jiang, S., Chen, Z., Li, A., Wang, Y.: Robust optic disc localization by large scale learning. In: Fu, H., Garvin, M.K., MacGillivray, T., Xu, Y., Zheng, Y. (eds.) OMIA 2019. LNCS, vol. 11855, pp. 95–103. Springer, Cham (2019). https://doi.org/10.1007/978-3-030-32956-3_12
8. Jiang, Y., et al.: JointRCNN: a region-based convolutional neural network for optic disc and cup segmentation. IEEE Trans. Biomed. Eng. **67**(2), 335–343 (2020). Conference Name: IEEE Transactions on Biomedical Engineering
9. Kamble, R., Samanta, P., Singhal, N.: Optic disc, cup and fovea detection from retinal images using U-Net++ with EfficientNet encoder. In: Fu, H., Garvin, M.K., MacGillivray, T., Xu, Y., Zheng, Y. (eds.) OMIA 2020. LNCS, vol. 12069, pp. 93–103. Springer, Cham (2020). https://doi.org/10.1007/978-3-030-63419-3_10
10. Meyer, M.I., Galdran, A., Mendonça, A.M., Campilho, A.: A pixel-wise distance regression approach for joint retinal optical disc and fovea detection. In: Frangi, A.F., Schnabel, J.A., Davatzikos, C., Alberola-López, C., Fichtinger, G. (eds.) MICCAI 2018. LNCS, vol. 11071, pp. 39–47. Springer, Cham (2018). https://doi.org/10.1007/978-3-030-00934-2_5
11. Orlando, J.I., et al.: Refuge challenge: a unified framework for evaluating automated methods for glaucoma assessment from fundus photographs. Med. Image Anal. **59**, 101570 (2020)
12. Porwal, P., , et al.: IDRiD: diabetic retinopathy - segmentation and grading challenge. Med. Image Anal. **59**, 101561 (2020)
13. Ramachandran, P., Parmar, N., Vaswani, A., Bello, I., Levskaya, A., Shlens, J.: Stand-alone self-attention in vision models. arXiv:1906.05909 [cs], June 2019. arXiv: 1906.05909
14. Ronneberger, O., Fischer, P., Brox, T.: U-Net: convolutional networks for biomedical image segmentation. In: Navab, N., Hornegger, J., Wells, W.M., Frangi, A.F. (eds.) MICCAI 2015. LNCS, vol. 9351, pp. 234–241. Springer, Cham (2015). https://doi.org/10.1007/978-3-319-24574-4_28
15. Sedai, S., Tennakoon, R., Roy, P., Cao, K., Garnavi, R.: Multi-stage segmentation of the fovea in retinal fundus images using fully Convolutional Neural Networks. In: 2017 IEEE 14th International Symposium on Biomedical Imaging (ISBI 2017), pp. 1083–1086, April 2017. iSSN 1945–8452

16. Srinivas, A., Lin, T.Y., Parmar, N., Shlens, J., Abbeel, P., Vaswani, A.: Bottleneck transformers for visual recognition. arXiv:2101.11605 [cs], January 2021. arXiv: 2101.11605

17. Sudre, C.H., Li, W., Vercauteren, T., Ourselin, S., Jorge Cardoso, M.: Generalised dice overlap as a deep learning loss function for highly unbalanced segmentations. In: Cardoso, M.J., et al. (eds.) DLMIA/ML-CDS -2017. LNCS, vol. 10553, pp. 240–248. Springer, Cham (2017). https://doi.org/10.1007/978-3-319-67558-9_28

18. Tan, M., Le, Q.V.: EfficientNet: rethinking model scaling for convolutional neural networks. arXiv:1905.11946 [cs, stat], September 2020. arXiv: 1905.11946

19. Vaswani, A., et al.: Attention is all you need. In: Advances in Neural Information Processing Systems, vol. 30 (2017)

20. Wang, S., Yu, L., Yang, X., Fu, C.W., Heng, P.A.: Patch-based output space adversarial learning for joint optic disc and cup segmentation. IEEE Trans. Med. Imaging **38**(11), 2485–2495 (2019). Conference Name: IEEE Transactions on Medical Imaging

21. Woo, S., Park, J., Lee, J., Kweon, I.S.: CBAM: convolutional block attention module. CoRR (2018)

22. Yu, H., et al.: Fast localization of optic disc and fovea in retinal images for eye disease screening. In: Medical Image Computing and Computer Assisted Intervention - MICCAI 2011, vol. 7963, p. 796317, March 2011

23. Zhang, Z., Fu, H., Dai, H., Shen, J., Pang, Y., Shao, L.: ET-Net: a generic edge-aTtention guidance network for medical image segmentation. In: Shen, D., et al. (eds.) MICCAI 2019. LNCS, vol. 11764, pp. 442–450. Springer, Cham (2019). https://doi.org/10.1007/978-3-030-32239-7_49

Radial U-Net: Improving DMEK Graft Detachment Segmentation in Radial AS-OCT Scans

Bram M. van der Velden[1](✉), Mitko Veta[1], Josien. P. W. Pluim[1,2],
Mark Alberti[2], and Friso G. Heslinga[1]

[1] Department of Biomedical Engineering, Eindhoven University of Technology,
Eindhoven, The Netherlands
[2] Ophthalmology Department, Rigshospitalet - Glostrup, Copenhagen, Denmark

Abstract. Descemet's membrane endothelial keratoplasty (DMEK) has become the preferred corneal transplantation technique for severe stages of corneal pathologies such as Fuchs' endothelial dystrophy. Postoperative assessment of DMEK graft attachment can be done using anterior segment optical coherence tomography (AS-OCT), but manual quantification of DMEK graft detachment is a time-consuming process. Recently, a deep learning-based pipeline was proposed to aid in the quantification of such detachments. The method includes a U-Net model for segmentation of the detached graft segments, which was applied on individual AS-OCT cross-sectional slices (B-scans), neglecting contextual information from neighbouring B-scans. In this work, a novel model architecture - Radial U-Net - is proposed that takes into account the radial acquisition of the AS-OCT data and that integrates contextual information from neighbouring B-scans to the input. We compare Radial U-Net with variants of U-Net previously described in literature. Models were trained and optimized using 960 B-scans from 50 patients that were annotated by corneal specialists. Performance of the models was evaluated on an independent test set of 320 B-scans of 18 other patients to compare the detachments with corneal specialist annotations. Incremental improvements in the Dice score were obtained in comparison with the baseline model (0.859 ± 0.009), with Radial U-Net performing best (0.872 ± 0.006). The design of Radial U-Net is easily customisable and can be adapted to other radially acquired data sets.

Keywords: Radial data · Segmentation · Deep learning · DMEK

1 Introduction

Descemet's Membrane Endothelial Keratoplasty (DMEK) has become the preferred corneal transplantation procedure for restoration of vision for patients affected by corneal pathology, such as Fuchs' dystrophy [7,13,15]. The most prevalent complication after a DMEK procedure is (partial) graft detachment.

© Springer Nature Switzerland AG 2021
H. Fu et al. (Eds.): OMIA 2021, LNCS 12970, pp. 72–81, 2021.
https://doi.org/10.1007/978-3-030-87000-3_8

Graft detachment occurs in 4% to 62% of cases depending on experience of the
surgeon and may require another gas bubble injection or a complete repeat of
the DMEK procedure [12,14,16,17]. Presence of (partial) graft detachment can
be determined using anterior segment optical coherence tomography (AS-OCT).
Using the AS-OCT, the physician can observe high resolution cross-sectional
images (B-scans) of the graft and cornea without invasive measures [3]. For
each eye, 16 radial B-scans are obtained, as schematically represented in Fig. 1.
However, the manual quantification of the detachments in all these B-scans is
tedious and time-consuming. In some B-scans, presence of graft detachment can
be ambiguous and the DMEK expert uses neighbouring B-scans to gather contextual information that can indicate detachment.

A fast and objective method to evaluate graft detachment has previously
been proposed by Heslinga et al. [8]. The authors developed an image analysis
pipeline that includes a segmentation model based on deep learning [11]. The
segmentation model was designed to automatically locate graft detachments in
individual B-scans. In contrast to evaluation by a physician, the existing segmentation model does not take into account neighbouring B-scans for contextual
information.

In this research, we aim to improve upon the previously developed segmentation model by incorporating contextual information from neighbouring B-scans.
We compare multiple modifications to the segmentation model and propose a
novel model architecture - Radial U-Net - that takes into account the radial
nature of the AS-OCT data.

1.1 Related Work

U-Net has become the de facto standard for deep learning-based biomedical
image segmentation [19]. The U-Net architecture consists of two pathways that
yield a U-shaped network. The first pathway is a downsampling path that reduces
the spatial information while increasing the feature information. The second
pathway is the upsampling path that uses upsampling layers to increase resolution while combining this with the extracted features from the downsampling

Fig. 1. A schematic representation of the B-scans and their radial nature [8].

path. A 3D variant of a U-Net can be used to segment 3D volumes. For example, Qamar et al. used a 3D U-Net to segment infant brain tissues in MRI data [18]. However, 3D layers are computationally expensive and 2D architectures that can process 3D input effectively are still actively being used. Examples include stacking of slices as if they were channels [22] and processing the 2D images separately before combining their feature maps later in the network [21].

Alternatively, Zhou et al. combined 2D and 3D layers into a single network, referred to as D-UNet [23]. The model consists of two downsampling pathways that both take the same 3D input. The first pathway, however, processes the input as if it were 2D while the second pathway processes the 3D input as 3D. The information extracted by the 3D layers is then concatenated to the 2D pathway which is made possible by a transformation block that reduces the dimension of the 3D data. The authors concluded that the D-UNet has similar results compared to a standard 3D U-Net while significantly reducing the computational costs.

2   Methods and Materials

2.1   Data

The data used in this research consists of swept-source AS-OCT scans (CASIA2; Tomey Corp. Nagoya, Japan) collected by the department of Ophthalmology in the Rigshospitalet Glostrup in Denmark as part of a randomized study that examined the difference between air and sulfur hexafluoride DMEK surgery [1]. Eighty AS-OCT scans from 68 patients were obtained either directly after or seven days after surgery. The dataset contains scans with and without graft detachment. In some scans the intraocular gas bubble was visible, which can have a similar appearance as the DMEK graft. Each AS-OCT scan consists of 16 radially acquired B-scans of 2133 by 1466 pixels (16 by 11 mm) with a separating angle of 11.25%. Details about the dataset, regarding participants age, sex, diagnosis and other characteristics can be found in [8]. For each B-scan, DMEK experts annotated the locations where the grafts were detached. Similar to [8] the B-scans were horizontally aligned, cropped and split into two halves to decrease the size of the training input. AS-OCT data was split on a patient-level into a set of 960 B-scans for training and validation, and a set for 320 B-scans for testing. Furthermore, the images were downsampled by a factor of two resulting in images of 480 by 384 pixels.

2.2   Models and Experiments

Baseline Model. Our baseline model is similar to the model described by Heslinga et al. [8], based on the U-Net architecture [19]. It consists of four down-sampling blocks and four upsampling blocks with skip connections between each block. The model takes a single grey-scale B-scan as input and produces its corresponding segmentation map. The baseline model and all adaptations were implemented using Python 3.7 and Keras 2.3.1 with TensorFlow 1.13.1 backend. All models were trained by optimizing the binary cross-entropy loss between the model predictions and the annotated masks with Adam [10]. Hyperparameters for each model were similar unless mentioned otherwise. The standard batch size was 10 and the initial learning rate 0.001. Training was continued for 200 epochs and the learning rate was updated every 60 epochs with a factor of 0.3.

Pseudo-3D U-Net. As a first alternative to the baseline model, contextual information is captured by including neighbouring B-scans as if they were channels [22]. We refer to this model as Pseudo-3D U-Net. A schematic representation of the model and its inputs is shown in Fig. 2. The model was tested with increasing numbers of neighbouring slices ranging from one to four on each side of the central slice. Based on the performance on the validation set the optimal number of neighbouring slices found to be two on each side.

Multi-Branch U-Net. A different approach for including contextual information is inspired by the work from Sun et al. [21]. The proposed network uses multiple downsampling branches where each neighbouring B-scan passes through its own individual branch before they are combined at a later stage in the network. A visual representation of this model, from here on referred to as the Multi-Branch model (MB), is depicted in Fig. 3. Based on the validation set, we determined that the optimal point of concatenation was just before the fourth max-pooling layer, using a single neighbouring slice on each side of the central slice.

3D U-Net. A 3D variant of U-Net was included [4], using the same input as for the Pseudo-3D model. In contrast to the aforementioned models, the 3D U-Net uses 3D kernels and outputs a 3D volume from which we select only the middle slice. Due to the higher computational costs of the 3D convolutions, this model was exclusively tested with a single neighbouring slice on each side of the central slice and 16 initial filters instead of 32. Because of the small number in the z-direction, max-pooling operation of the 3D U-Net were only applied in the x and y-direction, keeping the depth of the feature maps constant.

D-UNet. As a more efficient alternative to 3D U-Net, D-UNet [23] was implemented. Two separate downsampling branches process the input volume as 2D and 3D simultaneously. A transformation block that reduces the dimension of the 3D information made concatenation between the 2D and 3D branches possible. The upsampling path behaves in the same manner as the standard 2D U-Net. Since D-UNet is computationally more efficient than 3D U-Net, training was possible with two neighbouring slices on each side of the central slice rather than just one.

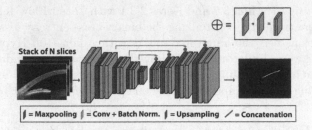

Fig. 2. Pseudo-3D U-Net. Neighbouring slices are stacked onto the central slice and act as a single input.

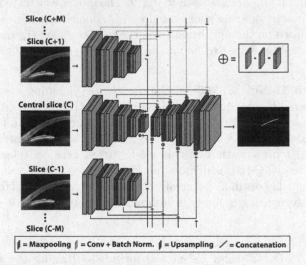

Fig. 3. Multi-Branch U-Net. The central (C) and neighbouring slices (C + 1, C − 1) will go through separate downsampling branches before concatenation and finally producing a segmentation map of the central slice (C).

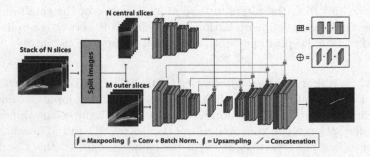

Fig. 4. Radial U-Net. Slices are preprocessed by cutting into two parts, resulting in two stacks of slices, central and outer slices. The number of neighbouring slices can be varied independently for the two stacks. The stacks go through separate downsampling branches before concatenation in the x-y plane.

Radial U-Net. All models so far did not take into account the radial nature of the AS-OCT data scans (Fig. 1). Since acquisition of neighbouring slices happens at a different angle, the slices are misaligned in the x-dimension when stacked, an effect that is more pronounced for x-coordinates more distant from the centre. The misalignment might have a negative effect on the convolutions of a deep neural network, where one assumes that the stacked data is directly sampled from 3D space. Moreover, due to the diverging nature of the radially acquired B-scans, the distance between neighbouring slices is larger at the outer part than in the central part. We therefore hypothesised that misaligned or distant information is less useful and potentially hampers model's performance. We therefore propose a new model (Fig. 4) that allows us to customize the addition of the number of neighbouring slices for different segments of the B-scan.

For our experiments we chose to have two image segments: a central stack and an outer stack, but the concept can be extended to a larger number of segments. Segments are obtained by simply dividing a B-scan along the x-dimension. To deal with the different input sizes of the different segments, each segment has its own downsampling branch. At the lowest level, just before the fourth max-pooling operation, the feature maps of the branches are concatenated in the x-y plane, along the x-dimension, restoring the relative spatial placing of the segments. Please note that this type of concatenation is different from the typical concatenation along the channel-dimension. This architecture allows us to easily control the number of neighbouring slices for central and outer part of the image. We refer to this model as the Radial U-Net. For our experiments, slices are vertically cut into a central and outer part that consist of 30% (2.16 mm) and 70% (5.04 mm) of the original slice width respectively. Specifically, the network uses a stack of nine central slices while limiting the stack of outer slices to three.

2.3 Metrics

Model performance was evaluated based on the *projected Dice score*, similar to [8]. The model's prediction and annotations were projected onto the x-axis and subsequently the Dice score for both projections was calculated [5]. Cases without detachment were excluded when calculating the mean Dice.

In addition, we analyzed the projected Dice score for the central and outer part of the image separately. The central part consists of the central 288 pixels (4.32 mm) and the outer part consists of the outer 672 pixels (10.08 mm). These separate Dice scores give us more insight regarding the differences due to the radial component of the data set, where we would expect more improvement in the central part of the segmentation map.

Every network was trained five times using random weight initialization to acquire an average Dice score that is representative of the model's performance. A one-tailed t-test for two independent means was used to determine the significance of the change in performance of each model in comparison with the baseline model.

3   Results

The segmentation results obtained by the different model types on the test set are shown in Table 1. The baseline model obtained the lowest Dice score (0.859 ± 0.009) followed by the 3D archetypes, 3D U-Net (0.861 ± 0.008) and D-UNet (0.863 ± 0.004). Pseudo-3D U-Net and Multi-Branch U-Net models performed similarly with Dice scores of $0.869 \, (\pm 0.008)$ and $0.868 \, (\pm 0.008)$ respectively. Radial U-Net performed best with a Dice score of $0.872 \, (\pm 0.006)$. Based on the one-tailed two independent means t-tests, Pseudo-3D U-Net and Radial U-Net were found to perform significantly better than the baseline model. Dice scores for the other models were not statistically different from the baseline model.

Similarly, the baseline model and 3D archetypes had the lowest Dice scores for the central part, while the Radial model performed best with a Dice score of $0.872 \, (\pm 0.006)$. Dice scores for the outer segments were similar for all models, ranging from $0.869 \, (\pm 0.009)$ to $0.874 \, (\pm 0.006)$ and were not statistically different from the baseline model. The difference in performance for the central part is visualized with an example in Fig. 5. Segmentation maps for a B-scan with substantial detachment is shown for the baseline, Pseudo-3D and Radial U-Net. As can be seen by the gaps in the segmentation map compared to the annotated mask, the baseline model under-segments some parts of the graft for this particular image. The Pseudo-3D model performs slightly better, but only the Radial U-Net seems to have detected the full extent of the detachments in the central part of the image.

Table 1. Results on the test. M indicates the number of neighbouring slices on each side. *For this particular model the first number states the amount of outer neighbouring slices and the second number states the amount of central neighbouring slices. Param. = number of trainable weights.

Model	M	Param.	Batch	Projected dice score		
				Full	Central	Outer
Baseline	0	7,766,369	10	0.859 ± 0.009	0.830 ± 0.023	0.869 ± 0.009
P3D	2	7,767,521	10	0.869 ± 0.008	0.865 ± 0.011	0.873 ± 0.007
MB	1	14,041,313	5	0.868 ± 0.008	0.858 ± 0.023	0.871 ± 0.011
3D	1	5,648,337	10	0.861 ± 0.008	0.843 ± 0.007	0.869 ± 0.007
D-UNET	2	8,633,667	10	0.863 ± 0.004	0.840 ± 0.010	0.870 ± 0.004
Radial	1/4*	8,942,849	10	0.872 ± 0.006	0.873 ± 0.009	0.874 ± 0.006

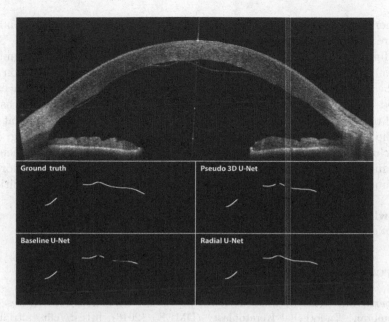

Fig. 5. Top: AS-OCT B-scan with substantial graft detachment. Bottom: segmentation maps for the baseline U-Net, pseudo-3D U-Net, radial U-Net and the ground truth.

4   Discussion

Manual quantification of DMEK graft detachments in AS-OCT images is tedious and time-consuming, and can be challenging for some cases. Automated segmentation using deep learning has been shown to yield good results, yet the baseline model sometimes missed some obvious detachments in the central region of the image that corneal specialists would have been unlikely to miss. Using neighbouring slice information to improve graft segmentation makes sense from a clinical perspective, as this is also standard practice by corneal specialists. However, how to effectively incorporate this contextual information into a deep learning framework for segmentation had not been addressed before. Our study compared multiple strategies to modify a U-Net and showed that incremental improvements could be achieved.

The proposed Radial U-Net achieved the largest improvement in segmentation performance in comparison with the baseline U-Net. The improvement is more pronounced in the central region where DMEK graft detachment is clinically most relevant and could be a direct result of the addition of more slices for this region. Radial U-Net also performed best for segmentation in the outer region, although this difference is not statistically significant when compared with the baseline model. For the full range, significant improvements were also obtained with the more straight-forward approach of Pseudo-3D U-Net. However, visual evaluation of B-scans with particularly high amounts of partial graft detachment in the central region indicated that the Radial U-Net outperformed the other models. A more extensive hyperparameter search could be conducted in future research to find the optimal configuration of the Radial U-Net. Specifically, finding the optimal x-location to cut the B-scans, and the number of neighbouring slices for both stacks. In addition, a more extensive ablation study could be performed to identify which hyperparameters and design choices contributed mostly to the results. The concept of Radial U-Net can also easily be applied to other applications that use radially acquired cross-sectional data sets, since the design is customisable. Within the field of ophthalmic imaging, examples include corneal layer segmentation [6], corneal thickness measurements [9], retinal fluid segmentation [20], and optic nerve head segmentation [2]. Moreover, radial image acquisition is used in several other medical imaging modalities.

Acknowledgments. This research is financially supported by the TTW Perspectief program and Philips Research.

References

1. Alberti, M., la Cour, M., Cabrerizo, J., et al.: Air versus sf6 for Descemet's Membrane Endothelial Keratoplasty (DMEK) (2016). https://clinicaltrials.gov/ct2/show/NCT03407755
2. Almobarak, F.A., et al.: Automated segmentation of optic nerve head structures with optical coherence tomography. Investig. Ophthalmol. Vis. Sci. **55**(2), 1161–1168 (2014)
3. Ang, M., et al. Anterior segment optical coherence tomography. Progr. Retinal Eye Res. **66**, 132–156 (2018)
4. Çiçek, Ö., Abdulkadir, A., Lienkamp, S.S., Brox, T., Ronneberger, O.: 3D U-Net: learning dense volumetric segmentation from sparse annotation. In: International Conference on Medical Image Computing and Computer-Assisted Intervention, pp. 424–432 (2016)
5. Dice, L.R.: Measures of the amount of ecologic association between species. Ecology **26**(3), 297–302 (1945)
6. Elsawy, A., Gregori, G., Eleiwa, T., Abdel-Mottaleb, M., Abou Shousha, M.: Pathological-corneas layer segmentation and thickness measurement in OCT images. Transl. Vis. Sci. Technol. **9**(24), 2164–25918 (2020)
7. Fuchs, E.: Dystrophia epithelialis corneae. Albrecht von Graefes Archiv für Ophthalmologie **76**(3), 478–508 (1910)
8. Heslinga, F.G., Alberti, M., Pluim, J.P., Cabrerizo, J., Veta, M.: Quantifying graft detachment after Descemet's membrane endothelial keratoplasty with deep convolutional neural networks. Transl. Vis. Sci. Technol. **9**(2), 48 (2020)
9. Heslinga, F.G., et al.: Corneal pachymetry by AS-OCT after Descemet's membrane endothelial keratoplasty. Sci. Rep. **11**(1), 13976 (2021)
10. Kingma, D.P., Ba, J.: Adam: a method for stochastic optimization. arXiv preprint - arXiv:1412.6980 (2014)
11. LeCun, Y., Bengio, Y., Hinton, G.: Deep learning. Nature **521**(7553), 436–444 (2015)
12. Maier, A.K.B., et al.: Rate and localization of graft detachment in Descemet membrane endothelial keratoplasty. Cornea **35**(3), 308–312 (2016)

13. Marques, R.E., Guerra, P.S., Sousa, D.C., Gonçalves, A.I., Quintas, A.M., Rodrigues, W.: DMEK versus DSAEK for Fuchs' endothelial dystrophy: a meta-analysis. Eur. J. Ophthalmol. **29**(1), 15–22 (2019)
14. Melles, G.R., San Ong, T., Ververs, B., van der Wees, J.: Descemet membrane endothelial keratoplasty (DMEK). Cornea **25**(8), 987–990 (2006)
15. Rodríguez-Calvo-de Mora, M., et al.: Clinical outcome of 500 consecutive cases undergoing Descemet's membrane endothelial keratoplasty. Ophthalmology **122**(3), 464–470 (2015)
16. Müller, T.M., et al.: Histopathologic features of Descemet membrane endothelial keratoplasty graft remnants, folds, and detachments. Ophthalmology **123**(12), 2489–2497 (2016)
17. Parekh, M., et al.: Graft detachment and rebubbling rate in Descemet membrane endothelial keratoplasty. Surv. Ophthalmol. **63**(2), 245–250 (2018)
18. Qamar, S., Jin, H., Zheng, R., Ahmad, P., Usama, M.: A variant form of 3D-UNet for infant brain segmentation. Future Gener. Comput. Syst. **108**, 613–623 (2020)
19. Ronneberger, O., Fischer, P., Brox, T.: U-net: convolutional networks for biomedical image segmentation. In: International Conference on Medical Image Computing and Computer-Assisted Intervention, pp. 234–241 (2015)
20. Roy, A.G., et al.: ReLayNct: retinal layer and fluid segmentation of macular optical coherence tomography using fully convolutional networks. Biomed. Opt. Express **8**(8), 3627–3642 (2017)
21. Sun, Y., Zhu, L., Wang, G., Zhao, F.: Multi-input convolutional neural network for flower grading. J. Electr. Comput. Eng. **2017** (2017)
22. Vu, M.H., Grimbergen, G., Nyholm, T., Löfstedt, T.: Evaluation of multislice inputs to convolutional neural networks for medical image segmentation. Med. Phys. (2020)
23. Zhou, Y., Huang, W., Dong, P., Xia, Y., Wang, S.: D-UNet: a dimension-fusion U shape network for chronic stroke lesion segmentation. IEEE/ACM Trans. Comput. Biol. Bioinform. (2019)

Guided Adversarial Adaptation Network for Retinal and Choroidal Layer Segmentation

Jingyu Zhao[1,2], Jiong Zhang[2], Bin Deng[1], Yalin Zheng[3], Jiang Liu[4],
Ran Song[5(✉)], and Yitian Zhao[2(✉)]

[1] School of Mechanical Engineering, Southwest Jiaotong University, Chengdu, China
[2] Cixi Institute of Biomedical Engineering, Ningbo Institute of Materials Technology
and Engineering, Chinese Academy of Sciences, Ningbo, China
yitian.zhao@nimte.ac.cn
[3] University of Liverpool, Liverpool, UK
[4] Department of Computer Science and Engineering,
Southern University of Science and Technology, Shenzhen, China
[5] School of Control Science and Engineering, Shandong University, Jinan, China
ransong@sdu.edu.cn

Abstract. Morphological changes, e.g. thickness of retinal or choroidal
layers in Optical coherence tomography (OCT), is of great importance
in clinic applications as they reveal some specific eye diseases and other
systemic conditions. However, there are many challenges in the accurate segmentation of retinal and choroidal layers, such as low contrast
between different tissue layers and variations between images acquired
from multiple devices. There is a strong demand on accurate and robust
segmentation models with high generalization ability to deal with images
from different devices. This paper proposes a new unsupervised guided
adversarial adaptation (GAA) network to segment both retinal layers
and the choroid in OCT images. To our best knowledge, this is the first
work to extract retinal and choroidal layers in a unified manner. It first
introduces a dual encoder structure to ensure that the encoding path of
the source domain image is independent of that of the target domain
image. By integrating the dual encoder into an adversarial framework,
the holistic GAA network significantly alleviates the performance degradation of the source domain image segmentation caused by parameter
entanglement with the encoder of the target domain and also improves
the segmentation performance of the target domain images. Experimental results show that the proposed network outperforms other state-of-
the-art methods in retinal and choroidal layer segmentation.

Keywords: OCT · Domain adaptation · Retinal and choroidal layer

1 Introduction

Optical coherence tomography (OCT) is an indispensable ocular imaging tool
and has been extensively used in clinics. Anatomically, the retina can be divided

H. Fu et al. (Eds.): OMIA 2021, LNCS 12970, pp. 82–91, 2021.
https://doi.org/10.1007/978-3-030-87000-3_9

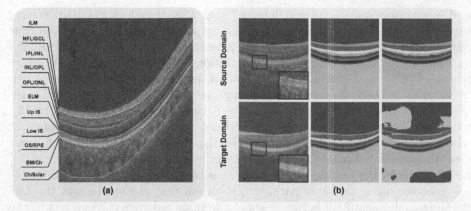

Fig. 1. Illustration of full layer segmentation of OCT images. (a) Boundaries of different layers manually annotated by an experienced clinician. ILM: internal limiting membrane, NFL: nerve fiber layer, GCL: ganglion cells layer, IPL: inner plexiform layer, INL: inner nuclear layer, OPL: outer plexiform layer, ONL: outer nuclear layer, ELM: external limiting membrane, IS: inner segment, OS: outer segment, RPE: retinal pigment epithelium, Ch: choroid. (b) Segmentation results by a pre-trained U-Net on images from the source and target domains. From left to right: example OCT B-scans, ground truth, and the segmentations by U-Net, which was trained on the source domain dataset.

into nine cellular layers with varying thickness [1–3]. The choroid is a densely vascularized layer lying between the retina and the sclera of the eye. Figure 1(a) illustrates the boundaries of different retinal and choroidal layers in a *B*-scan OCT image annotated manually by a senior ophthalmologist. In clinics, layer thickness is an important biomarkers for the diagnosis of many different types of eye diseases. For instance, glaucoma leads to the thinning of the nerve fiber layer (NFL) [4,5]. Age-related macular degeneration (AMD) causes a thinner choroid [6] whilst central serous chorioretinopathy [7] and polypoidal choroidal vasculopathy [6] may lead to choroidal thickening. In consequence, the accurate measurement of thickness of retinal and choroidal layers is vital for diagnosing and monitoring disease progression. However, manual annotation of a large number of images is an exhausting task for clinicians and vulnerable to human errors. Current proprietary segmentation programs of clinical OCT devices still lack accuracy and robustness.

With the rapid development of deep learning, many segmentation networks, such as FCN [8], U-Net [9], CS-Net [10,11] and CE-Net [3], have been employed for retinal layer segmentation tasks. However, to the best of our knowledge, no existing method is dedicated to the segmentation of retinal and choroidal layers in a unified model. In addition, although the retina and choroid of the human eye share similarity, different imaging devices could produce large domain discrepancy even of the same eye due to different noise distributions, i.e., domain gap between the training (source) and test (target) images. This often causes low generalization of a pre-trained model - high performance in the source domain and low performance in target domain, as demonstrated in Fig. 1(b). Hence, supervised model often requires re-annotating pixel-level ground truth and thus require high labour costs. To this end, it is essential to establish a model trained on an existing dataset with manual annotations and can be generalized to new test data from another domain (e.g. different device or with varying protocols).

In order to overcome these shortcomings, several unsupervised domain adaptation techniques [12] based on Generative Adversarial Network (GAN) [13–15], have been proposed to close the gap between the source and target domains, where manual labels are not available in the target domain. Although some typical approaches such as Adversarial Discriminative Domain Adaptation [16] achieved promising results, the input images of the source and target domains are encoded using the same path, which means that the source and the target domain segmentation networks share the same parameters. As a result, the parameters of the two networks will be entangled with each other and affect the overall performance of the model.

In this paper, we develop a Guided Adversarial Adaptive (GAA) framework for full layer segmentation in OCT images. We use the source domain encoder to guide the target domain encoder for learning segmentation network parameters. The dual encoder structure makes the encoding path of the source domain independent of that of the target domain, and thus does not produce parameter entanglement. Simultaneously, we carry out adversarial adaptation both in the feature and output space of the two domain images, to minimize the feature discrepancy between the source and target domains after encoding. Consequently, the target domain encoder can make continuous progress.

The contributions of our work can be summarized in three-fold: **1)** This is the first attempt to segment full layers (both retinal and choroidal layers) in OCT imagery by a single segmentation model, and it also demonstrates the ability of data adaptation for different imaging devices. **2)** We propose a guided dual-encoder joint structure to guarantee the mutual independence between the encoding paths of the source and target domains for parameter entanglement. **3)** We show that without the need of any manual annotations on the target domain, our method outperforms supervised learning using annotations in the target domain by a large margin.

2   Proposed Method

In this section, we first provide an overview to the proposed method, and then elaborate its two main components, i.e., the guided dual-encoding and the adversarial adaption, respectively.

2.1   Overview

As shown in the Fig. 2, our framework consists of five basic modules: a source domain encoder E_s, a target domain encoder E_t, a sharing decoder D_{sh}, a encoding discriminator Dis_{en} and a decoding discriminator Dis_{de}. Thus, E_s and D_{sh}

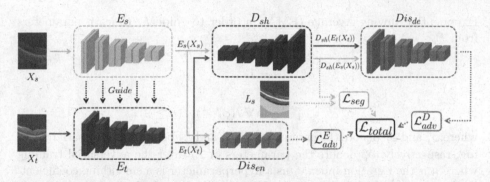

Fig. 2. Overview of the Guided Adversarial Adaptation (GAA) network. The yellow and the green arrows indicate the source and target domain paths, respectively. The black dashed arrows denote the parameter guidance and the red dashed arrows denote the adversarial learning. (Color figure online)

constitute the source domain segmentation network (SDSN), and E_t and D_{sh} constitute the target domain segmentation network (TDSN). The input OCT image from the source domain is denoted as $X_s \in R^{C \times H \times W}$ with its corresponding annotation L_s while the one from the target domain denoted as $X_t \in R^{C \times H \times W}$ has no annotation.

Adversarial methods can reduce the domain discrepancy [17] and thus make the output feature space of TDSN consistent with that of SDSN through training. However, for most adversarial methods, since the parameters of the two networks are shared which trigger the parameter entanglement, the SDSN couldn't gain the optimal solution, so that TDSN will often end with a compromise performance, which is better than that of the model trained only with the source domain data but worse than that of the model trained with the target domain data (assuming that the annotations are available). To alleviate this problem, our idea is to lift the performance of TDSN by allowing it more independence while still keeping its training guided by SDSN for domain adaption. Therefore, we propose a guided dual-encoding architecture where the two encoders of SDSN and TDSN are not shared and the domain adaption for transferring the segmentation knowledge from SDSN to TDSN is delivered through a parameter guidance process and an architecture of adversarial learning.

2.2 Guided Dual-Encoding

In this work, we use two individual encoders for X_s and X_t for SDSN and TDSN, respectively so that there is no parameter sharing in their encoding paths during the training. We build a teacher-student structure which aims to use E_s to guide E_t for encoding the input images of the same modality but acquired by different OCT devices into the same feature space.

Then, two levels of adversarial learning is adopted to promote the continuous progress of E_t and achieve the same encoding effect as E_s. Here, we apply the

Exponential Moving Average (EMA) in order to guide E_t to learn parameters from E_s:

$$\begin{cases} \phi_t^n = \gamma \hat{\phi}_t^{n-1} + (1-\gamma)\phi_s^n & (n \geq 2) \\ \phi_t^n = \phi_s^n & (n = 1) \end{cases} \tag{1}$$

$$\hat{\phi}_t^{n-1} = \phi_t^{n-1} - \alpha \nabla J(\phi_t^{n-1}) \quad (n \geq 2) \tag{2}$$

where ϕ_s^n and ϕ_t^n denote the parameters of E_s and E_t before the adversarial training, respectively. $\hat{\phi}_t^n$ denote the parameters of E_t after the adversarial training where n is the iteration index. γ as a hyperparameter is a smoothing coefficient. $J(\phi)$ represents the loss function of E_t and α denotes the learning rate.

2.3 Adversarial Adaptation

We regard the encoder and decoder of the segmentation network as two levels of generators, which conduct adversarial learning with different discriminators in the intermediary feature space and the output space of the whole model, respectively. In the encoding stage, we adopt the adversarial process between E_t and the Dis_{en} to reduce the gap between the feature spaces of $E_s(X_s)$ and $E_t(X_t)$, which aims to encode the X_s and X_t from E_s and E_t respectively to an identical feature space. The Dis_{en} loss $\mathcal{L}_d^E$ and the adversarial loss $\mathcal{L}_{adv}^E$ for E_t can be expressed as follows:

$$\begin{aligned} \mathcal{L}_d^E(X_s, X_t) = &- \sum z \, log(Dis_{en}(E_s(X_s))) \\ &+ (1-z)(1 - log(Dis_{en}(E_t(X_t)))) \end{aligned} \tag{3}$$

$$\mathcal{L}_{adv}^E(X_t) = - \sum log(Dis_{en}(D_{sh}(E_t(X_t)))) \tag{4}$$

where $z = 1$ if the encoding prediction is from S, and $z = 0$ if from T.

In the decoding stage, D_{sh} starts with the encoded features $E_s(X_s)$ and $E_t(X_t)$, and fuse the multi-scale features outputs from different levels of the two encoders concurrently through skip connections. Although such a popular network architecture is well know for improving the segmentation mainly due to the preservation of low-level features, it hinders the restoration of high-level features after the adversarial encoding. Therefore, we use Dis_{de} in the output space of D_{sh} to eliminate the potential impact of the skip connections. Dis_{de} can further enhance the effect of domain adaptation and make the output $D_{sh}(E_t(X_t))$ more similar to $D_{sh}(E_s(X_s))$. The Dis_{en} loss $\mathcal{L}_d^D$ and the adversarial loss $\mathcal{L}_{adv}^D$ for E_t are expressed as follows:

$$\begin{aligned} \mathcal{L}_d^D(X_s, X_t) = &- \sum z \, log(Dis_{de}(D_{sh}(E_s(X_s)))) \\ &+ (1-z)(1 - log(Dis_{de}(D_{sh}(E_t(X_t))))) \end{aligned} \tag{5}$$

$$\mathcal{L}_{adv}^D(X_t) = - \sum log(Dis_{de}(D_{sh}(E_t(X_t)))). \tag{6}$$

We adopt the mean square error (MSE) loss function to train SDSN with supervised learning.

$$\mathcal{L}_{seg}(X_s) = \frac{1}{2m} \sum_{i=1}^{m} \left(l_s^{(i)} - D_{sh}(E_s(x_s^{(i)})) \right)^2 \tag{7}$$

where $l_s^{(i)}$ and $x_s^{(i)} \in X_s$ denote the ith ground truth and the input image in the source domain, respectively. m is the total number of the source domain OCT images. The overall training objective for our framework is:

$$\mathcal{L}_{total}(X_s, X_t) = \mathcal{L}_{seg}(X_s) + \mathcal{L}_{adv}^{E}(X_t) + \mathcal{L}_{adv}^{D}(X_t). \tag{8}$$

Based on Eq. (8), we optimize the following min-max criterion:

$$\min_{G} \max_{D} = \mathcal{L}_{total}(X_s, X_t). \tag{9}$$

where G denotes the generator and D denotes the discriminator. The ultimate objective is to minimize the segmentation loss for source image, while fooling the discriminators Dis_{en} and Dis_{de} by maximizing the probability of $E_t(X_t)$ and $D_{sh}(E_t(X_t))$ being considered as $E_s(X_s)$ and $D_{sh}(E_s(X_s))$ in the feature and the output spaces, respectively.

3   Experimental Results

3.1   Datasets

Our experiments are performed on two OCT image datasets acquired by two different devices. The first dataset provides layer segmentation annotations and thus is considered as the *source* dataset to train SDSN in a supervised manner. The images in the second dataset are used as *target* domain images and will be used to evaluate the model generalization ability.

Source: **Topcon** dataset consists of 1,280 OCT B-scans with the resolution of 992 × 512 pixels. All the images were captured by a Topcon DRI-OCT-1 system from 20 subjects. Each image has a corresponding pixel-level manual annotation of the retinal and choroidal layers provided by experts. We make use of 640 images for training and 640 images for testing.

Target: **Optovue** dataset comprises 670 OCT B-scans in total taken by an Optovue RTVue-XR device, with the resolution of 640 × 400 pixels. In particular, 640 images (without layer manual annotations) were used for training, and 30 images (with manual annotations) were used for testing. All the images were acquired with regulatory approvals and patient consents as appropriate.

3.2   Implementation Details

In this experiment, DCGAN [13] and ResNet [18] were employed as the encoding and decoding discriminator, respectively. Both the source and target domain images were cropped to 512 × 400 pixels automatically, where all the cropped images contain retinal and choroidal layers in either source or target domain. During the training, batch size was set to 4 and we adopt the Adam optimizer with a weight decay of $5e^{-4}$ to train the entire network end-to-end. The smoothing coefficient γ of EMA was set to 0.8.

3.3   Evaluation Metrics

In order to quantitatively evaluate the performance of our framework, the following metrics were calculated: the Dice coefficient (Dice) and the Intersection over Union (IoU). In addition, we introduce the mean absolute error of the boundaries (MAE (pixels)) to evaluate boundary segmentation performance. It is defined as the mean error of retinal and choroidal interfaces:

$$MAE_{R/C} = \frac{1}{M \times N} \sum_{i=1}^{N} \sum_{j=1}^{M} \left| l_j^{(i)} - y_j^{(i)} \right| \tag{10}$$

where $l_j^{(i)}$ and $y_j^{(i)}$ denote the jth boundary mean coordinates of the ground truth label and the prediction of the ith testing OCT image, respectively. We choose $M = 10$ when computing the MAE of the retina layers, and $M = 2$ of the choroid layer.

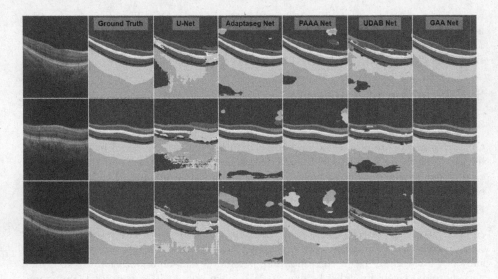

Fig. 3. Visual results of different segmentation networks with domain adaptation.

3.4   Results

In the following sections, we report the segmentation performance under different scenarios, i.e., different segmentation models with and without our adaptation module. For comparisons, we use the well-known network architectures such as U-Net [9], CE-Net [3] and CS-Net [10,11] as SDSN and TDSN.

Domain Adaptation. To justify the superiority of the proposed method in domain adaptation, we compared our GAA Net with state-of-the-art domain adaptation methods: Adapt Structured Output Space for Semantic Segmentation (AdaptSeg Net) [19], Perceptual-assisted Adversarial Adaptation(PAAA Net) [20], Unsupervised domain adaptation by backpropagation (UDAB Net) [17], with the U-Net applied as backbone for the segmentation of the target domain images.

Table 1 shows the evaluation results of the proposed GAA Net against the state-of-the-art methods. Compared to utilizing U-Net to segment the target domain images directly, the Dice and the IoU of domain adaptation methods have great improvements in the retina and choroid segmentation. The GAA Net outperforms all competing methods consistently in terms of all evaluation metrics. In particular, we calculate the MAE of all domain adaptation methods after post-processing, our method achieves a much lower MAE in both retina and choroid segmentation, which indicates that it is an accurate and reliable method for measuring the retinal layers and choroid thickness. Figure 3 shows some visual results for retina and choroid segmentation. Moreover, we also set CE-Net and CS-Net as the segmentation backbone to verify the versatility of our method. The results in Table 1 show that compared to the pre-trained CE-Net and CS-Net, our method leads to a roughly 18% improvement in terms of Dice score for both segmentation backbones.

Table 1. Layer segmentation performances over **target domain** image by different domain adaptation methods with different segmentation networks.

Method	Retinal layer			Choroidal layer		
	IoU ↑	Dice ↑	MAE ↓	IoU ↑	Dice ↑	MAE ↓
U-Net [9]	64.09%	77.96%	—	71.32%	83.26%	—
Adaptseg Net (U) [19]	82.22%	90.15%	2.918	77.93%	87.40%	8.928
PAAA Net (U) [20]	83.56%	91.00%	2.141	70.21%	82.34%	10.689
UDAB Net (U) [17]	82.55%	90.40%	3.334	74.12%	85.04%	10.614
GAA Net(U)	**92.41%**	**96.05%**	**1.099**	**85.01%**	**91.84%**	**5.374**
CE-Net [3]	65.52%	79.17%	—	57.09%	72.69%	—
GAA Net(CE)	**93.74%**	**96.76%**	**0.939**	**87.01%**	**93.06%**	**4.124**
CS-Net [10]	62.06%	76.53%	—	76.51%	86.01%	—
GAA Net(CS)	**90.12%**	**94.79%**	**1.026**	**83.37%**	**90.84%**	**5.610**

* Adaptseg Net (U) denotes the Adaptseg Net uses U-Net as the segmentation backbone, and so on.

Table 2. Performance degradation between U-Net and domain adaptation methods over **source domain** image.

Method	Retinal layer			Choroidal layer		
	E_{IoU} ↓	E_{Dice} ↓	E_{MAE} ↓	E_{IoU} ↓	E_{Dice} ↓	E_{MAE} ↓
U-Net [9]	—	—		—	—	—
Adaptseg Net [19]	4.37%	2.44%	1.285	0.55%	0.32%	1.699
PAAA Net [20]	5.06%	2.80%	1.145	0.96%	0.56%	2.474
UDAB Net [17]	6.17%	3.44%	1.145	2.93%	1.69%	2.592
GAA Net	**0.68%**	**0.70%**	**0.70**	**0.10%**	**0.05%**	**0.178**

Parameter Entanglement. We also evaluate the effect of parameter entanglement (i.e. SDSN and TDSN share the same encoder). In order to reasonably verify the performance degradation caused by parameter entanglement in the source domain, the SDSN and TDSN of the five competing methods listed in Table 2 all adopt U-Net with the same setting. The parameters of the SDSN and TDSN are shared in AdaptSeg Net, PAAA Net and UDAB Net but not in the GAA Net that we propose. We take the performance mertics of U-Net as the baseline, and computed the error of IoU (E_{IoU}), Dice (E_{Dice}) and MAE (E_{MAE}) between U-Net and the other methods. It can be seen from Table 2 that the metrics of retinal layer segmentation of all methods whose parameters are shared, have significant margin when compared to U-Net. By contrast, our GAA Net achieves a comparable performance with the original U-Net. This indicates that the SDSN module in our method is capable of retaining the segmentation performance of the source domain images, while the TDSN module can alleviate the performance degradation caused by the parameter sharing. For the choroidal layer segmentation, similarly, GAA Net performs better than all other competing methods in terms of all metrics. The results demonstrate that the parameter entanglement generally leads to the performance degradation of the SDSN, such that the TDSN cannot gain the best performance when combined with SDSN together.

4   Conclusion

This paper have proposed a guided adversarial adaptation (GAA) framework for the segmentation of retinal and choroidal layers in OCT images acquired from different devices. By using a dual-encoder structure, the source domain encoder guides the learning of the target domain encoder. This helps to avoid the degradation of source domain segmentation caused by parameter entanglement. In addition, through an adversarial scheme, the target domain segmentations are also enhanced with good performance as the source domain segmentations. In the future work, we will focus on applying the GAA framework to the diagnosis of various ophthalmic diseases.

Acknowledgments. This work was supported in part by the Zhejiang Provincial Natural Science Foundation of China (LZ19F010001), in part by the Youth Innovation Promotion Association CAS (2021298), in part by the Ningbo 2025 S&T Megaprojects (2019B10033 and 2019B1006). This work was also supported in part by Ningbo Natural Science Foundation (202003N4039).

References

1. Liu, X., et al.: Macular thickness profiles of intraretinal layers in myopia evaluated by ultrahigh-resolution optical coherence tomography. Am. J. Ophthalmol. **160**(1), 53–61 (2015)
2. Cheng, J., et al.: Speckle reduction in 3D optical coherence tomography of retina by a-scan reconstruction. IEEE Trans. Med. Imaging **35**(10), 2270–2279 (2016)
3. Gu, Z., et al.: CE-Net: context encoder network for 2D medical image segmentation. IEEE Trans. Med. Imaging **38**(10), 2281–2292 (2019)
4. Bowd, C., Weinreb, R.N., Williams, J.M., Zangwill, L.M.: The retinal nerve fiber layer thickness in ocular hypertensive, normal, and glaucomatous eyes with optical coherence tomography. Arch. Phthalmol. **118**(1), 22–26 (2000)

5. Charng, J., et al.: Age-dependent regional retinal nerve fibre changes in six1/six6 polymorphism. Sci. Rep. **10**(1), 1–7 (2020)
6. Chung, S.E., Kang, S.W., Lee, J.H., Kim, Y.T.: Choroidal thickness in polypoidal choroidal vasculopathy and exudative age-related macular degeneration. Ophthalmology **118**(5), 840–845 (2011)
7. Yang, L., Jonas, J.B., Wei, W.: Choroidal vessel diameter in central serous chorioretinopathy. Acta Ophthalmol. **91**(5), e358–e362 (2013)
8. Long, J., Shelhamer, E., Darrell, T.: Fully convolutional networks for semantic segmentation. In: Proceedings of the IEEE 33rd Conference on Computer Vision and Pattern Recognition, pp. 3431–3440 (2015)
9. Ronneberger, O., Fischer, P., Brox, T.: U-net: Convolutional networks for biomedical image segmentation. In: Navab, N., Hornegger, J., Wells, W., Frangi, A. (eds.) MICCAI 2015. LNCS, vol. 9351, pp. 234–241. Springer, Cham (2015). https://doi.org/10.1007/978-3-319-24574-4_28
10. Mou, L., et al.: CS-Net: channel and spatial attention network for curvilinear structure segmentation. In: Shen, D., et al. (eds.) MICCAI 2019. LNCS, vol. 11764, pp. 721–730. Springer, Cham (2019). https://doi.org/10.1007/978-3-030-32239-7_80
11. Mou, L., et al.: CS2-Net: deep learning segmentation of curvilinear structures in medical imaging. Med. Image Anal. **67**, 101874 (2021)
12. Kouw, W.M., Loog, M.: A review of domain adaptation without target labels. IEEE Trans. Pattern Anal. Mach. Intell. **43**(3), 766–785 (2021)
13. Isola, P., Zhu, J.Y., Zhou, T., Efros, A.A.: Image-to-image translation with conditional adversarial networks. In: Proceedings of the IEEE 35th Conference on Computer Vision and Pattern Recognition, pp. 1125–1134 (2017)
14. Yi, X., Walia, E., Babyn, P.: Generative adversarial network in medical imaging: a review. Med. Image Anal. **58**, 101552 (2019)
15. Ma, X., et al.: Understanding adversarial attacks on deep learning based medical image analysis systems. Pattern Recogn. **110**, 107332 (2021)
16. Tzeng, E., Hoffman, J., Saenko, K., Darrell, T.: Adversarial discriminative domain adaptation. In: Proceedings of the IEEE 35th Conference on Computer Vision and Pattern Recognition, pp. 7167–7176 (2017)
17. Ganin, Y., Lempitsky, V.: Unsupervised domain adaptation by backpropagation. In: Proceedings of the 32nd International Conference on Machine Learning, pp. 1180–1189 (2015)
18. He, K., Zhang, X., Ren, S., Sun, J.: Deep residual learning for image recognition. In: Proceedings of the IEEE 34th Conference on Computer Vision and Pattern Recognition, pp. 770–778 (2016)
19. Tsai, Y.H., Hung, W.C., Schulter, S., Sohn, K., Yang, M.H., Chandraker, M.: Learning to adapt structured output space for semantic segmentation. In: Proceedings of the IEEE 36th Conference on Computer Vision and Pattern Recognition, pp. 7472–7481 (2018)
20. Chai, Z., et al.: Perceptual-assisted adversarial adaptation for choroid segmentation in optical coherence tomography. In: Proceedings of the 2020 IEEE 17th International Symposium on Biomedical Imaging, pp. 1966–1970 (2020)

Juvenile Refractive Power Prediction Based on Corneal Curvature and Axial Length via a Domain Knowledge Embedding Network

Yang Zhang[1,2], Risa Higashita[1,3(✉)], Yanwu Xu[4], Daisuke Santo[3], Yan Hu[1], Guodong Long[2], and Jiang Liu[1,4,5,6(✉)]

[1] Department of Computer Science and Engineering, Southern University of Science and Technology, Shenzhen 518055, China
k-chen@tomey.co.jp
[2] University of Technology Sydney, Sydney, Australia
[3] Tomey Corporation, Nagoya, Japan
[4] Cixi Institute of Biomedical Engineering, Chinese Academy of Sciences, Beijing, China
[5] Research Institute of Trustworthy Autonomous Systems, Southern University of Science and Technology, Shenzhen, China
[6] Guangdong Provincial Key Laboratory of Brain-Inspired Intelligent Computation, Department of Computer Science and Engineering, Southern University of Science and Technology, Shenzhen, China
liuj@sustech.edu.cn

Abstract. Traditional cycloplegic refractive power detection with specific lotions dropping may cause side-effects, e.g., the pupillary retraction disorder, on juvenile eyes. In this paper, we develop a novel neural network algorithm to predict the refractive power, which is assessed by the Spherical Equivalent (SE), using real-world clinical non-cycloplegic refraction records. Participants underwent a comprehensive ophthalmic examination to obtain several related parameters, including sphere degree, cylinder degree, axial length, flat keratometry, and steep keratometry. Based on these quantitative biomedical parameters, a novel neural network model is trained to predict the SE. On the whole age test dataset, the domain knowledge embedding network (DKE-Net) prediction accuracies of SE achieve 59.82% (between $\pm 0.5D$), 86.85% (between $\pm 1D$), 95.54% (between $\pm 1.5D$), and 98.57% (between $\pm 2D$), which demonstrate superior performance over conventional machine learning algorithms on real-world clinical electronic refraction records. Also, the SE prediction accuracies on the excluded examples that are disqualified for model training, are 2.16% (between $\pm 0.5D$), 3.76% (between $\pm 1D$), 6.15% (between $\pm 1.5D$), and 8.78% (between $\pm 2D$). This is the leading application to predict refraction power using a neural network and domain knowledge, to the best of our knowledge, with a satisfactory accuracy level. Moreover, the model can also assist in diagnosing some specific kinds of ocular disorders.

H. Fu et al. (Eds.): OMIA 2021, LNCS 12970, pp. 92–100, 2021.
https://doi.org/10.1007/978-3-030-87000-3_10

Keywords: Refractive power prediction · Neural network · Non-cycloplegic detection

1 Introduction

Over the past two decades, myopia has increased rapidly among juvenile students, which is also the leading cause of correctable vision impairment [1,2], and presented a significant burden on the public healthcare system [3]. The innate character of myopia is the excessive elongation of ocular axial length far away from the normal integrated optical power of the corneal and crystalline lens. Previous research has recognized the refractive error as a significant predictor of myopia. The refractive detection can be measured after a comprehensive eye examination, conducted by ophthalmologists and optometrists in eye hospitals or ophthalmic centers [4,5]. In general, myopia can be defined as having a refractive error of Spherical Equivalent (SE) of less than −0.50 diopter (D), which is equivalent to the Sphere degree (S) plus half of the Cylinder degree (C).

Previous epidemiological research has established an apparent high prevalence of myopia in younger, female, and parental-myopia adolescents [6–10]. Besides, education background, living area (rural or city), and ethnicity are also important risk profiles of myopia [8]. Comparison between near work, mid-distance, and distance activities has shown that the longer time spent outdoor activity may effectively prevent myopia progression. Moreover, different environments and lifestyles may contribute to various myopia presentations among the same ethnic people, not to mention among the other races and ethnicities [8]. Above all, while some studies have been carried out on refractive errors analysis, most of the studies focused on identifying and evaluating the myopia distribution characteristics through classical statistical and meta-analysis methods or linear modeling approach (e.g., Generalized estimating equations).

Generally, the refractive error is measured by subjective refraction and objective refraction procedure. Due to the children's strong accommodation ability, the objective refraction detection of schoolchildren is usually conducted by cycloplegic autorefraction, which is regarded as the gold standard for refraction measurement, to obtain the informative ocular optic and structural biometric variables. Above all, (I) such detection operation is unsatisfactory, which may have side-effects and cause sequelae, such as the pupillary retraction disorder. (II) the existence of fundus lesions, amblyopia, small pupil, strong nystagmus, and crystal turbidity will impede correctly measure the refractive power with a low-credibility. This paper has proposed a novel domain knowledge embedding network (DKE-Net), leveraging the axial length (AL) and corneal curvature to investigate the feasibility of predicting the refractive power, i.e., spherical equivalent, to avoid the aforementioned problems (I) and (II). Also, this study has investigated the prediction ability of the refractive power and provided a significant opportunity to advance the diagnosis of poor-refractive eyes according to the output of the proposed prediction model. It has revealed that the forecast result of the refractive power of participants with ocular pathological changes is far away from the ground-truth value, which enables us to distinguish healthy eyes from diseased ones with great potential for future clinical application.

2 Methodology

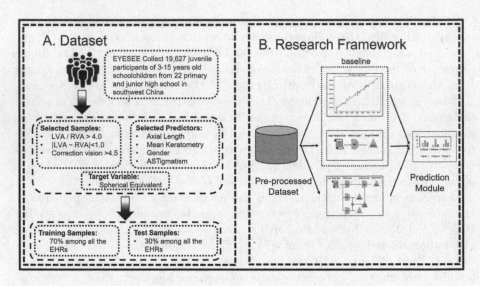

Fig. 1. An overview of the research framework. The examples inclusion criteria are as follows: Left/Right Vision Acuity (L/RVA) higher than 4.0; the absolute difference between LVA and RVA less than 1.0; and the correction vision higher than 4.5, which was our pre-processing standard in this experiment to select health ocular subjects.

The study is a multidisciplinary, cross-sectional research project. Three quantitative analysis machine learning approaches are conducted to evaluate the refractive power prediction performance on a clinical data collection after pre-processing. An overview of the three research pipelines is shown in Fig. 1(B). The refractive power prediction experiment is first conducted on the standard linear regression for the high-interpretability available. Then, the naïve forward neural network is selected as the second pipeline to create another baseline. After that, we propose a novel network architecture to utilize the cylinder degree and sphere degree as the assisted branches to predict the spherical equivalent. Specifically, we first transfer the refractive power prediction problem to a regression task based on the initial step's clinical electronic health records (EHRs). Following the regression task, the test samples can be classified according to the predicted error between the model output and the ground truth value.

2.1 Data Collection and Pre-processing

The clinical EHRs of 19,627 recruited participants from 22 schools (including kindergartens, primary schools, and middle schools) were collected by the same equipment and investigators from the EYESEE hospital. All of the participants enrolled in our research have signed the clinical informed consent form. An auto-refractometer (RM-800, TOPCON, Japan) was used to perform non-cycloplegic autorefraction to measure S and C. The AL, Flat Keratometry (KF), and Steep Keratometry (KS) were collected by an optical biometer (AL-SCAN, NIDEK, Japan). Besides, some other intuitive parameters were recorded in the tabular format, such as age, school, grade, etc. In Fig. 1, Part A on the left side is the data collection procedure by EYESEE. We performed quality control for the original tabular data by filtering inappropriate participant examples and disqualified biomedical parameters described in Fig. 1(A), through which 7,142 participant records were excluded (12,485 records left).

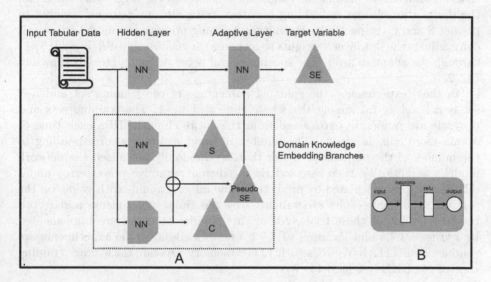

Fig. 2. The network architecture of DKE-Net. The Part A provides the whole structure of DKE-Net. Part B shows the detail of the hidden layer and adaptive layer, which all consist of input subject, specific number of neurons, relu activation function, and output subject.

Depending on the clinical fact, the vision correction by orthokeratology and contact lens participants were excluded from the original examples. Based on the biomedical knowledge, we averaged the KF and KS to calculate Mean Keratometry (KM) and exploited the absolute value of KS minus KF to obtain ASTigmatism (AST). To keep the magnitude consistency, we take AL's reciprocal value as an additional parameter. Among these biomedical variables, we chose gender, axial length, Mean Keratometry (KM), and ASTigmatism (AST) to be the parameters according to clinical practice. The target variable is spherical equivalent (SE), which represents the refractive power in clinical.

The final parameters are AL's reciprocal value, KM, Gender, and AST in our study. As the clinical record of one participant contains two eyes' measurement data, thus one record is split into two examples to create a more abundant database. Thus, the study includes 24,970 preprocessed real-world clinical samples covering a total of 12,485 participants, between 3 and 15 years of age, from 22 primary and junior high schools in Southwest China.

2.2 Domain Knowledge Embedding Network (DKE-Net)

Although the multi-layer feedforward neural network can recognize the non-linear data pattern, we consider S and C's existence would presumably further improve the refractive power prediction performance. This paper has proposed a novel domain knowledge embedding network (DKE-Net), which embeds two assisted branches to predict the target variable. When the target variable is SE, the domain knowledge embedding branches train distinct neurons' weights to predict S and C, respectively. During the training process, the model automatically adjusts the last layer's weights to leverage the relationship $SE = S + 0.5 \times C$ through the adaptive layer. The specific neural network architecture is shown in Fig. 2.

In these experiments, the splitting percentage of the training set and test set is defined as 7:3 among the whole clinical dataset. The training sets and test sets are randomly partitioned from the entire clinical EHRs each time to obtain more reliable results. The number of input neurons is corresponding to the number of the parameters. After that, we randomly initialized the network model's weights. We then assessed the predicted refractive power error under different scopes, calculated by predicted value minus ground-truth value, on the test set. The final results are validated by ten times experiments and record the mean value of these trials. All of the experiment codes are implemented by Python v3.7.5 and PyTorch v1.4.0 framework. Besides, the experiments are conducted on TITAN V GPUs with 12 GB memory. Overall, the average training time of the DKE-Net model is 75 s.

3   Experimental Results

We conduct two quantitative analysis machine learning algorithms, i.e. linear regression (LR) and multi-layer perceptron (MLP), to compare with out method. The prediction accuracy of SE of the complete experiment results are exhibited in the Tables 1 and 2. Based on clinical evaluation metrics, the scopes were defined as $\pm 0.5D$, $\pm 1D$, $\pm 1.5D$, and $\pm 2D$, containing results of both unilateral and bilateral. It can be seen from the table that DKE-Net's performance has achieved the best accuracy, which is better than all of the previous approaches. Especially in the $-0.5D \sim 0.5D$, the occurrence rate of prediction error under 0.5D is 59.82% and the performance improvement has achieved 1.6% than MLP, which is about 100 patients in our research. The centralized trends of SE's prediction error for different scopes are significant throughout the projection period, as shown in the Table 2. The proposed network outperform other baseline rivals with the max patient numbers in the lowest error scope.

Table 1. Performance of spherical equivalent prediction task

	LR	MLP	DKE-Net
−0.5D~0.5D	3,580 (47.79%)	4,382 (58.23%)	**4,481 (59.82%)**
−1D~1D	5,930 (79.16%)	6,535 (87.24%)	6,506 (86.85%)
−1.5D~1.5D	6,992 (93.34%)	7,170 (95.71%)	7,157 (95.54%)
−2D~2D	7,307 (97.54%)	7,396 (98.73%)	7,384 (98.57%)
All	7,491 (100%)	7,491 (100%)	7,491 (100%)

Table 2. Stratified performance of spherical equivalent prediction task

	LR	MLP	DKE-Net
Less −2D	35 (0.47%)	31 (0.41%)	38 (0.51%)
−2D~−1.5D	136 (1.82%)	51 (0.68%)	56 (0.75%)
−1.5D~−1D	623 (8.32%)	293 (3.91%)	260 (3.47%)
−1D~−0.5D	1,491 (19.90%)	1,120 (14.95%)	994 (13.27%)
−0.5D~0D	1,997 (26.66%)	2,319 (30.96%)	**2,355 (31.44%)**
0D~0.5D	1,583 (21.13%)	2,043 (27.27%)	**2,126 (28.38%)**
0.5D~1D	859 (11.47%)	1,053 (14.06%)	1,031 (13.76%)
1D~1.5D	439 (5.86%)	342 (4.57%)	391 (5.22%)
1.5D~2D	179 (2.39%)	175 (2.34%)	171 (2.28%)
More 2D	149 (1.99%)	64 (0.85%)	69 (0.92%)

Subsequently, a unilateral and bilateral summary of the comparison of SE's prediction performance distribution of the three kinds of quantitative approaches is revealed in Fig. 3, where the refraction power absolute error is aligned with the ascend diopter scope, from 0.5D to all. In these figures, the X-axial represents the absolute prediction error under 0.5D (diopter), 1D, 1.5D, 2D, and all. Meanwhile, the Y-axial represents the total number of people under various scope. Clear evidence of a higher prediction trend has existed in our DKE-Net. As shown in Fig. 3, most of the DKE-Net prediction output value is higher than the real ground truth value (hyperopia). In contrast, the output of standard linear regression exhibits an opposite result (myopia).

4   Discussion

To the best of our knowledge, until now, there has been little quantitative analysis based on machine learning algorithms in the refractive power prediction area. Recently, investigators have examined the effects of the random forests algorithm on predicting high-level myopia in a specific future time point, achieving a satisfactory forecasting performance. Such an approach deals with the longitudinal electronic medical records collected from several large ophthalmic centres

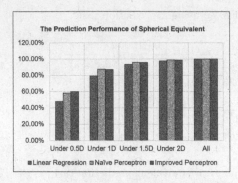 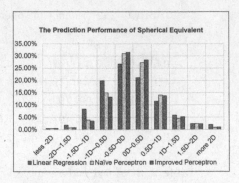

Fig. 3. The unilateral and bilateral prediction performance of the spherical equivalent

in China. Different from the task of previous research, this paper attempts to illuminate the prediction of spherical equivalent on cross-sectional large-scale non-cycloplegic autorefraction clinical data by developing an improved perceptron neural network. The experiments have been conducted on standard linear regression, naive multi-layer feedforward neural network, and DKE-Net, among which the DKE-Net has achieved the best prediction performance.

4.1   Main Findings

Our study has estimated refraction power, i.e., spherical equivalent, through a newly proposed DKE-Net, which has achieved a satisfactory accuracy (prediction diopter error under 0.5D) of 59.82%. Consistently throughout our linear model for SE prediction, the axial length's reciprocal value is most associated with the target variables in the prediction tasks, which is in agreement with the previous findings [4]. This is also relevant for the KM and gender, which are significant determinate of refraction prediction. Compared with that, the AST and the intercept term are relatively less critical risk factors in the specific linear model. In the beginning, we have considered age as one of the candidature parameters to predict the refraction power. In contrast, the prediction performance had no significant improvement with the existence of age. According to Occam's Razor principle, the model structure should be as simple as possible. Thus, we excluded the variable age from our basic pipelines. Apart from the SE prediction, we also have conducted the sphere degree prediction experiment with obtaining 60.75% accuracy (diopter error under 0.5D) by DKE-Net, which is better than other approaches.

However, to distinguish the gender-specific influence has generated on the regression model, distinctive linear regression of male and female in the whole age records have been conducted. After the linear regression of different age subgroups, there is a significant trend toward higher coefficients of the gender with increasing age. The detailed coefficients of gender are displayed in the Table 3 when the standard linear regression is conducted to predict sphere equivalent in each different age subgroup. We found that the coefficient of gender was

Table 3. Stratified gender coefficients of linear regression model

Age	3	4	5	6	7	8	9
Coefficients	−0.0211	−0.0268	−0.145	−0.244	−0.374	−0.409	−0.485
Age	10	11	12	13	14	15	All
Coefficients	−0.527	−0.554	−0.553	−0.498	−0.699	−0.581	−0.401

gradually increasing with age arising. It means gender plays a more important role in the refraction power prediction among older participants.

After that, we built the linear regression model on male and female participant examples separately to compare the gender's influence on the refraction power. The co-efficients of the age in these two prediction equations are 0.0162 (P < 0.0001, 95% CI, 0.009∼0.024) and 0.0514 (P < 0.0001, 95% CI, 0.044∼0.059) for female and male, respectively. The statistical analysis reflects a significant lifestyle discrepancy in male and female students among our participants, which means the male juvenile is more prone to be myopia. This phenomenon may be associated with different daily outdoor behavior patterns and study/reading habits.

To further investigate the best prediction performance, we have tried some tricks on the DKE-Net architecture. For example, the double hidden layers of naïve feedforward neural network architecture and dropout modules are separately applied to the task. Besides, independent S, SE, and C output structures without the adaptive layer are also tested for the SE prediction. However, the experimental results show that the double hidden-layers structure, the presence of dropout, and simply average the last layer lead to a performance degeneration about 2% of the accuracy of ±0.5D. This suggests the DKE-Net may have achieved the best performance among all similar network architecture.

An interesting aspect of these health records are the differences in the effect of risk factors between normal examples and redundant instances, which were excluded in the pre-processing unit. In addition, the experiments evaluated the refractive power prediction performance of the excluded instances. The results show that when the prediction error is below 0.5D, the percentage of instances among all test datasets is only 2.16% for SE, when testing with excluded eyes. Therefore, the results conclude that the abnormal participant examples do not follow the same data distribution with normal participants. This study has important implications for simple scrooning or disorder warning prediction, such as fundus lesions, amblyopia, small pupil, strong nystagmus, and crystal turbidity.

4.2   Strengths and Limitations

The strengths of the study include extensive population-based clinical EHRs of refraction detection. Data on a cohort of 19627 participants enrolled in the study between 3 to 15 years old children were collected in the present investigation. As the samples are randomly selected, the analyzed sub-cohort is representative of the entire research population. Moreover, this large Southwest China schoolchildren population-based research has provided strong evidence of the effectiveness and accuracy of our new proposed approach for SE prediction with satisfactory performance.

However, our study has some defects which can be improved later. The first is the relatively limited chosen biomedical parameters. Anterior chamber depth and lens thickness are vital candidate risk factors that could be added to the analysis to boost the prediction accuracy and aid lesion localization. Moreover, previous research has revealed a strong association between myopia's relevance in Children and some common risk factors, such as outdoor activity time, parental myopia, parental employment, and parental education, which are absent in this study. Second, cross-sectional research based on the specific time point's clinical HERs cannot reflect the potential trend of refractive power changes over time. The longitudinal data collection is also one of the improved directions.

Acknowledgments. This work was supported in part by Guangdong Provincial Department of Education (2020ZDZX3043), Guangdong Provincial Key Laboratory (2020B121201001), and Shenzhen Natural Science Fund (JCYJ20200109140820699 and the Stable Support Plan Program 20200925174052004).

References

1. Dolgin E.: The myopia boom. Nature **519**, 276–278 (2015)
2. Chen, M., Wu, A., Zhang, L., et al.: The increasing prevalence of myopia and high myopia among high school students in Fenghua city, eastern China: a 15-year population-based survey. BMC Ophthalmol. **18**, 1–10 (2018)
3. Vitale, S., Cotch, M.F., Sperduto, R., Ellwein, L.: Costs of refractive correction of distance vision impairment in the United States, 1999–2002. Ophthalmology **113**, 2163–2170 (2006)
4. Zadnik, K., Mutti, D.O., Friedman, N.E., et al.: Ocular predictors of the onset of juvenile myopia. Investig. Ophthalmol. Vis. Sci. **40**, 1936–1943 (1999)
5. Mutti, D.O., Hayes, J.R., Mitchell, G.L., et al.: Refractive error, axial length, and relative peripheral refractive error before and after the onset of myopia. Investig. Ophthalmol. Vis. Sci. **47**, 2510–2519 (2007)
6. Attebo, K., Ivers, R.Q., Mitchell, P.: Refractive errors in an older population. Ophthalmology **106**, 1066–1072 (1999)
7. Saw, S.M., Chua, W.H., Gazzard, G., et al.: Eye growth changes in myopic children in Singapore. Br. J. Ophthalmol. **89**, 1489–1494 (2005)
8. Saw, S.M., Chan, Y.H., Wong, W.L., et al.: Prevalence and risk factors for refractive errors in the Singapore Malay eye survey. Ophthalmology **115**, 1713–1719 (2008)
9. Lou, L., Liu, X.I., Tang, X., et al.: Gender inequality in global burden of uncorrected refractive error. Am. J. Ophthalmol. **198**, 1–7 (2018)
10. Vainer, I., Mimouni, M., Rabina, G., et al.: Age- and gender-related characteristics of corneal refractive parameters in a large cohort study. Am. J. Ophthalmol. **209**, 45–54 (2020)

Peripapillary Atrophy Segmentation with Boundary Guidance

Mengxuan Li[1], He Zhao[1], Jie Xu[2], and Huiqi Li[1](✉)

[1] Beijing Institute of Technology, Beijing, China
huiqili@bit.edu.cn
[2] Beijing Tongren Hospital, Beijing, China

Abstract. Peripapillary atrophy (PPA) is a clinical finding that reflects atrophy of the retinal layer and retinal pigment epithelium. It is very important to segment PPA area as it indicates the progress of eye diseases such as myopia and glaucoma, while it is a challenging task to segment PPA due to the irregular and ambiguous boundaries. In this paper, a boundary guidance deep learning method is introduced to segment PPA area to obtain precise shape. We propose a boundary guidance block together with a contour loss function to improve the PPA segmentation performance on boundaries. Our approach is evaluated on a clinical dataset. The F1-score, IOU and Hausdorff distance of our method performance is 80.06%, 67.29%, 5.4934 respectively. Compared with other methods, our method achieves the best performance both qualitatively and quantitatively. Our proposed method can work well on retinal images with narrow PPA even with small training set.

Keywords: Peripapillary atrophy (PPA) · Boundary guidance · Segmentation

1 Introduction

Peripapillary atrophy (PPA) is a clinical finding associated with chorioretinal thinning and disruption of the retinal pigment epithelium (RPE) in the area surrounding optic disc [1]. Clinical studies show that the presence of PPA often associates with myopia or glaucoma [2]. Therefore, monitoring PPA area is very helpful for myopia and glaucoma screening. In recent years, PPA segmentation has been investigated. Most methods segment the area of optic disc (OD) and PPA together (i.e. PPAOD) following by subtracting the OD region due to the difficulty of direct PPA segmentation [3]. Constraint on the shape of PPA or OD with a simple ellipse fitting is also considered in some work, but it leads to a limited improvement.

In this paper, we propose a novel deep learning method to segment PPA regions. Different from other work, we segment the PPA area directly, which reduces the model complexity compared with methods based on PPAOD subtraction. Furthermore, a new module is engaged in our network to provide the boundary guidance together with a contour constraint. The contributions of our approach can be summarized as follows. (1) A novel end-to-end PPA segmentation method is proposed to directly extract PPA region with a precise boundary in retinal images. (2) A boundary guidance block is

© Springer Nature Switzerland AG 2021
H. Fu et al. (Eds.): OMIA 2021, LNCS 12970, pp. 101–108, 2021.
https://doi.org/10.1007/978-3-030-87000-3_11

proposed to provide boundary information and work as a guidance for the network. (3) We utilize the contour loss to constrain the pixels around the boundary to further improve performance. (4) We have carried out extensive experiments with the clinical data to evaluate our approach. The results suggest that our approach achieves the superior performance compared with the state-of-the-art methods, and the performance is significantly improved even with small training set.

2 Related Work

Image segmentation is a classic problem in computer vision and there are many methods used in image segmentation, which are mainly divided into two categories: conventional segmentation methods and deep-learning based segmentation algorithms. Conventional segmentation methods vary from threshold-based, region-based and edge detection-based methods [4] to the wavelet analysis and active contour models [5]. With the development of deep learning, more and more convolutional neural network models have been proposed for segmentation task and achieve satisfactory performance, such as Unet [6] and SegNet [7].

Many methods are also proposed for retinal fundus image segmentation. Joshi et al. [8] proposed a novel OD segmentation method which integrates the local image information around each point of interest in multidimensional feature space. The method proposed by Yu et al. [9] used alternating sequential filtering (ASF) and morphological reconstruction to remove vessels and bright region distractors followed by level set model with both region information and local edge vector to segment OD. Bharkad et al. [10] proposed to segment the OD region using a combination of the equiripple low pass finite impulse response filter, thresholding, and grayscale morphological dilation and median filtering operation. Maninis et al. [11] proposed a network structure based on VGG network to segment both retinal vessel and OD. Wang et al. [12] proposed a coarse-to-fine pipeline which segments OD based on a U-net structure and the segmentation map from color funds images and corresponding grayscale vessel density maps.

As to retinal PPA segmentation, Lu et al. [3] proposed to extract PPA using region growing and modified Chan-Vese model with a shape constraint. This method searches for the local optimum, so it is seriously affected by initialization. Li et al. [13] used evenly-oriented radial lines to detect the candidate boundary points of OD and PPAOD, followed by outlier removal and ellipses fitting. The complicated illuminance situation around optical disk will lead to failure due to the unreliable point determination which relies on brightness curve on the radiation line. Chai et al. [14] proposed a novel PPA area segmentation using a multi-task fully convolutional Network, which simultaneously divided the OD and PPAOD regions and subtracted the two to obtain the final result.

3 Methodology

In this paper, we propose a boundary guidance PPA segmentation method, which contains a boundary guidance block with contour loss. These two components are helpful to learn

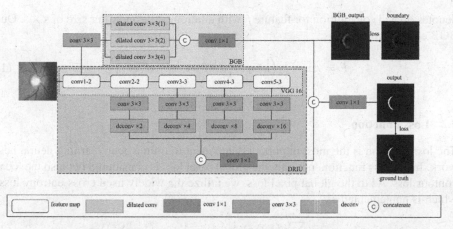

Fig. 1. The overview framework for PPA segmentation.

low-level boundary features and generate precise PPA shape. The overall architecture is illustrated in Fig. 1, which is designed based on backbone of DRIU [10]. Feature maps are extracted by VGG convolutional blocks and the proposed boundary guidance block, which are fused for the final segmentation result and provides an auxiliary boundary constraint. The boundary guidance block generates the refined feature maps maintaining boundary information. Combining the features from multiple scales provided by DRIU, the model can finally give the prediction of a full size segmentation map. In what follows, we will give detailed information on the main components of our approach.

3.1 Boundary Guidance Block (BGB)

Facing the problem of ambiguous shape in the segmentation map, we introduce a sharp-aware component to alleviate the issue by enhancing the power of boundary information extraction. If only the backbone network is used for segmentation, the segmentation map sometimes has a confusing shape at the boundary. Therefore, a boundary guidance block is proposed to help the network improve the segmentation performance. We believe that by adding this block, the network can learn more information at the boundary area, and the output of this block is integrated with the output of the backbone to guide the process of segmentation.

The proposed boundary guidance block (BGB) is shown as the light green box in Fig. 1, which is only applied on the low-level feature maps of VGG containing the sufficient boundary information. In practice, feature maps from the second layer of the first convolutional block in VGG (i.e. conv1–2) are used as the input of BGB. Our BGB consists of three dilated convolution kernels with different dilation rates, where dilated convolutions can control the receptive field and resolution without increasing the number of parameters. The generated feature maps are concatenated followed by a 1×1 convolutional layer to extract richer boundary information. As a result, let $d_r^s(f)$

denotes dilated convolution for feature f with dilation rate r and filter size of s × s. Our BGB can be expressed as:

$$F = conv_{1 \times 1}\left(concat\left(d_1^3(f), d_2^3(f), d_4^3(f)\right)\right) \tag{1}$$

3.2 Loss Function

The loss function is the most important component to train a deep learning neural network. In our loss function, not only the global pixel loss is considered but also the local contour loss. As to the global pixel loss, we utilize the widely used cross-entropy loss, which is implemented as:

$$L_{CE} = -\sum_i \left(Y_i log Y_i^* + (1 - Y_i)log\left(1 - Y_i^*\right)\right), \tag{2}$$

where Y_i, Y_i^* represent ground truth label and predicted probability value of pixel i. Besides, we propose a contour loss on the surrounding pixels of PPA to improve the poor performance around the edge. This local punishment forces the model pay more attention on the region where the more errors are going to happen. A weighted mask is obtained by dilation and erosion operations on the ground truth followed by a Gaussian filter, the purpose of this is to give more attention to the pixels closer to the boundary area, with the expression as follows:

$$M = Gauss\left(\left((Y; S)^+ - (Y; S)^-\right)\right), \tag{3}$$

where $(Y; S)^+$ and $(Y; S)^-$ represent dilation and erosion operations to the ground truth Y respectively, and S is the operation kernel size. The reason for Gaussian filtering is that pixels closer to the boundary should be given higher weights due to the high influence to the shape. The loss function of the boundary area consists of two parts: 1) the loss between the ground truth boundary area and the corresponding area of the output; 2) the loss between the BGB module output image and the ground truth boundary area. The loss function can be expressed as:

$$L_{contour} = \begin{array}{l} -\sum_i M_i\left(Y_i log Y_i^* + (1 - Y_i)log\left(1 - Y_i^*\right)\right) \\ -\sum_i \left(B_i log B_i^* + (1 - B_i)log\left(1 - B_i^*\right)\right) \end{array} \tag{4}$$

where M_i, Y_i and Y_i^* represent the mask, ground truth label and predicted probability value of pixel i respectively, B_i, B_i^* represent ground truth boundary label and BGB predicted probability value of pixel i. Finally, the total loss to train our model is:

$$L = L_{CE} + K \times L_{contour}, \tag{5}$$

where K is a hyperparameter to balance the weights. In our experiments, K is empirically set to 1.

4   Experiment and Results

4.1   Dataset and Evaluation

Retinal fundus PPA images can be divided into two categories: crescent-shaped and ring-shaped. In most cases, the shape of PPA is crescent-shaped, so we focus on the crescent-shaped PPA in our experiment. The dataset we use is provided by the Beijing Tongren Hospital, which contains 200 clinical data. For this dataset the PPA area is narrow which occupies an average of 2.37% of the ROI area and the age range of the data collectors is 6 to 14 years old. Because the target region is narrow, segmentation is difficult.

We randomly select 50 images as the testing set, and the rest as the training set. The preprocessing including eye alignment and ROI extraction is performed before resizing the images to a unified size of 512×512. Eye alignment mainly refers to the normalization of all data to the right eye. ROI extraction first uses the [15] method to locate the optic disc, and then the cropping side length is determined by 0.4 times the height of the fundus image.

We use F1-score and IOU as the main metrics to evaluate PPA segmentation performance. Both F1-score and IOU are metrics to measure the similarity between two sets. In the field of image segmentation, they are used to measure the similarity between the segmentation result and ground truth (GT). To evaluate the performance on the boundary, we apply Hausdorff distance as it is more sensitive to the boundary changes.

Our model is implemented using PyTorch. During training, our model is optimized using Adam optimizer with batch size of 8 and learning rate of 0.0001. The training stop condition adopts early stopping mechanism which selects the model with the smallest loss, if there is no lower point than the current point in the next 50 epochs, the current model is the final result. When constructing mask M in contour loss, the kernel size S is selected as 5×5, and the kernel size of the Gaussian filer is equal to 5×5.

4.2   Comparison with State-of-Arts

We compare our method with Li et al. [13], Unet [6], SegNet [7] and DRIU [11]. Figure 2 shows the visual comparison between our method and other methods. Our method achieves better results which are the closest to the ground truth especially on the boundaries. The reason for the analysis is that the method proposed in this paper adds boundary constraints, which makes the network pay more attention to boundary information in learning, thereby improving the performance of the entire network.

Table 1 show the quantitative results of our method and other methods on the clinical datasets. It can be observed from Table 1 that our method has an improvement in quantitative evaluation compared with other methods. Although Li's method [13] has superior performance in traditional methods, there is still a gap compared with the performance of algorithms based on deep learning.

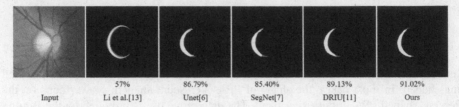

	57%	86.79%	85.40%	89.13%	91.02%
Input	Li et al.[13]	Unet[6]	SegNet[7]	DRIU[11]	Ours

Fig. 2. Comparison with other methods. The corresponding number below the image is the F1-score corresponding to the result. In the result, the red is the ground truth, the green is the segmentation result, and the yellow is the overlap area. (Color figure online)

Table 1. Comparison with the-state-of-art methods.

	Li et al. [13]	Unet [6]	SegNet [7]	DRIU [11]	Ours
F1-score	63.70%	79.11% ±0.70%	76.57% ±1.25%	79.43% ±0.67%	**80.06% ±0.39%**
Precision	63.19%	**79.89% ±1.08%**	75.71% ±1.45%	78.69% ±1.16%	79.06% ±0.86%
Recall	68.13%	79.67% ±1.15%	79.42% ±1.16%	81.57% ±0.33%	**82.25% ±0. 82%**
Accuracy	97.93%	99.01% ±0.04%	98.86% ±0.06%	99.01% ±0.05%	**99.04% ±0.02%**
IoU	48.59%	65.99% ±0.91%	62.91% ±1.36%	66.46% ±0.86%	**67.29% ±0.54%**
Hausdorff distance	5.9699	5.7504 ±0.2489	5.8039 ±0.3182	5.5596 ±0.2154	**5.4934 ±0.1384**

4.3 Ablation Study

In order to validate the contribution of our BGB block and the contour loss, we have conducted the experiments on the models trained with or without each component. Table 2 summarizes the results of three models. We use DRIU and SegNet respectively as the baseline model. It can be seen from the results that whether the baseline uses DRIU or SegNet, the dataset has been greatly improved. For the dataset, the segmentation task is difficult for narrow PPA, mainly because narrow PPA occupies a small area in the image, which will be ignored without carefully loss design in deep learning. Adding only the BGB or CL module improves F1-score and IoU, but may cause the Hausdorff distance to decrease. The reason is that in addition to the boundary information being extracted and processed in the feature map generated by the BGB module, the blood vessels and optic disc regions will also be slightly affected. The CL focuses on the boundary area of the ground truth, so adding CL may cause discontinuities or holes in the segmentation. In such cases, the addition of BGB and CL can significantly improve the performance.

Take baseline method DRIU as an example, it can be seen from Fig. 3 that each added part has a certain constraint effect on the boundary.

Table 2. Ablation study on boundary guidance block and contour loss.

		Baseline	Baseline + BGB	Baseline + CL	Baseline + BGB + CL
DRIU	F1-score	79.43% ±0.67%	79.79% ±0.10%	79.60% ±0.42%	**80.06%** **±0.39%**
	IoU	66.46% ±0.86%	66.91% ±0.13%	66.70% ±0.55%	**67.29%** **±0.54%**
	Hausdorff distance	5.5596 ±0.2154	5.6067 ±0.0891	**5.4373** **±0.1366**	5.4934 ±0.1384
SegNet	F1-score	76.57% ±1.25%	76.72% ±1.17%	76.94% ±2.04%	**77.16%** **±1.04%**
	IoU	62.91% ±1.36%	63.00% ±1.40%	63.23% ±2.58	**63.50%** **±1.29%**
	Hausdorff distance	5.8039 ±0.3182	6.0630 ±0.2331	5.9227 ±0.4811	**5.6910** **±0.1638**

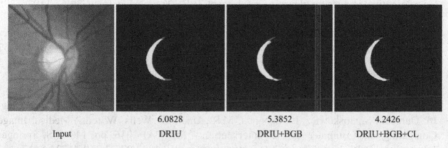

Input	6.0828 DRIU	5.3852 DRIU+BGB	4.2426 DRIU+BGB+CL

Fig. 3. Comparison of the ablation study with DRIU baseline method. Corresponding number below the image is the Hausdorff distance corresponding to the result. In the result, the red is the ground truth, the green is the segmentation result, and the yellow is the overlap area. (Color figure online)

5   Conclusion

In this paper, we propose a deep convolution neural network to segment PPA area automatically from retinal images. To solve the problem of irregular and blurry boundaries of PPA, we propose a boundary guidance block and introduce a contour loss to improve the PPA segmentation performance on the boundary. The proposed model is trained and evaluated based on clinical data. Our model achieves 80.06% F1-score, 67.29% IoU, Hausdorff distance of 5.4934, outperforming the state-of-art model. In the future, we will further analyze multiple situations of PPA such as ring-shaped area.

Acknowledgment. The research work is supported by the National Natural Science Foundation of China (NSFC) (Grant No. 82072007) and China Postdoctoral Science Foundation (No. 2020M680387).

References

1. Manjunath, V., Shah, H., Fujimoto, J.G., Duker, J.S.: Analysis of peripapillary atrophy using spectral domain optical coherence tomography. Ophthalmology **118**(3), 531–536 (2011)
2. Jonas, J.B., Gusek, G.C., Naumann, G.O.H.: Optic disk morphometry in high myopia. Graefe's Arch. Clin. Exp. Ophthalmol. **226**(6), 587–590 (1988)
3. Lu, C.K., Tang, T.B., Alan, F.M., Lauda, A., Dhillon, B.: Automatic parapapillary atrophy shape detection and quantification in colour fundus images. In: 2010 Biomedical Circuits and Systems Conference (BioCAS), pp. 86–89. Paphos (2010)
4. Patil, D.D., Deore, S.G.: Medical image segmentation: a review. Int. J. Comput. Sci. Mob. Comput. **2**(1), 22–27 (2013)
5. Narkhede, H.P.: Review of image segmentation techniques. Int. J. Sci. Modern Eng. **1**(8), 54–61 (2013)
6. Ronneberger, O., Fischer, P., Brox, T.: U-Net: convolutional networks for biomedical image segmentation. In: International Conference on Medical Image Computing and Computer-Assisted Intervention, pp. 234–241. Springer, Cham (2015)
7. Badrinarayanan, V., Kendal, A., Cipolla, R.: SegNet: a deep convolutional encoder-decoder architecture for image segmentation. IEEE Trans. Pattern Anal. Mach. Intell. **39**(12), 2481–2495 (2017)
8. Joshi, G.D., Sivaswamy, J., Krishnadas, S.R.: Optic disk and cup segmentation from monocular color retinal images for glaucoma assessment. IEEE Trans. Med. Imag. **30**(6), 1192–1205 (2011)
9. Yu, H., et al.: Fast localization and segmentation of optic disk in retinal images using directional matched filtering and level sets. IEEE Trans. Inform. Technol. Biomed. **16**(4), 644–657 (2012)
10. Bharkad, S.: Automatic segmentation of optic disk in retinal images. Biomed. Signal Process. Control **31**, 483–498 (2017)
11. Maninis, K.-K., Pont-Tuset, J., Arbeláez, P., Van Gool, L.: Deep Retinal Image Understanding. In: Ourselin, S., Joskowicz, L., Sabuncu, M.R., Unal, G., Wells, W. (eds.) Medical Image Computing and Computer-Assisted Intervention – MICCAI 2016, pp. 140–148. Springer International Publishing, Cham (2016). https://doi.org/10.1007/978-3-319-46723-8_17
12. Wang, L., Liu, H., Lu, Y., Chen, H., Zhang, J., Pu, J.: A coarse-to-fine deep learning framework for optic disc segmentation in fundus images. Biomed. Signal Process. Control **51**, 82–89 (2019)
13. Li, H., Li, H., Kang, J., Feng, Y., Xu, J.: Automatic detection of parapapillary atrophy and its association with children myopia. Comput. Methods Programs Biomed. **183**, 105090 (2020)
14. Chai, Y., Liu, H., Xu, J.: A new convolutional neural network model for peripapillary atrophy area segmentation from retinal fundus images. Appl. Soft Comput. J. **86**, 1–11 (2020)
15. Li, H., et al.: Automatic location of optic disk in retinal images. In: Proceedings 2001 International Conference on Image Processing, vol. 2, pp. 837–840 (2001)

Are Cardiovascular Risk Scores from Genome and Retinal Image Complementary? A Deep Learning Investigation in a Diabetic Cohort

Mohammad Ghouse Syed[1,2](✉) [iD], Alexander Doney[2] [iD], Gittu George[2] [iD], Ify Mordi[2] [iD], and Emanuele Trucco[1] [iD]

[1] VAMPIRE Project, Computing (SSEN), University of Dundee, Dundee, Scotland, UK
m.g.syed@dundee.ac.uk
[2] Ninewells Hospital and Medical School, University of Dundee, Dundee, Scotland, UK

Abstract. Risk of cardiovascular diseases (CVD) is driven by both genetic and environmental factors. Deep learning (DL) has shown that retinal images contain latent information indicating CVD risk. At the same time, genome-wide polygenic risk scores have demonstrated CVD risk prediction accuracy similar to conventional clinical factor-based risk scores. We speculated that information conveying CVD risk in retinal images may predominantly indicate environment factors rather than genetic factors, i.e., provide complementary information. Hence, we developed a DL model applied to diabetes retinal screening photographs from patients with type 2 diabetes based on EfficientNetB2 for predicting clinical atherosclerotic cardiovascular disease (ASCVD) risk score and a genome-wide polygenic risk score (PRS) for CVD. Results from 6656 photographs suggest a correlation between the actual and predicted ASCVD risk score ($R^2 = 0.534$, 95% CI [0.504, 0.563]; MAE = 0.109 [0.105, 0.112]), but not so for actual and predicted PRS ($R^2 = -0.005$ [-0.02, 0.01]; MAE = 0.484 [0.467, 0.5]. This suggests that retinal and genetic information are potentially complementary within an individual's cardiovascular risk, hence their combination may provide an efficient and powerful approach to screening for CVD risk. To our best knowledge, this is the first time that DL is used to investigate the complementarity of retinal and genetic information for CVD risk.

Keywords: CVD risk · Genetic risk · Retinal fundus imaging · EfficientNet

1 Introduction and Motivation

With the growing burden of cardiovascular disease (CVD) globally, there is an urgent need to be able to identify rapidly and inexpensively individuals at risk, to maximize the potential for cost-effective prevention at both individual and population level. Currently clinical risk assessment, such as the PCE ASCVD risk score, perform moderately at best

Electronic supplementary material The online version of this chapter (https://doi.org/10.1007/978-3-030-87000-3_12) contains supplementary material, which is available to authorized users.

© Springer Nature Switzerland AG 2021
H. Fu et al. (Eds.): OMIA 2021, LNCS 12970, pp. 109–118, 2021.
https://doi.org/10.1007/978-3-030-87000-3_12

in practice and do not incorporate many well-established markers of cardiovascular (CV) risk, e.g. body mass index, leading to over-estimation of the risk in some populations and under-estimation in others [22]. There is therefore a need for refinements of CV risk prediction tools in clinical practice.

We present a deep learning (DL) investigation of the potential for complementarity of the retinome (the totality of potentially clinically relevant information embedded in the retina; here, in retinal fundus images) and genome to predict clinical and genomic risk of atherosclerotic cardiovascular disease (ASCVD) risk. To our best knowledge, this is the first ever report of such a DL study.

CVD is largely preventable through lifestyle and medical management, so the ability to accurately predict risk at an early stage simply and conveniently would enable timely intervention, with important clinical benefits. Like other chronic complex conditions, CVD risk is determined by a combination of inherited (genetic) factors and environmental and lifestyle factors. Recently genome-wide polygenic risk scores (GW-PRS) have been reported to predict CVD risk with similar accuracy to conventional clinical risk scoring approaches such as the Pooled Cohort Equations ASCVD risk score [9]. Combining a clinical score with a GW-PRS may further increase prediction accuracy [6]. GW-PRS can today be determined relatively easily and cheaply from genome-wide chip-based assays but determining a clinical risk score is by comparison logistically more complex and costly in terms of time and resources: it requires a clinic visit to obtain a range of clinical measures to be combined with other patient information.

There is increasing interest in the retina as a potential source of information indicating CVD risk, supported by recent DL approaches [2, 8, 24, 25]. Importantly, images of the retina can be captured simply and efficiently, including with portable devices exploiting mobile-phone technology. Crucially, the extent to which information in the retina is complementary to clinical risk and information in the genome for predicting risk has not yet been established. We therefore investigated, for the first time to our best knowledge, to what extent a DL approach applied to retinal images would be able to predict clinical risk score and a GW-PRS for CVD.

2   Related Work

DL algorithms for image analysis of fundus camera retinal images have been appearing at a fast rate in recent years, addressing mostly vessel segmentation and artery-vein classification [13, 19, 32], vessel morphology quantification and abnormalities/lesion detection in the context of diseases [31]. For recent reviews we refer the reader to [20, 31]. Vascular measurements pre-defined by clinicians have been computed semi-automatically by systems like QUARTZ [32], SIVA [16] and VAMPIRE [21] to explore retinal biomarkers for systemic conditions like diabetes and its complication, dementia and CVD risk [3, 4, 7, 11]. There has long been interest in the association of retinal parameters and CV risk. Several studies have shown that specific retinal vascular measures, such as vessel diameter, tortuosity and fractal dimension, are all associated with CV markers and CVD events [17, 18].

Recently, DL approaches have identified retinal information related to CV risk, e.g. [24, 25]. DL has enabled an approach to biomarkers research complementary to pre-defined dictionaries of clinical features. The DL approach seeks to classify retinal images directly by outcome (e.g. an adverse cardiovascular event happened within a given time from imaging the retinal); if successful, the DL network must be mined for a representation of the image information driving the classification [28, 29]. Several groups have reported results with large image sets [8, 15, 24, 25], exploring the association of the retina with various diseases as well as patient information like age and gender.

3 Materials

3.1 Dataset

Genetics of Diabetes Audit and Research in Tayside Scotland (GoDARTS) is a cohort study started in 1998 for investigating genetics of type 2 diabetes, progression and response to treatment. Full details have been described previously [12]. GoDARTS is accessible by negotiated agreement with the access committee. GoDARTS medical records for patients with type 2 diabetes have been linked to retinal images from the Scottish diabetic retinopathy screening program; here we use the baseline (earliest available) image available for each patient. We selected a primary prevention cohort, i.e. individuals who had no previous history of hospitalization for myocardial infarction (MI) or stroke using ICD-10 codes I21–I23 and I60–I63. We used a total of 13964 retinal images from n = 6656 individuals. The increased number of images reflect the availability of left and right eye photographs. Image capture followed the standard Scottish diabetes retinal screening protocol [27] that includes 45° field of view, macula centered. Multiple images are available for some individuals for quality assessment reasons. A statistical description of the data is shown in Table 1 for the whole cohort as well as the data splits.

3.2 Outcome Variables: Risk Scores

Clinical risk of ASCVD was calculated using the Pooled Cohort Equations (PCE) ASCVD risk score [9]. The PCE risk score includes the following clinical variables: age, sex, systolic and diastolic blood pressure, total and high-density lipoprotein cholesterol, diabetes history and smoking status. The equation gives the percentage risk of ASCVD at 10 years. Using available electronic health record data, we captured these variables at the time of the retinal photograph for each individual and calculated the PCE risk score at the time of the photograph. The GW-PRS was constructed from the genome-wide genotyping data available in the GoDARTS bioresource using previously published data provided [14]. The score was z-standardised

4 Methods

4.1 Image Pre-processing

The 13964 images used have 14 different resolution levels; 2236 × 3504 (12936 images, 92.6%) and with 2304 × 3456 (560, 4%) form the vast majority of the images. Smaller resolutions account for only 3.4% of the images. The images present significant variations

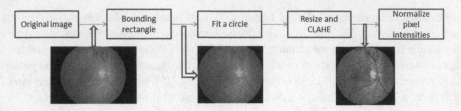

Fig. 1. Block diagram for image pre-processing.

in terms of luminosity, pigmentation, focus, and in general quality. To compensate we apply the pre-processing sketched in Fig. 1. We automatically locate the circular retinal region (briefly: color to grey levels, thresholding to binary, bounding rectangle), drop the peripheral black regions and fit a circle to remove the artefacts on the retina. We then resize the images to 512×512 and perform contrast-limited adaptive histogram equalization (CLAHE) on each color channel (R, G, B) and normalized the intensities to [0,1].

Table 1. Baseline characteristics (full cohort and data splits): *std* = standard deviation; *n* = total; *n available* = used for the feature in boldface. Gene risk score values are z-standardised.

	Overall	Train	Validation	Test
n	6656	4659	665	1332
Images	13964	9786	1392	2786
Of which right eye (%)	6928(49.61)	4852(49.58)	690(49.57)	1386(49.75)
Age at imaging				
n available	6655	4659	665	1331
Mean (std)	67.21(11.18)	67.0(11.1)	67.32(11.3)	67.88(11.4)
Sex				
n available	6655	4659	665	1331
Male (%)	3721(55.91)	2610(56.02)	349(52.48)	762(57.25)
ASCVD clinical risk score				
n available	6638	4647	663	1328
Mean (std)	0.34(0.2)	0.34(0.2)	0.34(0.21)	0.35(0.2)
Genetic risk score				
n available	6441	4508	645	1288
Mean (std)	6.95(0.61)	6.95(0.61)	6.94(0.62)	6.93(0.63)

4.2 Deep Learning Architecture and Training

We adopted the EfficientNetB2 [30] DL model, a family of deep convolutional architectures that achieved excellent performance in the ImageNet challenge [26] with 1000
object classes. We used 260×260 input images following the authors' recommenda-
tions [30] for best performance based on the compound scaling mechanism. We replaced
the EfficientNetB2 fully connected layer with a global average pooling layer followed
by a single output node with linear activation. The total number of trainable parameters
in the model is ~7.7M.

We initialized the model with pre-trained weights from ImageNet. The image set was
split randomly into 70% training, 10% validation and 20% testing. Care was taken not
to have retinal images of the same individual in different splits to avoid information leak
during training. We trained all the model parameters for a total of 50 epochs and batch size
32 for fine-tuning with retinal image as input and corresponding CVD risk score as output
label. For image augmentations on the train dataset during training we applied horizontal
flip and random rotation. We used mean squared error loss, Adam optimization and
Nesterov Accelerated Gradient momentum with initial learning rate 0.001, reduced by a
factor 0.1 if the validation loss did not improve within 5 consecutive epochs (minimum
learning rate 10^{-5}). Further, to avoid overfitting, the training stopped if there was no
improvement in the validation loss for 20 epochs. The weights with best validation
performance were saved. The learning curves are provided in the supplementary material
(SM) (Sect. 1).

Experiments were carried out in the safe haven (SH) environment provided by our
local health informatics center (HIC) services following the University of Dundee, UK
guidelines [10] on a NVIDIA TITAN Xp GPU. We used Python 3.6 for code development
with libraries opencv [1], scikit-learn [23] for image processing, and Keras 2.2.2 [5] with
tensorflow 1.9.0 as back-end for training and testing DL model.

4.3 Evaluation Metrics

Following recent reports of DL studies on retinal biomarkers [8, 15, 24, 25], we computed
the mean absolute error (MAE, Eq. (1)), and the coefficient of determination (R^2, Eq. (2)),
as both risk scores (ASCVD, PRS) are real numbers. Note that R^2 can sometime give
negative values, suggesting that the mean provides a better fit than the function fitted.
Below, y_i is the true value, $\overline{y}$ the mean true value and $\hat{y}_i$ the predicted value of the i-th
sample.

$$MAE = 1/n \sum\nolimits_{i=1}^{n} |y_i - \hat{y}_i| \tag{1}$$

$$R^2 = 1 - \frac{\sum_{i=1}^{n}(y_i - \hat{y}_i)^2}{\sum_{i=1}^{n}(y_i - \overline{y})^2} \tag{2}$$

4.4 Statistical Significance

Non-parametric bootstrap sampling was used to assess the statistical significance of the
model performance on test data. We used 2000 random samples with replacement from

the test data where each sample size was the same as that of the test data and computed MAE, R^2 from each bootstrap sample. Following [24], we define the 95% confidence interval (CI) from the distributions of the performance metrics as the range between the 2.5 and 97.5 percentile points.

4.5 Activation Visualization

We used gradient-based class activation mapping (grad-CAM) [28] to visualize the regions of the input images that contains key information for the classifier. Grad-CAM uses the gradient of the loss function with respect to the feature maps (in the intermediate layers, like convolutional layer) as weights. The weighted averaged feature maps in the layers of interest can be then upscaled to the original input size to visualize the critical regions identified.

We applied grad-CAM to the last convolutional layer which is followed by a batch normalization layer, an activation layer, a global average pooling layer and the output layer of EfficientNetB2. The spatial dimensions of the feature maps at these layers are $9 \times 9 \times 1048$, where 1048 is the number of channels. The 9×9 weighted feature maps are rescaled to input image dimensions (260×260) to obtain heatmaps. The substantial upscaling can generate artifacts. We computed non-normalized heatmaps for all the input images in the test data from the visible circular retinal region. Figure 3 shows examples of images and grad-CAM heatmaps.

5 Results

We used 9786 retinal images for training, 1392 images for validation to avoid overfitting and 2786 for testing. Two models for estimating the PCE ASCVD risk score and the genetic risk score were trained, validated and tested individually. The respective bootstrap results of MAE and R^2 for the test data are reported in Table 2. The model achieved an R^2 of 0.5338 (95% CI 0.5036, 0.5628) and MAE of 0.1085 (0.1053, 0.1116) for estimating the PCE ASCVD risk score. The R^2 achieved when estimating the PRS is -0.0053 (-0.0198, 0.009) with MAE of 0.4837 (0.4670, 0.5).

Table 2. Model performance on the estimating risk scores in the test dataset. 95% CI values computed using 2000 bootstrap samples.

Feature	Image number	Metric	Metric value
PCE ASCVD risk score	2778	R^2 (95%CI)	0.5338 (0.5036, 0.5628)
		MAE (95%CI)	0.1085 (0.1053, 0.1116)
Genetic risk score	2690	R^2 (95%CI)	-0.0053 (-0.0198, 0.009)
		MAE (95%CI)	0.4837 (0.4670, 0.5)

The scatter plot for PCE ASCVD risk score estimation (Fig. 2 left) shows a positive correlation between the actual and predicted labels which represents that the model learned to estimate PCE ASCVD risk score from the retinal images. The model has not learnt any associations between retinal image and genetic risk score, simply learning the average of the actual genetic risk score (value: 7).

Further, we generated grad-CAM heatmaps at the last convolutional layers from the model trained for estimating PCE ASCVD risk score using the test images. Figure 3 shows two sample retinal images along with the heatmap generated for the prediction made. More example heatmaps are provided in SM (Sect. 2). The optic disc, macula and vasculature emerge as the most important for classifying the PCE ASCVD risk score from retinas.

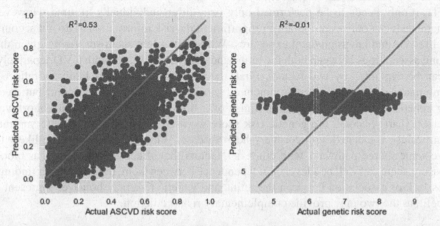

Fig. 2. Scatter plots for actual and predicted risk scores in the test data. Left: actual and predicted ASCVD risk score. Right: actual and predicted genetic risk score. Green line: main diagonal. (Color figure online)

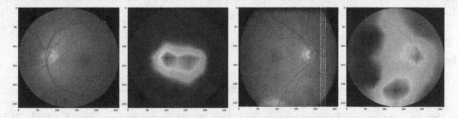

Fig. 3. Two examples of grad-CAM heatmaps for ASCVD risk score (original image, overlaid heat map). Left: actual label 0.05, predicted 0.09. Right: actual label 0.95, predicted 0.67.

6   Discussions and Conclusions

We applied a DL model to 13964 conventional digital photographs from 6656 patients with type 2 diabetes. Our main result is that the retina seems to contain information that can indicate clinical risk as defined by the PCE ASCVD risk score, but we found no indication that it contained information relating to genetic risk as defined by the GW-PRS. This finding suggests that the retina may provide valuable information relating to CVD risk that is largely complementary to a powerful genome-wide polygenic risk score. For instance, the PRS used in our study was shown to be capable of identifying individuals in the population with equivalent risk to monogenic mutations [14] and indeed in our GoDARTS population we have demonstrated a 68% increase in risk of CVD per standard deviation increase in the PRS used for this study (data not shown).

Genome-wide data is becoming increasingly cheap and easy to obtain, for example from a saliva sample or mouth scraping. The cost keeps falling and is currently similar to that of a standard laboratory blood test. Furthermore, unlike many clinical tests for CVD, it only needs to be performed only once in an individual's lifetime. However genetic tests can only ever contain a proportion of the risk information as do not account for lifestyle and environmental exposures. While this might seem surprising given the strong associations between both the retina and genetic risk scores with CVD separately, it can be explained by two factors. First, the retinal assessment is likely to reflect a combination of genetic and environmental factors, which means that the contribution of any genetic pathways is likely to diminish over time; the mean age in our cohort was over 60 years. Second, the genetic risk score we used was based on genetic variants significantly associated with coronary heart disease. While these variants are likely to have some shared pathways with other risk factors that affect the retina such as blood pressure, there can well be a level of independence between them, reflected in our finding. This lack of association between the retina and genetic risk may however represent a benefit, as the two may provide complementary risk prediction.

Acknowledgements. This research was funded by the National Institute for Health Research (NIHR) (INSPIRED 16/136/102) using UK aid from the UK Government to support global health research. The views expressed in this publication are those of the author(s) and not necessarily those of the NIHR or the UK\Department of Health and Social Care. We would like to thank VAMPIRE and INSPIRED project teams, Computing (SSEN), University of Dundee, especially Muthu Mookiah and Stephen Hogg for relevant, useful discussions.

References

1. Bradski, G.: The OpenCV Library. Dr. Dobb's Journal of Software Tools (2000)
2. Chang, J., Ko, A., Park, S.M., et al.: Association of cardiovascular mortality and deep learning-funduscopic atherosclerosis score derived from retinal fundus images. Am. J. Ophth. **217**, 121–130 (2020)
3. Cheung, C.Y.I., Zheng, Y., Hsu, W., et al.: Retinal vascular tortuosity, blood pressure, and cardiovascular risk factors. Ophthalmology **118**(5), 812–818 (2011)
4. Cheung, C.Y.I., Chan V.T., Mok V.C., et al.: Potential retinal biomarkers for dementia: what is new? Curr. Opin. Neurol. **32**(1), 82–91 (2019)
5. Chollet, F., et al.: Keras. https://keras.io (2015). Last accessed 2 March 2021
6. Elliott, J., Bodinier, B., Bond, T.A., et al.: Predictive accuracy of a polygenic risk score-enhanced prediction model vs a clinical risk score for coronary artery disease. JAMA **323**(7), 636–645 (2020). https://doi.org/10.1001/jama.2019.22241
7. Fetit, A., Doney, A.S., Hogg, S., et al.: A multimodal approach to cardiovascular risk stratification in patients with type 2 diabetes incorporating retinal, genomic and clinical features. Sci. Rep. **9**(1), 3591 (2019). https://doi.org/10.1038/s41598-019-40403-1

8. Gerrits, N., Elen, B., Van Craenendonck, T., et al.: Age and sex affect deep learning prediction of cardiometabolic risk factors from retinal images. Sci. Rep. **10**(1), 1–9 (2020)
9. Goff, D., Lloyd-Jones, D.M., Bennett, G., et al.: 2013 ACC/AHA guideline on the assessment of cardiovascular risk: a report of the American College of Cardiology/American Heart Association Task Force on Practice Guidelines. Circulation **129**(25_suppl_2), S49–S73 (2014). https://doi.org/10.1161/01.cir.0000437741.48606.98
10. Health Informatics Center (HIC) Services: Homepage, https://www.dundee.ac.uk/hic/hicservices/. Last accessed 21 July 2021
11. Ho, H., Cheung, C.Y., Sabanayagam, C., Yip, W., et al.: Retinopathy signs improved prediction and reclassification of cardiovascular disease risk in diabetes: a prospective cohort study. Sci. Rep. **7**(1), 1–8 (2017). https://doi.org/10.1038/srep41492
12. Hébert, H.L., Shepherd, B., Milburn, K., et al.: Cohort profile: genetics of diabetes audit and research in tayside scotland (godarts). Int. J. Epidemiol. **47**(2), 380–381j (2018). https://doi.org/10.1093/ije/dyx140
13. Hemelings, R., Elen, B., Stalmans, I., et al.: Artery-vein segmentation in fundus images using a fully convolutional network. Comp. Med. Img. Graph. **76**, 101636 (2019)
14. Khera, A.V., Chaffin, M., Aragam, K.G., et al.: Genome-wide polygenic scores for common diseases identify individuals with risk equivalent to monogenic mutations. Nat. Genet. **50**(9), 1219–1224 (2018). https://doi.org/10.1038/s41588-018-0183-z
15. Kim, Y.D., Noh, K.J., Byun, S.J., et al.: Effects of hypertension, diabetes, and smoking on age and sex prediction from retinal fundus images. Sci. Rep. **10**, 4623 (2020)
16. Lau, Q.P., Lee, M.L., Hsu, W., Wong, T.Y.: Simultaneously identifying all true vessels from segmented retinal images. IEEE Trans. Biomed. Eng. **60**(7), 1851–1858 (2013)
17. Liew, G., Mitchell, P., Rochtchina, E., et al.: Fractal analysis of retinal microvasculature and coronary heart disease mortality. Eur. Heart J. **32**(4), 422–429 (2011). https://doi.org/10.1093/eurheartj/ehq431
18. McGeechan, K., Liew, G., Macaskill, P., et al.: Meta-analysis: retinal vessel caliber and risk for coronary heart disease. Ann. Intern. Med. **151**(6), 404 413 (2009). https://doi.org/10.7326/0003-4819-151-6-200909150-00005
19. Ma, W., Shuang, Y., Ma, K., Wang, J., Ding, X., Zheng, Y.: Multi-task Neural Networks with Spatial Activation for Retinal Vessel Segmentation and Artery/Vein Classification. In: Shen, D., et al. (eds.) Medical Image Computing and Computer Assisted Intervention – MICCAI 2019: 22nd International Conference, Shenzhen, China, October 13–17, 2019, Proceedings, Part I, pp. 769–778. Springer International Publishing, Cham (2019). https://doi.org/10.1007/978-3-030-32239-7_85
20. Mookiah, M.R.K., Hogg, S., MacGillivray, T.J., et al.: A review of machine learning methods for retinal blood vessel segmentation and artery/vein classification. Med. Image Anal. **68**, 101905 (2021). https://doi.org/10.1016/j.media.2020.101905
21. Mookiah, M.R.K., Hogg, S., MacGillivray, T., Trucco, E., et al.: On the quantitative effects of compression of retinal fundus images on morphometric vascular measurements in vampire. Comp. Meth. Progr. Biomed., 105969 (2021)
22. Mora, S., Wenger, N.K., Cook, N.R., et al.: Evaluation of the pooled cohort risk equations for cardiovascular risk prediction in a multiethnic cohort from the women's health initiative. JAMA Intern. Med. **178**(9), 1231–1240 (2018)
23. Pedregosa, F., Varoquaux, G., Gramfort, A., et al.: Scikit-learn: machine learning in Python. J. Mach. Learn. Res. **12**, 2825–2830 (2011)
24. Poplin, R., Varadarajan, A.V., Blumer, K., et al.: Prediction of cardiovascular risk factors from retinal fundus photographs via deep learning. Nat. Biomed. Eng. **2**(3), 158–164 (2018)
25. Rim, T.H., Lee, G., Kim, Y.,, et al.: Prediction of systemic biomarkers from retinal photographs: development and validation of deep-learning algorithms. Lancet Digital Health **2**(10), e526–e536 (2020)

26. Russakovsky, O., Deng, J., Su, H., et al.: ImageNet large scale visual recognition challenge. Int. J. Comput. Vis. **115**(3), 211–252 (2015). https://doi.org/10.1007/s11263-015-0816-y
27. Scottish Diabetic Retinopathy Screening Homepage: https://www.ndrs.scot.nhs.uk/. Last accessed 2 March 2021
28. Selvaraju, R.R., Cogswell, M., Das, A., et al.: Grad-cam: visual explanations from deep networks via gradient-based localization. Int. J. Comput. Vis. **128**(2), 336–359 (2019). https://doi.org/10.1007/s11263-019-01228-7
29. Singh, A., Sengupta, S., Lakshminarayan, V.: Explainable deep learning models in medical image analysis, https://arxiv.org/pdf/2005.13799.pdf (2020)
30. Tan, M., Le, Q.: Efficientnet: rethinking model scaling for convolutional neural networks. In: Proc. Int. Conf. on Machine Learning (ICML), pp. 6105–6114. PMLR (2017)
31. Trucco, E., MacGillivray, T.J., Xu, Y.W.: Computational Retinal Image Analysis. Academic Press, ISBN 9780081028162 (2019)
32. Welikala, R.A., Foster, P.J., Whincup, P.H., et al.: Automated arteriole and venule classification using deep learning for retinal images from the UK Biobank cohort. Comput. Biol. Med. **90**, 23–32 (2017)

Dual-Branch Attention Network and Atrous Spatial Pyramid Pooling for Diabetic Retinopathy Classification Using Ultra-Widefield Images

Zhihui Tian[1], Haijun Lei[1], Hai Xie[2], Xianlu Zeng[3], Xinyu Zhao[3], Miaohong Chen[3], Guoming Zhang[3(✉)], and Baiying Lei[2(✉)]

[1] Key Laboratory of Service Computing and Applications, Guangdong Province Key Laboratory of Popular High Performance Computers, College of Computer Science and Software Engineering, Shenzhen University, Shenzhen, China
[2] National-Regional Key Technology Engineering Laboratory for Medical Ultrasound, Guangdong Key Laboratory for Biomedical Measurements and Ultrasound Imaging, School of Biomedical Engineering, Health Science Center, Shenzhen University, Shenzhen, China
leiby@szu.edu.cn
[3] Shenzhen Eye Hospital, Shenzhen Key Ophthalmic Laboratory, The Second Affiliated Hospital of Jinan University, Shenzhen, China

Abstract. Diabetic Retinopathy (DR) is a very common retinal disease in the world, which can affect vision and even cause blindness. Early diagnosis can effectively prevent the disease, or at least delay the progression of DR. However, most methods are based on regular single-view images, which would lack complete information of lesions. In this paper, a novel method is proposed to achieve DR classification using ultra-widefield images (UWF). The proposed network includes a dual-branch network, an efficient channel attention (ECA) module, a spatial attention (SA) module, and an atrous spatial pyramid pooling (ASPP) module. Specifically, the dual-branch network uses ResNet-34 model as the backbone. The ASPP module enlarges the receptive field to extract rich feature information by setting different dilated rates. To emphasize the useful information and suppress the useless information, the ECA and SA modules are utilized to extract important channel information and spatial information respectively. To reduce the parameters of the network, we use a global average pooling (GAP) layer to compress the features. The experimental results on the UWF images collected by a local hospital show that our model performs very well.

Keywords: Diabetic retinopathy · Dual-branch network · Efficient channel and spatial attention · Atrous spatial pyramid pooling

1 Introduction

Diabetic retinopathy (DR) originates from diabetes and is a relatively common fundus disease that can cause blindness. It is estimated that about 93 million people worldwide

© Springer Nature Switzerland AG 2021
H. Fu et al. (Eds.): OMIA 2021, LNCS 12970, pp. 119–128, 2021.
https://doi.org/10.1007/978-3-030-87000-3_13

suffer from DR [1], and this number continues to rise. Since DR can be detected by the morphological changes of the retina, many researchers are devoted to the research of disease detection based on fundus images to assist ophthalmologists for diagnosis. However, most methods are based on single-view fundus images, which lead to incomplete information of lesions. So some researchers chose ultra-widefield (UWF) images as their studying objects [2–4]. In clinical, compared with conventional single-view scanning images, the UWF images have a vision of 180–200° and contain more region information, which is beneficial for the accurate diagnosis. For instance, Nagasato et al. proposed a central retinal vein occlusion detection method based on UWF fundus images [5]. Pellegrini et al. presented an method for artery/vein classification using UWF images [6].

The UWF fundus images of patients with DR and those of normal people are shown in Fig. 1. It shows that there is little contrast between the lesion area and the normal area, with differences in lesion size and inhomogeneous distribution, which brings great challenges to the processing and analysis of the UWF images.

Fig. 1. Display of the UWF images with two categories. The two images on the left are DR images, and the two on the right are normal images.

Deep learning performs well in medical image processing and analysis and many researchers have applied it to automatically diagnose various diseases. For example, Brown et al. designed an automatic detection method for retinopathy of prematurity using deep convolutional network [7]. Li et al. used a deep learning method to detect DR and diabetic macular oedema [8]. Diaz-Pinto et al. presented a method based on deep learning to detect and classify glaucoma [9]. Xie et al. used a cross-attention network for fundus diseases classification [10]. However, compared to the background area, some lesion areas are small and the background area is more obvious than the target area (especially in UWF images). Some researchers tried to use more complex models or design multiple networks to extract the discriminative features. For instance, Hamwood et al. used a fully convolutional network to determine the positions of cone photoreceptors [11]. Ruan et al. achieved kidney tumor segmentation on CT images by using a multi-branch feature sharing network [12]. However, these networks have advantages in extracting global features, but easily overlook the important local information, which is disadvantageous for the expression of discriminative detailed features. To address this situation, some researchers have turned to attention mechanism [13–16]. The attention mechanism can obtain more detailed information of the target, which is very helpful for the detection and discrimination of lesion.

In this paper, a dual-branch network with ResNet-34 [17] as the backbone is proposed to extract features. We use atrous spatial pyramid pooling module (ASPP) to enlarges the receptive field and obtain rich semantic information. According to the dependence of spatial and channel information between the features, the efficient channel attention (ECA) and spatial attention (SA) modules are utilized to emphasize the useful information after multiple convolutional layers of the network. Finally, we use a global average pooling (GAP) layer to compress the features and concatenate the features from two branches to complete the final classification task.

2 Methodology

The architecture of our proposed method is shown in Fig. 2. We propose a dual-branch network to extract features and enlarge the receptive field by ASPP to obtain richer semantic information. At the same time, the ECA and SA modules are employed to emphasize some important information. After obtaining discriminative features by GAP, the features from the two branches are concatenated and used for the prediction. The detailed information of modules will be described below.

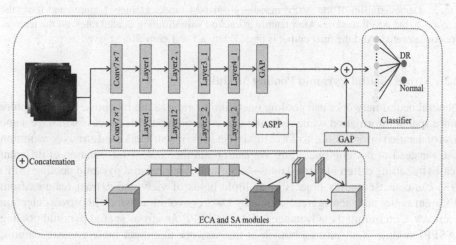

Fig. 2. The architecture of proposed method. The ResNet-34 model is the backbone and is used in both two branches. The features extracted from the ASPP module are fed into the ECA and SA modules to interact the high-dimensional features and compressed by GAP.

2.1 Dual-Branch Network

Inspired by [9], we propose a dual-branch network to extract depth features. Each branch of the model is based on the ResNet-34 model, which solves the gradient disappearance problem in deep networks through residual connection. It is worth noting that the first three layers of the two branch networks share parameters, so the scale of the model parameters is reduced. We use the UWF images as the input of the dual-branch network, and the extracted rich deep semantic features can be used in the subsequent modules.

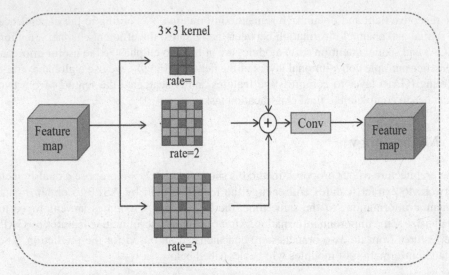

Fig. 3. Demonstration of the ASPP module. Resnet-34 model extracts features and feeds the features to the ASPP module. After feature extraction with different dilated rates, all the features are concatenated. And the firral output is obtained by a 1 × 1 convolution layer.

2.2 Atrous Spatial Pyramid Pooling Module

General neural networks use pooling operation to enlarge the receptive field to capture more spatial information while reducing the resolution, but this process will have some loss of detailed information. To solve this issue, some researchers used atrous convolution (AC) instead of pooling operation. We can obtain the context information of different scales by setting different dilated rates. At the same time, spatial pyramid pooling (SPP) [18] can detect complex objects in multiple fields of view and extract features from different angles and then aggregate them by 1 × 1 convolution, which improves detection accuracy. Combining the advantages of AC and SPP, an atrous spatial pyramid pooling (ASPP) module is added to a branch of the network to extract more context features, which can further improves the classification performance on UWF images without increasing parameters. Specifically, we use three different dilated rates to perform atrous convolution operation and all the extracted features are integrated by a 1 × 1 convolution layer. The structure of ASPP module is demonstrated in Fig. 3 in which we set the dilated rate to 1, 2, and 3 respectively. Because the extraction of information with a large dilated rate may only have an obvious effect on the detection of some large objects, while the focus area of most fundus diseases is relatively small compared with the global background area.

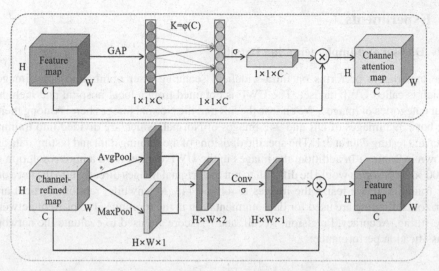

Fig. 4. The structure of ECA and SA modules. After a GAP layer, ECA generates channel attention weights matrix by a one-dimensional convolution of size K, where K is adaptively determined by the number of channels. The channel attention map is obtained by multiplying the channel attention weight matrix with the original feature map. After AP and MP, we use a convolutional layer and an sigmoid function to integrate the concatenated features as the spatial attention weight matrix. Finally, the channel-refined map is multiplied by the spatial attention weights to get the final output.

2.3 Efficient Channel Attention Module and Spatial Attention Module

Inspired by [19–21], we use the attention mechanism of efficient channel attention (ECA) and spatial attention (SA) to enhance the feature representation ability. The ECA and SA modules are shown in Fig. 4. We perform a GAP operation on the feature map and capture the cross-channel information from each channel and its K neighbors, which can be achieved by a one-dimensional convolution of size K. Then use a matrix multiplication operation to integrate the output of the previous step with the original feature map. After that, we perform average pooling (AP) operation and max pooling (MP) operation, and the spatial attention coefficients matrix are obtained by a simple convolutional layer and sigmoid operation. Finally, all features are integrated and become the output of this module. Moreover, an adaptive selection method of one-dimensional convolution kernel size in ECA is employed to find the suitable receptive region of kernel. The formula is described as follows.

$$K = \phi(C) = |\frac{\log_2(C) + b}{\gamma}|, \tag{1}$$

where K is the kernel size of one-dimensional convolution, C is the number of channels, b and γ are manually parameters, which are set as 1 and 2 respectively.

3 Experiments

3.1 Dataset and Implementation Details

The experiment performs on ultra-widefield scanning laser ophthalmoscopy images which is called UWF dataset. The UWF is obtained from a local hospital and includes four categories of images. We choose the DR and the Normal images here. Among them, we have 398 images of DR and 948 images of Normal, which are divided into training data and testing data at 3:1. The specific divisions of the training data and testing data are shown in Table 1. In addition, the images in the UWF dataset have a high resolution of 2600×2048 which would be difficult to put the original images directly into the network for training. So we resize the images to 448×448. Meanwhile, random vertical and horizontal flipping are used for data augmentation in the training set to prevent network overfitting. Accuracy, Precision, Recall, and F1-score are used to evaluate the network classification performance.

Table 1. The specific distribution of the training data and testing data.

	DR	Normal
Training data	298	708
Test data	100	240
Total	398	948

We implement our work with PyTorch and use GPUs to accelerate the training process. The pre-trained ResNet-34 model is used for the first three layers of the network, and the second two layers are initialized randomly. During training, we choose the Adam with default values as the optimizer. We set the max epoch to 80, set the size of every training batch to 8 and set the size of every testing batch to 1. In addition, the learning rate is 0.0001 and decays by 10% per 50 epochs.

3.2 Experimental Results

The experimental results of different methods is shown in Table 2. We choose VGG16 [22], ResNet-34 [17], ResNet-50 [17], InceptionV3 [23], and DenseNet121 [24] for comparison. The VGG16, ResNet-34, ResNet-50, and DenseNet121 contain the characteristics of deep networks, while InceptionV3 has the characteristics of multiple branches and great feature extraction ability. So these networks are good baselines for research.

From Table 2, we can see that among the backbone networks, InceptionV3 has the best performance, followed by ResNet-34. So we know the multi-branch has an impact in the stage of feature extraction. From line 2, line 3, and line 5, it shows that the deep networks perform not as good as other networks. Generally, the deeper networks are easily overfitting and difficult to train. The proposed method extracts multi-scale features and uses the attention mechanism to strengthen the degree of attention to some

Table 2. Performance of different models (%).

Method	Accuracy	Precision	Recall	F1-score
VGG16	95.00	95.60	87.00	91.10
ResNet34	95.88	89.81	97.00	93.27
ResNet50	93.53	84.21	96.00	89.72
InceptionV3	96.18	93.34	93.00	93.47
DenseNet121	95.59	88.99	97.00	92.82
Proposed	**98.82**	**96.15**	**100.00**	**98.04**

important information. From Table 2, our model performs well compared with the other backbone networks and achieves the highest accuracy of 98.82%.

Ablation experiments are conducted to estimate the modules in our model. Specifically, we select the following networks for comparison: ResNet-34 model (ResNet34), dual-branch model (DB), dual-branch model with ASPP (DB-ASPP), dual-branch model with attention modules (DB-AM), and dual-branch network with all complete modules (Proposed). The experimental results are shown in Table 3. We can know that adding corresponding modules to the backbone can slightly strengthen the classification performance. From the experimental results, the score of dual-branch model with ECA and SA on Recall is lower than backbone, because both ECA and SA modules operate with deep features. Without strengthening the global feature extraction capability, the use of ECA and SA alone will produce biased errors in the classification results. So the result has a slight decrease in Recall.

Table 3. Evaluation of every module of our method (%).

Method	Accuracy	Precision	Recall	F1-score
ResNet34	95.88	89.81	97.00	93.27
DB	95.88	90.83	98.00	93.33
DB-ASPP	97.06	92.45	98.00	95.15
DB-AM	96.47	92.31	96.00	94.12
Proposed	**98.82**	**96.15**	**100.00**	**98.04**

To more intuitively evaluate our method, we plot the receiver operating characteristic (ROC) curves and the area under curve (AUC) is used as the evaluation metric. The ROC curves are shown in Fig. 5 in which we can observe our model has very good performance.

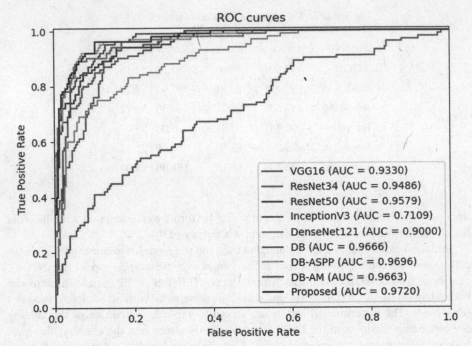

Fig. 5. Demonstration of ROC curves. We can see that the AUC value of our proposed model is 0.9720, which is the highest compared to other methods.

4 Conclusions

We propose a novel dual-branch network for DR classification. Two branches use ResNet-34 as the backbone, which can strengthen the extraction ability. ASPP enlarges the receptive field and integrates more features. ECA and SA emphasize the important information of feature space to obtain more discriminative features. The experimental results show our method performs better than other methods on the UWF dataset.

Acknowledgements. This work was supported partly by National Natural Science Foundation of China (Nos. 61871274, 61801305 and 81571758), National Natural Science Foundation of Guangdong Province (No. 2020A1515010649 and No. 2019A1515111205), Guangdong Province Key Laboratory of Popular High Performance Computers (No. 2017B030314073), Guangdong Laboratory of Artificial-Intelligence and Cyber-Economics (SZ), the China Postdoctoral Science Foundation (2021M692196), Shenzhen Peacock Plan (Nos. KQTD2016053112051497 and KQTD2015033016104926), Shenzhen Key Basic Research Project (Nos. JCYJ20190808165209410, 20190808145011259, JCYJ20180507184647636, GJHZ20190822095414576 and JCYJ20170302153337765, JCYJ20170302150411789, JCYJ20170302142515949, GCZX2017040715180580, GJHZ20180418190529516, and JSGG20180507183215520), NTUT-SZU Joint Research Program (No. 2020003), Special Project in Key Areas of Ordinary Universities of Guangdong Province (No. 2019KZDZX1015), Shenzhen Key Medical Discipline Construction Fund (No. SZXK038), Shenzhen Fund for Guangdong Provincial High-level Clinical Key Speciaties (No. SZGSP014), Shenzhen-Hong Kong Co-financing Project (No. SGDX20190920110403741).

References

1. Yau, J.W., et al.: Global prevalence and major risk factors of diabetic retinopathy. Diabetes Care **35**(3), 556–564 (2012)
2. Webb, R.H., Hughes, G.W.: Scanning laser ophthalmoscope. IEEE Trans. Biomed. Eng. **7**, 488–492 (1981)
3. Haleem, M.S., Han, L., van Hemert, J., Li, B., Fleming, A.: Retinal area detector from scanning laser ophthalmoscope (SLO) images for diagnosing retinal diseases. IEEE J. Biomed. Health Inform. **19**(4), 1472–1482 (2014)
4. Ashok, V., Murugesan, G.: Detection of retinal area from scanning laser ophthalmoscope images (SLO) using deep neural network. Int. J. Biomed. Eng. Technol. **23**(2–4), 303–314 (2017)
5. Nagasato, D., et al.: Deep neural network-based method for detecting central retinal vein occlusion using ultrawide-field fundus ophthalmoscopy. Ophthalmology **2018** (2018)
6. Pellegrini, E., et al.: A graph cut approach to artery/vein classification in ultra-widefield scanning laser ophthalmoscopy. IEEE Trans. Med. Imag. **37**(2), 516–526 (2017)
7. Brown, J.M., et al.: Automated diagnosis of plus disease in retinopathy of prematurity using deep convolutional neural networks. JAMA Ophthalmol. **136**(7), 803–810 (2018)
8. Li, F., et al.: Deep learning-based automated detection for diabetic retinopathy and diabetic macular oedema in retinal fundus photographs. Eye, 1–9 (2021)
9. Diaz-Pinto, A., et al.: Retinal image synthesis and semi-supervised learning for glaucoma assessment. IEEE Trans. Med. Imag. **38**(9), 2211–2218 (2019)
10. Xie, H., et al.: Cross-attention multi-branch network for fundus diseases classification using SLO images. Med. Image Anal. **71**, 102031 (2021)
11. Hamwood, J., et al.: Automatic detection of cone photoreceptors with fully convolutional networks. Transl. Vis. Sci. Technol. **8**(6), 10 (2019)
12. Ruan, Y., et al.: MB-FSGAN: joint segmentation and quantification of kidney tumor on CT by the multi-branch feature sharing generative adversarial network. Med. Image Anal. **64**, 101721 (2020)
13. Mou, L., et al.: CS-Net: Channel and Spatial Attention Network for Curvilinear Structure Segmentation. In: Shen, D., et al. (eds.) MICCAI 2019. LNCS, vol. 11764, pp. 721–730. Springer, Cham (2019). https://doi.org/10.1007/978-3-030-32239-7_80
14. Nie, D., Wang, L., Xiang, L., Zhou, S., Adeli, E., Shen, D.: Difficulty-aware attention network with confidence learning for medical image segmentation. In: AAAI, pp. 1085–1092 (2019)
15. Shaikh, M., Kollerathu, V.A., Krishnamurthi, G.: Recurrent attention mechanism networks for enhanced classification of biomedical images. In: IEEE ISBI, pp. 1260–1264 (2019)
16. Zhang, J., Xie, Y., Xia, Y., Shen, C.: Attention residual learning for skin lesion classification. IEEE Trans. Med. Imag. **38**(9), 2092–2103 (2019)
17. He, K., Zhang, X., Ren, S., Sun, J.: Deep residual learning for image recognition. In: CVPR, pp. 770–778 (2016)
18. Gu, Z., et al.: DeepDisc: optic disc segmentation based on atrous convolution and spatial pyramid pooling. In: Stoyanov, D., et al. (eds.) OMIA/COMPAY 2018, LNCS, vol. 11039, pp. 253–260. Springer, Cham (2018)

19. Schlemper, J., et al.: Attention gated networks: learning to leverage salient regions in medical images. Med. Image Anal. **53**, 197–207 (2019)
20. Xu, K., et al.: Show, attend and tell: neural image caption generation with visual attention. In: Bach, F.R., Blei, D.M. (eds.) International Conference on Machine Learning 2015, PMLR, vol. 37, pp. 2048–2057. PMLR, Lille (2015)
21. Wang, Q., et al.: ECA-Net: efficient channel attention for deep convolutional neural networks. In: CVPR (2020)
22. Simonyan, K., Zisserman, A.: Very deep convolutional networks for large-scale image recognition. In: ICLR (2015)
23. Szegedy, C., Vanhoucke, V., Ioffe, S., Shlens, J., Wojna, Z.: Rethinking the inception architecture for computer vision. In: CVPR, pp. 2818–2826 (2016)
24. Huang, G., et al.: Densely connected convolutional networks. In: CVPR, pp. 4700–4708 (2017)

Self-adaptive Transfer Learning for Multicenter Glaucoma Classification in Fundus Retina Images

Yiming Bao[1], Jun Wang[1], Tong Li[1], Linyan Wang[2], Jianwei Xu[1], Juan Ye[2], and Dahong Qian[1(✉)]

[1] Institute of Medical Robotics, Shanghai Jiao Tong University, Shanghai, China
dahong.qian@sjtu.edu.cn
[2] The Department of Ophthalmology, The Second Affiliated Hospital of Zhejiang University, College of Medicine, Hangzhou, China

Abstract. The early screening of glaucoma is important for patients to receive treatment in time and maintain eyesight. Deep learning (DL) based models have been successfully used for computer-aided diagnosis (CAD) of glaucoma. However, a DL model pre-trained on certain dataset from one hospital may have poor performance on other hospital data, therefore its applications in the real scene are limited. In this paper, we propose a self-adaptive transfer learning (SATL) strategy to fill the domain gap between multi-center datasets. Specifically, the encoder of a DL model that is pre-trained on the source domain is used to initialize the encoder of a reconstruction model. Then, this reconstruction model is trained using only unlabeled image data from the target domain, which makes the encoder in the model adapt itself to extract useful features both for target domain images encoding and glaucoma classification, simultaneously. Experimental results on a private and two public glaucoma diagnosis datasets demonstrate that the proposed SATL strategy is effective. Also, it meets the real scene application and the privacy protection policy due to its independence from the source domain data.

Keywords: Glaucoma diagnosis · Transfer learning · Multi-center domain adaptation

1 Introduction

Glaucoma is one of the most primary leading causes of blindness [10]. The loss of sight due to glaucoma is irreversible while some other eye diseases such as myopia and presbyopia are not. Thus, early diagnosis of glaucoma for effective treatment and vision conservation matters a lot for patients.

However, the symptoms of glaucoma in the early stage are difficult to perceive. One of the standard methods widely used by eye specialists nowadays is

---

Y. Bao and J. Wang are co-first authors. J. Ye and D. Qian are co-corresponding authors.

© Springer Nature Switzerland AG 2021
H. Fu et al. (Eds.): OMIA 2021, LNCS 12970, pp. 129–138, 2021.
https://doi.org/10.1007/978-3-030-87000-3_14

the optic nerve head (ONH) assessment [10] in fundus retina images. Whereas, mastering the tricks of performing ONH assessment remains challenging. Therefore, some automatically calculated parameters were presented and popularized as quantitative clinical measurements, such as cup to disc ratio (CRD) which means the ratio of vertical cup diameter to vertical disc diameter in the fundus retina image. Generally, a larger CRD represents a higher possibility of glaucoma and vice verse. However, manually labeling the mask of the cup or disc region is labor-consuming, which makes image-level category labels necessary and reasonable for automatically screening glaucoma.

In the past several years, Deep Learning (DL) based methods have received unprecedented attention and achieved state-of-the-art performance in many fields, including medical image analysis [14]. Glaucoma can be screened from fundus retina images by DL models which are well trained on sufficient data and precise image-level labels [4]. However, DL models trained on one single site cannot be directly generalized and applied to other sites. The distributions of training and testing data are partially different so the pre-trained model may fail to fulfill the diagnosis task.

Commonly, the difference between datasets can be seen as a domain gap. For Example, the discrepancy between images from different dataset can be reflected in many image statistical traits, such as color style, contrast, resolution, and so on. Also, the joint distributions of images and labels may be quite different between the source and the target domain, i.e., $P(x^s, y^s) \neq P(x^t, y^t)$. This is mainly because the margin distributions are different, i.e., $P(x^s) \neq P(x^t)$ even if the conditional distributions, i.e., $P(y^s|x^s)$ and $P(y^t|x^t)$ are similar. Many methods have been proposed to solve this problem. Fine tuning [19] is most widely used in real practical applications. However, fine-tuning is unable to apply when the dataset from a new target domain is completely unlabeled.

To solve the domain adaptation problem, a novel *self-adaptive transfer learning* (SATL) framework is proposed in this paper for glaucoma diagnosis. Specifically, we train a convolutional neural network in the source domain with sufficient labeled data. Then, the feature extraction layers of this trained model is shared as the encoder of a reconstruction network. The reconstruction network is trained in the target domain using only unlabeled data. The encoder is adapted to fit the distribution of target data while maintains the ability for glaucoma diagnosis. The contributions of this paper can be concluded as follows:

(1) To the best of our knowledge, our work is the first to investigate the study of transfer adaptation learning for the classification of glaucoma with multicenter fundus retina images.
(2) Our framework only uses unlabeled date in the target domain and is independent from source domain data, so it has great potential for real scene applications and can meet privacy protection policy for medical data.
(3) Experimental results shows that our framework can preserve most of the classification ability of the off-shelf model and meanwhile improve its classification performance in target domain data. Even totally independent from source domain data, it outperforms other state-of-the-art domain adaptation

methods such as CycleGAN, which heavily relies on source domain data in adaptation stage.

2   Related Works

Transfer adaptation learning (TAL) [20,22] is the most relevant area with the proposed method. It is a combination of transfer learning (TL) and domain adaptation (DA) and can be categorized into three classes, which will be introduced respectively.

Instance Re-weighting Adaptation Learning (IRAL). Methods in this area assign weights to the source domain instances based on their similarity to the target domain instances [13,24]. Via re-sampling or importance weighting, the performance of the trained source classifier in the target domain can be enhanced. However, the estimation of the assigned weights is under a prior-decided parametric distribution assumption [22], which may differ from the true parametric distribution.

Feature Adaptation Learning (FAL). For adapting datasets from multiple domains, methods in this category are widely proposed to find a feature representation space where the projected features from target and source domain follow similar distributions [15,21]. In the past few years, the most famous FAL methods are GAN-based domain adaptation models. However, finding a general feature space for most domains remains challenging. Also, training a GAN-based domain adaptation model needs both source and target domain data, which is more and more impractical in the real scene due to the privacy protection policy for medical data.

Self-supervised Transfer Learning (SSTL). Algorithms in this category focus on training a supervised classifier on the source domain and then transfer its knowledge to the target domain via self-supervised learning [2,3,5,17]. For example, Cheplygina *et al.* [3] investigated a Gaussian texture features-based classification model of chronic obstructive pulmonary disease (COPD) in multi-center datasets. These methods integrate the data information from different domains by extracting some manually designed features from images, which limits the generalization ability of model. Ghifary *et al.* [5] is the most relative literature with our framework. Our method differs from [5] mainly in the network structure. Moreover, we explore application in glaucoma diagnosis in several datasets.

3   Method

The framework of the proposed method is illustrated in Fig. 1. The proposed SATL framework can transfer a pre-trained source classification model to a target domain without using neither source images nor labels.

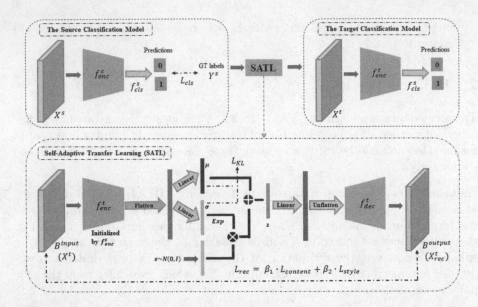

Fig. 1. Illustration of the self-adaptive transfer learning (SATL) strategy, which is independent of the source domain data and more suitable for the real scene applications.

Let $f^s : \mathcal{X}^s \to \mathcal{Y}^s$ be the source pre-trained classification model and $f^t : \mathcal{X}^t \to \mathcal{X}^t_{rec}$ be the target reconstruction model. The feature encoder is denoted as $f_{enc} : \mathcal{X} \to \mathcal{F}$ and the lightweight classification function $f_{cls} : \mathcal{F} \to \mathcal{Y}$. We denote one more function: an decoder $f_{dec} : \mathcal{F} \to \mathcal{X}$ in f^t. Then, given an input sample x, f^s and f^t can be formulated as:

$$f^s(x) = f^s_{cls}(f^s_{enc}(x)); f^t(x) = f^t_{dec}(f^t_{enc}(x)) \tag{1}$$

Once $f^t(x)$ is trained, we can build the self-adapted classification model $f^t_{SA}(x)$ for target domain image classification by $f^t_{SA}(x) = f^s_{cls}(f^t_{enc}(x))$

As shown in Fig. 1, the reconstruction model f^t_{dec} is implemented as a variational auto-encoder (VAE), which can compress the image information and sample a latent vector z. The encoder of it f^t_{enc} is initialized by the pre-trained source encoder f^s_{enc}.

The loss function used to optimize the proposed self-adaptive reconstruction model can be represented as:

$$L(f^t_{enc}, f^t_{dec}, x^t) = \alpha \cdot L_{KL} + \beta \cdot L_{rec}, \tag{2}$$

$$L_{KL} = -KL(f^t_{enc}(z|x^t)|f^t_{dec}(z|x^t)), \tag{3}$$

where the first term in the loss function L_{KL} is the KL divergency of the latent vector distribution and the true data distribution. The second term L_{rec} is the reconstruction loss between the output image and the input image.

Instead of using a single MSE loss, we perform a new designed combination of two loss functions following [9]. We argue that the self-adaptive reconstruction model should be guided to reconstruct high-level style information in the target domain images rather than just the pixel-wise texture. Thus, the reconstruction loss function designed in this paper is as:

$$L_{rec} = \beta_1 \cdot \sum_{i,j,k} (B_{ijk}^{output} - B_{ijk}^{input})^2 + \beta_2 \cdot \sum_{m,n} (G_{mn}^{output} - G_{mn}^{input})^2, \quad (4)$$

where B^{output} and B^{input} denote the output and input of the reconstruction model, respectively. i, j, k and m, n represent the position indexes. G^{output} and G^{input} are the Gram matrices of B^{output} and B^{input}. The gram matrix can be calculated as:

$$G = \frac{1}{n_i \times n_j \times n_k} \mathbf{v}\mathbf{v}^{\mathbf{T}}, \quad (5)$$

where $\mathbf{v}$ is the flattened column vector of B^{output} or B^{input}.

4   Experiments and Results

4.1   Datasets

Table 1. The statistical difference between three datasets

Dataset	Domain	Samples	Pos vs. Neg	Avg of image size
LAG (public)	Source/Target	4854	3143:1689	300×300
pri-RFG (private)	Source/Target	1881	1013:868	989×989
REFUGE (public)	Target only	400	40:360	1062×1062

We used two public datasets and one private dataset to validate the proposed SATL framework on glaucoma diagnosis task. The first public dataset is large-scale attention-based glaucoma (LAG) dataset [8] established by Li *et al.*. The second is from the REFUGE challenge [12]. Moreover, we also collected 1881 retina fundus images from one collaborated hospital and built a private dataset (pri-RFG) via labeling all the images by experienced ophthalmologists. The details of the above-mentioned three datasets (LAG, REFUGE, pri-RFG) are summarized and tabulated in Table 1. We can observe that the scales, the average size of images and the ratio of samples in different datasets are quite various, making transfer learning between them challenging. Due to the small number of samples in dataset REFUGE, we just used it as target domain dataset, while LAG and pri-RFG are used for cross-domain evaluation. In other words, we implemented a total of four groups of experiments. Based on the direction from source domain to target domain, they can be represented as LAG → pri-RFG, pri-RFG → LAG, LAG → REFUGE and pri-RFG → REFUGE. When used as a source domain dataset, we separated training and validation set. When used as a target domain dataset, all the images were fed into the reconstruction model to train and adapt the encoder layers.

4.2   Implement Details and Evaluation Metrics

Both the source classification model and the target reconstruction model were implemented using Pytorch (version 1.3.0) and trained on an NVIDIA RTX 2080Ti GPU. We implemented the source classification model as a VGG [16] and optimized it with cross entropy (CE) loss [11]. During the training stage of the source classification model, we set the learning rate as 10^{-6}, weight decay as 5×10^{-4}. All the samples in the source domain were split into training set and validation set using a ratio of 7:3 empirically, following stratified sampling method to ensure that the Pos vs. Neg ratios in each set are similar. At each iteration, a mini-batch of 16 samples were fed into the model. The number of training epochs was set as 50. To avoid the over-fitting issue, the model which achieved the maximum accuracy in the validation set was saved.

During the training stage of the self-adaptive reconstruction model on the target dataset, the learning rate of the encoder was set as 10^{-7} and that of the rest layers was set as 10^{-3}. To avoiding over-fitting on the reconstruction task and losing the ability to extract features that are useful for classification task, the target reconstruction model was trained for only 20 epochs. We empirically set the weights α, β_1 and β_2 in the reconstruction loss function as 0.3, 0.2, 0.5, and the channel number of the latent vector in the model as 32.

Once the target reconstruction model was trained, the self-adapted encoder of it was used as the feature extractor of a target classification model. The last lightweight FC layer of the source classification model played a role as classifier. This new combined target classification model was evaluated on target domain dataset by metrics in terms of Accuracy, Recall, Precision, F1 score and Area Under the ROC Curve (AUC).

4.3   Results and Discussion

As described in Sect. 4.2, based on the three available datasets, there are four executable domain adaptation directions denoted as LAG → pri-RFG, pri-RFG → LAG, LAG → REFUGE, and pri-RFG → REFUGE. For validating the effectiveness of the proposed SATL strategy, on each experiment direction we compared the performance of proposed method (**w/ SATL**) with the source classification model (**w/o SATL**) and a state-of-the-art CycleGAN-based domain adaptation method [23] (**w/ CGAN**). The CycleGAN-based method trains a generator to transfer the target images to the source domain by adversarial learning. The most noteworthy difference between CycleGAN and the proposed SATL strategy is that: our method is completely independent of the source domain data while CycleGAN is not. More specifically, training CycleGAN to perform domain

Table 2. The classification performance of four groups of experiments

Direction	LAG → pri-RFG			pri-RFG → LAG		
Strategy	w/o SATL	w/ CGAN	w/ SATL	w/o SATL	w/ CGAN	w/ SATL
Accuracy	0.799	0.672	**0.856**	0.352	**0.628**	0.579
Recall	0.659	0.422	**0.726**	**1.000**	0.707	0.779
Precision	0.807	**0.923**	0.855	0.352	**0.481**	0.445
F1 score	0.726	0.580	**0.785**	0.521	**0.573**	0.566
Direction	LAG → REFUGE			pri-RFG → REFUGE		
Strategy	w/o SATL	w/ CGAN	w/ SATL	w/o SATL	w/ CGAN	w/ SATL
Accuracy	0.933	0.913	**0.945**	0.240	0.540	**0.580**
Recall	0.425	**0.600**	0.500	**0.975**	0.825	0.850
Precision	0.810	0.558	**0.909**	0.114	0.157	**0.173**
F1 score	0.557	0.579	**0.645**	0.204	0.264	**0.288**

adaptation needs both source and target domain images. On the contrary, the proposed SATL strategy relies on only the target domain unlabeled images.

The experimental results of three strategies are tabulated in Table 2. Moreover, the ROC curves are also plotted and illustrated in Fig. 2. By observing the demonstrated results, two main conclusions can be drawn:

(1) Compared to the source model without SATL, which can be seen as a baseline, the model with SATL outperforms in all four domain adaptation directions in terms of Accuracy and F1 Score. Despite there exist a mass of differences between three used datasets, SATL shows to be effective for self-supervised domain adaptation regardless of the source and target domain data distribution. This phenomenon shows that the proposed SATL is valuable and reliable for the production of pseudo labels in data from a grand-new hospital.

(2) When testing the source model in the target domain images transferred by CycleGAN, the performance is comparable with the proposed SATL strategy in domain adaptation directions of pri-RFG → LAG and LAG → REFUGE. While in directions of LAG → pri-RFG and pri-RFG → REFUGE, the proposed SATL strategy surpasses the CycleGAN by a large margin. This phenomenon demonstrates that SATL is more robust and have more stable generalization ability in different domain adaptation scenes. Note that CycleGAN uses the source domain images in the domain adaptation stage while the proposed SATL does not. Thus, our method which is completely independent of the source domain is more feasible in real scene applications. It can ensure the isolation of multi-center datasets and meet the privacy protection policy.

Discussion. Despite the proposed method improves the performance of the classification model in the target domain via self-supervised training, there still remains some research worth exploring for enhancing the performance. For example, in this paper, we directly trained and validated the source classification model on the source domain. However, it may be a better option to initialize the source classification model by a model pre-trained on large scale nature image datasets such as ImageNet. Besides, the backbone used in this paper is VGG for the convenience of building the reconstruction VAE model. In the future, it can also be replaced by other state-of-the-art backbone such as Inception [18] or SENet [6]. Last but not least, the features adapted by SATL framework in the target domain need to be explore and compare with that before SATL. Further improvement in glaucoma diagnosis may be achieved by learning features which can better represent ONH traits.

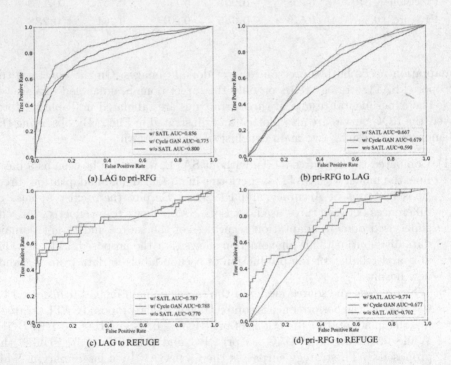

Fig. 2. ROC curves of the models evaluated in all four domain adaptation directions.

5   Conclusion

In this paper, we present a self-adaptive transfer learning (SATL) strategy to fill the domain gap between multicenter datasets and perform the evaluation in glaucoma classification based on three fundus retina image datasets. Specifically, a reconstruction model is trained using only target domain unlabeled images.

The encoder of this reconstruction model is initialized from a pre-trained source classification model and self-adapted in the target domain. Experimental results demonstrate that the proposed SATL strategy enhances the classification performance in the target domain and outperforms another state-of-the-art domain adaptation method which even utilizes source domain images for training, as well. In the near future, more efforts will be devoted to exploring how to furthermore lifting the performance of the self-supervised domain adaptation method via designing new reconstruction losses. Moreover, we will extend this strategy to other medical image analysis problems.

Acknowledgments. This work was supported in part by Department of Science and Technology of Zhejiang Province - Key Research and Development Program under Grant 2017C03029 and the Biomedical Engineering Interdisciplinary Research Fund of Shanghai Jiao Tong University under Grant YG2020YQ17.

References

1. Ahn, E., Kumar, A., Fulham, M.J., Feng, D., Kim, J.: Unsupervised domain adaptation to classify medical images using zero-bias convolutional auto-encoders and context-based feature augmentation. IEEE Trans. Med. Imag. **39**, 1 (2020)
2. Cheng, B., Liu, M., Suk, H., Shen, D., Zhang, D.: Multimodal manifold-regularized transfer learning for MCI conversion prediction. Brain Imag. Behav. **9**(4), 913–926 (2015)
3. Cheplygina, V., Pena, I.P., Pedersen, J.H., Lynch, D.A., Sorensen, L., De Bruijne, M.: Transfer learning for multicenter classification of chronic obstructive pulmonary disease. IEEE J. Biomed. Health Inform. **22**(5), 1486–1496 (2018)
4. Fu, H., et al.: Disc-aware ensemble network for glaucoma screening from fundus image. IEEE Trans. Med. Imag. **37**(11), 2493–2501 (2018)
5. Ghifary, M., Kleijn, W.B., Zhang, M., Balduzzi, D., Li, W.: Deep reconstruction-classification networks for unsupervised domain adaptation. In: Leibe, B., Matas, J., Sebe, N., Welling, M. (eds.) ECCV 2016. LNCS, vol. 9908, pp. 597–613. Springer, Cham (2016). https://doi.org/10.1007/978-3-319-46493-0_36
6. Hu, J., Shen, L., Albanie, S., Sun, G., Wu, E.: Squeeze-and-excitation networks. IEEE Trans. Pattern Anal. Mach. Intell. **43**, 1 (2019)
7. Kingma, D.P., Welling, M.: Auto-encoding variational Bayes. Machine Learning (2013)
8. Li, L., Xu, M., Wang, X., Jiang, L., Liu, H.: Attention based glaucoma detection: a large-scale database and CNN model. Computer Vision and Pattern Recognition (2019)
9. Li, Y., Wang, N., Liu, J., Hou, X.: Demystifying neural style transfer. Computer Vision and Pattern Recognition (2017)
10. Mary, M.C.V.S., Rajsingh, E.B., Naik, G.R.: Retinal fundus image analysis for diagnosis of glaucoma: a comprehensive survey. IEEE Access **4**, 4327–4354 (2016)
11. Ng, S., Perron, P.: Lag length selection and the construction of unit root tests with good size and power. Econometrica **69**(6), 1519–1554 (2001)
12. Orlando, J.I., et al.: Refuge challenge: a unified framework for evaluating automated methods for glaucoma assessment from fundus photographs. Med. Image Anal. **59**, 101570 (2020)

13. Qi, Q., et al.: Label-efficient breast cancer histopathological image classification. IEEE J. Biomed. Health Inform. **23**(5), 2108–2116 (2019)
14. Ravi, D., et al.: Deep learning for health informatics **21**(1), 4–21 (2017)
15. Shen, Y., et al.: Domain-invariant interpretable fundus image quality assessment. Med. Image Anal. **61**, 101654 (2020)
16. Simonyan, K., Zisserman, A.: Very deep convolutional networks for large-scale image recognition (2014)
17. Sun, Y., Yang, G., Ding, D., Cheng, G., Xu, J., Li, X.: A GAN-based domain adaptation method for glaucoma diagnosis. In: 2020 International Joint Conference on Neural Networks (IJCNN), pp. 1–8. IEEE (2020)
18. Szegedy, C., Ioffe, S., Vanhoucke, V., Alemi, A.A.: Inception-v4, inception-ResNet and the impact of residual connections on learning, pp. 4278–4284 (2016)
19. Tajbakhsh, N., et al.: Convolutional neural networks for medical image analysis: full training or fine tuning? IEEE Trans. Med. Imag. **35**(5), 1299–1312 (2016)
20. Wang, M., Deng, W.: Deep visual domain adaptation: a survey. Neurocomputing **312**, 135–153 (2018)
21. Wang, S., Yu, L., Yang, X., Fu, C., Heng, P.: Patch-based output space adversarial learning for joint optic disc and cup segmentation. IEEE Trans. Med. Imag. **38**(11), 2485–2495 (2019)
22. Zhang, L.: Transfer adaptation learning: a decade survey. Computer Vision and Pattern Recognition (2019)
23. Zhu, J., Park, T., Isola, P., Efros, A.A.: Unpaired image-to-image translation using cycle-consistent adversarial networks, pp. 2242–2251 (2017)
24. Zhu, Q., Du, B., Yan, P.: Boundary-weighted domain adaptive neural network for prostate MR image segmentation. IEEE Trans. Med. Imag. **39**(3), 753–763 (2020)

Multi-modality Images Analysis: A Baseline for Glaucoma Grading via Deep Learning

Huihui Fang[1], Fangxin Shang[1], Huazhu Fu[3], Fei Li[2], Xiulan Zhang[2(✉)], and Yanwu Xu[1(✉)]

[1] Intelligent Healthcare Unit, Baidu Inc., Beijing, China
ywxu@ieee.org
[2] State Key Laboratory of Ophthalmology, Zhongshan Ophthalmic Center, Sun Yat-sen University, Guangzhou, China
zhangxl2@mail.sysu.edu.cn
[3] Inception Institute of Artificial Intelligence, Abu Dhabi, United Arab Emirates

Abstract. Glaucoma is one of the leading causes of blindness in humans, which is not reversible, but early detection and treatment can save helpful vision. Clinicians classify glaucoma into early, moderate, and advanced stages based on the extent of the patient's visual field deficit. The treatment of glaucoma varies with the course of the disease. With the development of deep learning technology, more and more studies focus on the automatic diagnosis of glaucoma. Most of them are based on color fundus images or OCT images. However, there are limitations in using only one modality images to analyze glaucoma due to the complexity of glaucoma. Therefore, in this paper, two modalities of images, color fundus image and 3D OCT image provided by the GAMMA Challenge, were used to design baseline algorithms for glaucoma grading. On the preliminary dataset of the GAMMA Challenge, the kappa value of the glaucoma grading results based on the two modalities of image input were improved by 0.092 and 0.075, respectively, compared with those of the model with single fundus image and single OCT image input. And on the final datasets, the corresponding improvement were 0.029 and 0.127. At the same time, considering that optic disc changes are the main features of glaucoma, we added local information of optic disc into the input module, so that the kappa values were improved respectively by 0.075 and 0.068 in the preliminary dataset and final dataset of the model based on the images of two modalities as input. In addition, this study used an ordinal regression strategy on the classification task to increase the kappa value of the results of automatic classification of glaucoma based on multi-modality images by 0.097 and 0.050 on the preliminary and final datasets of the GAMMA Challenge.

Keywords: Multi-modality images classification · Glaucoma grading · 3D OCT · Color fundus photography · GAMMA challenge

© Springer Nature Switzerland AG 2021
H. Fu et al. (Eds.): OMIA 2021, LNCS 12970, pp. 139–147, 2021.
https://doi.org/10.1007/978-3-030-87000-3_15

1 Introduction

Glaucoma is one of the leading causes of irreversible but preventable blindness in the world [11]. Clinically, glaucoma is categorized into early, moderate, and advanced stages based on visual field defects. Visual field defects are determined by visual field tests, which can calculate the mean deviation (MD) of the patient's visual field compared to the normal person. According to [6], the MD is less than 6 dB for early glaucoma, between 6 dB and 12 dB for moderate glaucoma, and greater than 12 dB for advanced glaucoma. However, visual field tests require patient cooperation. Moreover, the tests are time-consuming, and poor reproducibility due to numerous influencing factors. With the development of deep learning technology, medical image processing has been paid more attention. Many researchers focused on diagnosing of glaucoma based on the color fundus images [1,4,9]. Meanwhile, some researchers first used 3D OCT images to obtain the thickness of optic nerve fiber layer or ganglion cell complex layer, and then made the diagnosis of glaucoma [2]. However, glaucoma can cause a variety of structural changes in the fundus that are difficult to observe only in color fundus photography. And, the task of glaucoma grading has been rarely studied.

Therefore, in this paper, we studied glaucoma grading by using color fundus photography and OCT images. Instead of calculating optic fiber layer thickness or ganglion cell complex layer thickness from OCT images in advance, we designed the models for the glaucoma grading directly using images. We used 100 pairs of color fundus images and 3D OCT images released in GAMMA Challenge for training. And, the preliminary and final datasets of GAMMA Challenge were used for testing. To improve the effect of glaucoma grading, this paper used the ordinal regression strategy [7], and discussed its influence on the results and its significance. The major contributions of this paper are threefold.

- The effect differences of automatic glaucoma grading using different modality images was analyzed.
- The importance of optic disc region to glaucoma grading was considered in the model.
- An ordinal regression strategy was performed to improve the performance of glaucoma grading.

2 Methodology

In this paper, the baselines of the automatic glaucoma grading task were designed using color fundus images only, OCT images only, and the above two modalities of images. The samples are divided into three categories: non-glaucoma, early glaucoma, and moderate and advanced glaucoma. We designed baselines based on the images of different modalities. In addition, considering that the optic disc region may be degenerate due to glaucoma, we extracted the optic disc region and added it into the models as input. Moreover, since the images of early, moderate and advanced glaucoma are all glaucoma samples, we divided

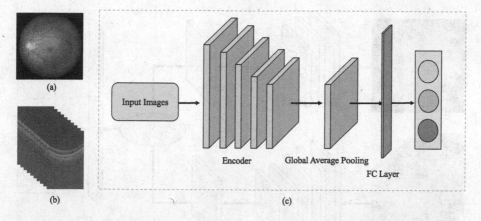

Fig. 1. The networks for the baselines based on one modality images, such as color fundus photography and OCT images. (a) color fundus photography, (b) OCT image slices, (c) the network structure. In the baselines based on the different modality images, the input images module of the network will be color fundus photography and OCT slices respectively.

the tripartite classification task into two binary classification tasks by referring to the ordinal regression strategy [7]. In this strategy, we judge whether the images belong to non-glaucoma or glaucoma samples, and then judge whether they belong to early or moderate/advanced stages.

2.1 Baselines

As shown in Fig. 1, the network structure of the baseline model adopts the form of a single branch for single-modality image input. For the fundus images or OCT images, the encoding network is used to extract features first, and the network structure used in this paper is ResNet34 [5]. Then the input images are divided into three categories according to their features by using the full connection layer. As shown in Fig. 2, for the two modalities of image input, the baseline is in the form of two branches. We used two ResNet34 networks to extract features from the input fundus images and OCT images respectively, and then concatenated these features, and finally classified these features using the full connection layer. The loss functions used in these model training processes are the cross-entropy loss which is commonly used in the classification task.

2.2 Local Information of Optic Disc

Since glaucoma leads to lesions in the optic disc region, such as cup-disc ratio enlargement, and optic disc hemorrhage [8], we considered extracting the optic

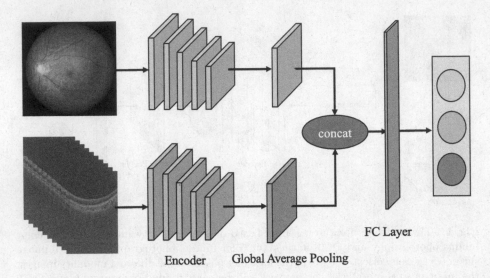

Fig. 2. The networks for the baseline based on the images of two modalities (color fundus photography and OCT images). The network simultaneously extracts the features of two modalities, and then synthesizes the two features through concat, finally realize the tri-classification task.

disc region of fundus images as local information to supplement the network input module. According to paper [12], we took the center of optic disc region as the center, and 2 times the maximum diameter of the optic disc as the side length. Square patches were cropped from fundus images as local information (see Fig. 3). Specifically, the optic disc region can be obtained through common deep learning methods such as U-Net [10] and M-Net [3]. In this paper, the optic disc regions are segmented by the U-Net network. The features of the local information were also extracted by the ResNet34 network, and then the features were combined with the features of other input images in the concat way, and then used for glaucoma grading.

2.3   Ordinal Regression Strategy

In the training process, if the model identifies advanced glaucoma as early glaucoma or identifies advanced glaucoma as non-glaucoma, the losses of these two situations are the same according to the cross-entropy loss, which is commonly used in the classification task. In fact, identifying advanced glaucoma as non-glaucoma deviates more from the gold standard than identifying as early glaucoma. Therefore, we need to consider not only the classification loss, but also the ranking relationship between the misclassified category and the true category, where the loss should be smaller if the classification is closer. Ordinal regression strategy can solve the above problems. As shown in Fig. 4, we used the output features to perform two binary classifications respectively. The first classifier divides the sample into 0 and 1, that is, to judge whether the input image is

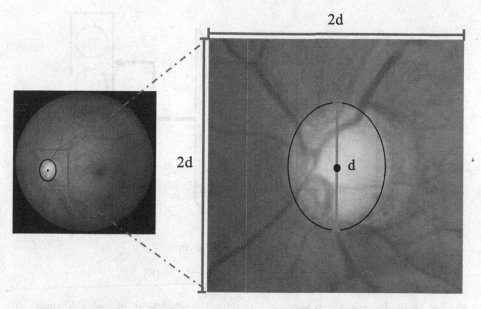

Fig. 3. Local information of optic disc. The square patch was extracted with the center of optic disc as the center, and the side length was 2 times the maximum diameter of optic disc.

a glaucoma sample. The second classifier divides the sample into 0 and 1 to identify the input image as moderate/advanced glaucoma sample or not. The labels of the original tripartite classification task were converted according to the two binary classification tasks, that is, the labels of the original non-glaucoma samples were changed to (0, 0), the labels of the original early glaucoma samples were changed to (1, 0), and those of the original moderate and advanced glaucoma samples were changed to (1, 1). The loss function used in this model training processes is the sum of the two binary cross-entropy losses.

3   Experiments and Discussion

Dataset. A total of 300 paired data of 3D OCT and 2D color fundus images were released in GAMMA Challenge. Among them, 100 samples are training data (with gold standard), 100 samples are preliminary data and 100 samples are final data. Among them, every 3D OCT contains 256 slices, each slice size is 512×992. The fundus image sizes are 2992×2000 or 1956×1934. The dataset was provided by Sun Yat-sen Ophthalmic Center, Sun Yat-sen University, Guangzhou, China. The ground truth of glaucoma grading for each sample was obtained from the clinical visual field testing results (early glaucoma: Mean deviation > -6 dB, advanced glaucoma: Mean deviation < -12 dB, and the rest were moderate glaucoma). Table 1 shows the distribution of glaucoma samples in each period in the dataset.

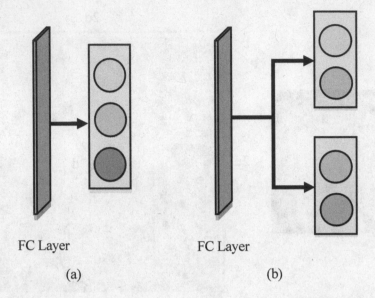

FC Layer   FC Layer

(a)   (b)

Fig. 4. Ordinal regression schematic. (a) tripartite classification task schematic, (b) two binary classification tasks with ordinal regression strategy.

Table 1. The distribution of glaucoma samples in each period in the dataset.

	Total	Non	Early	Moderate and advanced
Training	100	50	26	24
Preliminary	100	50	26	24
Final	100	51	25	24

Metrics. Cohen's kappa coefficient was used to evaluate the glaucoma grading results. Cohen's kappa is the standard evaluation metric for the multi-category classification task. The kappa coefficient is calculated based on the confusion matrix, with the value between -1 and 1, usually greater than 0. The calculation formula of kappa coefficient based on confusion matrix is as follows:

$$\kappa = \frac{p_0 - p_e}{1 - p_e} \tag{1}$$

where, p_0 is accuracy; p_e is the sum of the products of the actual and predicted numbers corresponding to each category, divided by the square of the total number of samples.

Implementation Details. The training procedure consists of 1000 iteration with a Nvidia Tesla V100-SXM2 GPU. Pre-trained ResNet34 was selected for all the models, Adam was selected for all the optimizers, and the number of iterations was 1000. The batch sizes were 4 and the initial learning rates were 1e−4. In our experiments, the 2D color fundus images were resized to 256×256, and the 3D OCT slices were resized to 512×512. The final full connection layer of all the pre-training ResNet was removed and the channel of the first convolution layer in the 3D slice branch was changed to 256. The codes of the baselines will be publicly available with the PaddlePaddle deep learning platform.

3.1   Overall Performances

Table 2 shows the experimental results of this paper. As can be seen from the table, seven models are designed in this paper. Among them, experiments 1, 3 and 5 were designed for glaucoma grading models under three conditions of single fundus image input, single OCT image input, and two modalities of image input. On the preliminary dataset of the GAMMA Challenge, the kappa values of the glaucoma grading model based on the two modalities of image input were improved by 0.092 and 0.075, respectively, compared with those of the model with single fundus image and single OCT image input. Similarly, in the final dataset of the GAMMA Challenge, the kappa values of the models for grading glaucoma using the two modalities were improved by 0.029 and 0.127.

Table 2. Performances of the baselines for glaucoma grading.

No.	Color fundus photography	3D OCT	Disc region	Ordinary regression	Preliminary	Final
1	✓	-	-	-	0.625	0.673
2	✓	-	✓	-	0.654	0.677
3	-	✓	-	-	0.642	0.575
4	-	✓	✓	-	0.703	0.732
5	✓	✓	-	-	0.717	0.702
6	✓	✓	✓	-	0.792	0.770
7	✓	✓	-	✓	0.814	0.752
8	✓	✓	✓	✓	**0.863**	**0.812**

Experiments 2, 4 and 6 were the experiments of supplementing the input module of Experiment 1, 3 and 5 with local information of optic disc from color fundus photograph. It can be seen from the table that the glaucoma grading results supplemented with local information of optic disc were better than the original models in both the preliminary and final GAMMA datasets. Especially for the model with only OCT images as the input, after supplementing the local information of optic disc, the kappa value of glaucoma grading results increased by 0.061 in the preliminary dataset and 0.157 in the final dataset. This is mainly because the original OCT data is the scanning volume data centered on the macula and lacks the features of optic disc. Therefore, the model effect is greatly improved after adding the local information of optic disc region.

Experiment 7 was an experiment using an ordinal regression strategy on the model which is based on the two modalities of image as input. By comparing Experiment 7 and Experiment 5, it can be seen that the model using the ordinal regression strategy is superior to the model using the traditional three-classification concept in terms of performance, and the kappa value of the grading results in the preliminary and final datasets can be improved by 0.097 and 0.050 respectively. As can be seen from Table 2, in the preliminary dataset, the model based on the input of two modalities images and using the ordinal regression strategy had the best effect, and the kappa value of the grading result was 0.814. In the final dataset, the model based on the input of two modalities images and supplemented local information of optic disc had the best effect, and the corresponding kappa value was 0.770. The above experimental results indicate that the effect of the glaucoma grading model with the input of two modalities is better than that with the input of a single modality. Experiment 8 was adding the local information of optic disc region and using an ordinal regression strategy on the model of Experiment 5. It can be seen from Table 2, Experiment 8 can achieve the highest kappa value on both preliminary and final datasets. The experimental results show that the local information of optic disc and the ordinal regression strategy can effectively improve the glaucoma grading performance of the model.

4   Conclusion

In this paper, to discuss the effect of automatic glaucoma grading by using deep learning algorithm based on different modality images, we designed several baselines for glaucoma grading based on 2D color fundus photography and 3D OCT images. We used the common ResNet-34 as the network structure of the baselines. 100 pairs of training data provided by GAMMA Challenge were used to train models based on 2D color fundus photographs, 3D OCT images, and these two modalities images. The experimental results show that the effect of automatic glaucoma grading achieved by using the images of two modalities is better than those by using the images of only one modality. In addition, since glaucoma causes many variations in the optic disc region, we cropped optic disc patch from the 2D color fundus photography and added it to the input module of the baselines, and found that the experimental results of supplementing local information of optic disc were better. Furthermore, we also found that the performance of the model based on multi-modality images can be improved by using the strategy of ordinal regression. In the future work, we will explore more effective methods of multi-modality image feature fusion to further improve the performance of glaucoma grading.

References

1. Ahn, J.M., Kim, S., Ahn, K.S., Cho, S.H., Lee, K.B., Kim, U.S.: A deep learning model for the detection of both advanced and early glaucoma using fundus photography. PLoS One **13**(11), e0207982 (2018)

2. An, G., et al.: Glaucoma diagnosis with machine learning based on optical coherence tomography and color fundus images. J. Healthcare Eng. **2019** (2019)

3. Fu, H., Cheng, J., Xu, Y., Wong, D.W.K., Liu, J., Cao, X.: Joint optic disc and cup segmentation based on multi-label deep network and polar transformation. IEEE Trans. Med. Imag. **37**(7), 1597–1605 (2018)

4. Gómez-Valverde, J.J., et al.: Automatic glaucoma classification using color fundus images based on convolutional neural networks and transfer learning. Biomed. Optics Express **10**(2), 892–913 (2019)

5. He, K., Zhang, X., Ren, S., Sun, J.: Deep residual learning for image recognition. In: Proceedings of the IEEE Conference on Computer Vision and Pattern Recognition, pp. 770–778 (2016)

6. Hodapp, E., Parrish, R.K., Anderson, D.R.: Clinical Decisions in Glaucoma. Mosby Incorporated, Chicago (1993)

7. Niu, Z., Zhou, M., Wang, L., Gao, X., Hua, G.: Ordinal regression with multiple output CNN for age estimation. In: Proceedings of the IEEE Conference on Computer Vision and Pattern Recognition, pp. 4920–4928 (2016)

8. Orlando, J.I., et al.: Refuge challenge: a unified framework for evaluating automated methods for glaucoma assessment from fundus photographs. Med. Image Anal. **59**, 101570 (2020)

9. Phene, S., et al.: Deep learning and glaucoma specialists: the relative importance of optic disc features to predict glaucoma referral in fundus photographs. Ophthalmology **126**(12), 1627–1639 (2019)

10. Ronneberger, Olaf, Fischer, Philipp, Brox, Thomas: U-Net: convolutional networks for biomedical image segmentation. In: Navab, Nassir, Hornegger, Joachim, Wells, William M.., Frangi, Alejandro F.. (eds.) MICCAI 2015. LNCS, vol. 9351, pp. 234–241. Springer, Cham (2015). https://doi.org/10.1007/978-3-319-24574-4_28

11. Tham, Y.C., Li, X., Wong, T.Y., Quigley, H.A., Aung, T., Cheng, C.Y.: Global prevalence of glaucoma and projections of glaucoma burden through 2040: a systematic review and meta-analysis. Ophthalmology **121**(11), 2081–2090 (2014)

12. Xiulan, Z., Yanwu, X., Weihua, Y.: Annotation and quality control specifications for fundus color photograph. Intelligent Medicine (2021)

Impact of Data Augmentation on Retinal OCT Image Segmentation for Diabetic Macular Edema Analysis

Daniel Bar-David[1](✉), Laura Bar-David[2], Shiri Soudry[2,3,4], and Anath Fischer[1]

[1] Faculty of Mechanical Engineering, Technion Israel Institute of Technology, Haifa, Israel
`danielba@technion.ac.il`
[2] Department of Ophthalmology, Rambam Health Care Campus, Haifa, Israel
[3] Clinical Research Institute at Rambam, Rambam Health Care Campus, Haifa, Israel
[4] Ruth and Bruce Faculty of Medicine, Technion Israel Institute of Technology, Haifa, Israel

Abstract. Deep learning models have become increasingly popular for analysis of optical coherence tomography (OCT), an ophthalmological imaging modality considered standard practice in the management of diabetic macular edema (DME). Despite the need for large image training datasets, only limited number of annotated OCT images are publicly available. Data augmentation is an essential element of the training process which provides an effective approach to expand and diversify existing datasets. Such methods are even more valuable for segmentation tasks since manually annotated medical images are time-consuming and costly. Surprisingly, current research interests are primarily focused on architectural innovation, often leaving aside details of the training methodology. Here, we investigated the impact of data augmentation on OCT image segmentation and assessed its value in detection of two prevalent features of DME: intraretinal fluid cysts and lipids. We explored the relative effectiveness of various types of transformations carefully designed to preserve the realism of the OCT image. We also evaluated the effect of data augmentation on the performance of similar architectures differing by depth. Our results highlight the effectiveness of data augmentation and underscore the merit of elastic deformation, for OCT image segmentation, reducing the dice score error by up to 23.66%. These results also show that data augmentation strategies are competitive to architecture modifications without any added complexity.

Keywords: Deep learning · Data augmentation · Elastic deformation · OCT · DME

1 Introduction

Diabetic retinopathy (DR) and one of its major sight-threatening complications, diabetic macular edema (DME), are the leading causes of vision loss in individuals with diabetes

Electronic supplementary material The online version of this chapter (https://doi.org/10.1007/978-3-030-87000-3_16) contains supplementary material, which is available to authorized users.

The original version of this chapter was revised: an author's last name has been corrected. The correction to this chapter is available at https://doi.org/10.1007/978-3-030-87000-3_21

H. Fu et al. (Eds.): OMIA 2021, LNCS 12970, pp. 148–158, 2021.
https://doi.org/10.1007/978-3-030-87000-3_16

mellitus. Early diagnosis and prompt treatment of DME are critical to prevent permanent vision loss [1]. The clinical features of DME include retinal thickening or fluid retention, sometimes with a cystic pattern, which may be accompanied by deposition of protein or lipid within the central retinal tissue.

Optical coherence tomography (OCT) is an ophthalmological imaging modality based on optical reflectivity, which can provide cross-sectional images and three-dimensional volumetric data of the retina [2]. Because of its simplicity, availability, and ability to provide abundance of information, OCT has become essential in the clinical practice, enabling better diagnosis and management of various retinal conditions, including DME.

Interpretation of OCT images requires trained retina experts and can be complex even for experienced clinicians. Moreover, human readings are notably time-consuming, with variable repeatability and interobserver agreement [3]. The application of computer-aided diagnosis (CAD) systems to medical imaging can significantly facilitate their interpretation, including detection of ophthalmic diseases such as DME. In the past few years, the use of deep-learning models in CAD has greatly improved the ability to detect clinical abnormalities in medical imaging, resulting in improved results [4]. To date, however, no retinal CAD system has become commercially available for routine clinical use, largely due to methodological challenges [5].

A major obstacle to the implementation of deep-learning algorithms for medical image analysis is the absence of large, annotated datasets required for training of neural networks. This partly stems from the level of expertise and extent of effort required for proper data interpretation and labeling, but also from ethical considerations required by data protection laws. Consequently, there are only a few publicly available OCT datasets collected from multiple imaging devices, most of which often comprise a relatively limited number of scans and represented pathologies [6].

The performance of deep-learning models in computer vision depends on the neural networks training, architecture and model scaling [7]. Moreover, architectural innovation is broadly regarded as the main focus of research interest, leaving aside critical details of the training methodology [8]. Specifically, only a few studies investigated the efficiency of data augmentation in convolutional neural network training for image classification and segmentation. The data augmentation type is often stated, but little is explained about the method, range, and frequency of the process [9].

Presently, for most computer vision problems, basic transformations such as random flipping, rotating, scaling, shifting or adjusting contrast are valuable regularizers which can generalize the model and reduce overfitting by expanding and diversifying datasets without acquiring new images [10].

Elastic deformation is a more complex approach for data augmentation, introducing higher-order transformation. Utilization of elastic deformation for training of convolutional neural networks was first introduced on the MNIST handwritten digit dataset [11] where after deformation the image still appeared sufficiently plausible to represent a real digit. Along with basic transformations, elastic deformation is particularly suitable for non-rigid objects, yet at the same time it is complicated to construct since it alters the inner elements of the image. Medical images deal with objects which can inherently undergo natural transformations that can be described as elastic deformations. Indeed, different methods of elastic deformation have been applied for medical image registration [12]. Yet, due to the difficulty of achieving elastic deformation methods for images with complex morphology, and perhaps also due to the indeterminate value of this approach thus far, elastic transformation for data augmentation has been less commonly used. A previously reported elastic deformation technique for data augmentation was applied on OCT scans of the optic nerve head to render the network invariant with atypical morphology [13]. Recently, an elastic deformation method was clinically validated for OCT images of patients suffering from DME [14]. However, to date, the impact of transformations on neural network performance for OCT image analysis, and particularly the benefit of elastic deformation, has been relatively understudied.

Here, to provide a systematic approach for OCT data segmentation for DME, we explored the benefits of data augmentation with a particular examination of the added value of elastic deformation. We first investigated the impact of diverse data augmentation methods on an established neural network for segmentation of OCT images from subjects with DME, and determined the relative effectiveness of the different approaches. We then evaluated the impact of data augmentation in relation with the depth of the neural networks by comparing the performance of two similar architectures differing by depth in OCT image segmentation.

2 Methods

2.1 Data Augmentation

Basic transformations are augmentation techniques commonly applied to most learning algorithms, as they are intuitive, easy to understand, and straightforward to implement. The inner composition of the image is essentially unaffected, but represents a variation in the image acquisition process such as the subject position or a physical property of the photographic system. Several basic transformation methods were evaluated on OCT scans and are described in Table 1.

Table 1. Description of the augmentations applied during neural network training

	Augmentation	Description
A	No transformation	Original OCT scan
B	Horizontal flip	Horizontally flip the OCT scan
C	Rotation	Randomly rotate the OCT scan in the range $\pm 15°$
D	Shift	Randomly translate horizontally and vertically by up to 10% of the image height and width
E	Scale	Randomly scale sampled from the interval [0.9,1.1]
F	Brightness, contrast, saturation	Modify the brightness, contrast and saturation by a random factor [0.75, 1.25]
G	Noise	Add gaussian noise with a variance of 0.07
H	Basic transformations	Combine and apply transformations A to G together
I	Elastic deformation	Apply elastic transformation with an intensity $\sigma = 9$
J	All transformations	Combine and apply transformations B to G and I together

Elastic deformation is a higher level of data augmentation that modifies the inner elements of the image, thus potentially affecting its intrinsic pattern and altering its realism. OCT retina images often represent anatomically complex features and thus following the introduction of additional distortion to the inner structure, practicing retina specialists highly-familiar with typical features of clinical OCT images can evaluate their authenticity to avoid potential bias. A recent study reported a process of clinical validation of the degree of elastic deformation that can be applied to OCT scans with DME while preserving their realistic value [14].

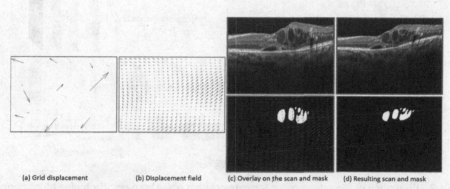

(a) Grid displacement   (b) Displacement field   (c) Overlay on the scan and mask   (d) Resulting scan and mask

Fig. 1. Elastic deformation process (a) Generate a displacement grid; (b) then a smooth displacement field is interpolated using spline interpolation on the grid displacement; (c) Superimposing the displacement field on the mask and OCT scan by using bilinear interpolation; (d) Result: deformed OCT scan and mask

The outline of the elastic deformation method is as follow. First, a uniform 2D grid of 3×3 control points is generated from a normal distribution of mean $\mu = 0$ and standard deviation σ (Fig. 1(a)). Then a displacement field is created by using spline interpolation between values of the 3×3 grid (Fig. 1(b)). Finally, the displacement grid is applied on the original OCT scan and on the mask by using bilinear interpolation (Fig. 1(c)), resulting in a deformed OCT image and mask (Fig. 1(d)). To keep the elastic deformation realistic for OCT images with DME, the maximum deformation intensity σ is equal to 9 [14].

2.2 Segmentation Network

To assess the impact of various types of transformations on segmentation tasks, we use a convolutional neural network (CNN) based on U-net architecture [15]. We choose the U-net model since it has gaineds tremendous recognition and popularity in recent years in medical image segmentation. Indeed, most of segmentation neural networks of OCT scans, rely on its encoder decoder design removing or adding layers [16], adding skip connection [17], modifying convolution [13] or pooling [18].

The segmentation network receives as input an OCT scan, and outputs a segmentation map that predicts for each pixel if it belongs to intraretinal fluid cysts (IRF), intraretinal lipid (IRL) or background. The symmetric structure of the network is shown in Fig. 2 including the contracting path for analyzing context information, the expanding path for synthesizing the output of the contracting and merging path that transfers local and accurate information. The proposed architecture differs from the original U-net in the following manner: batch normalization is added after each block of convolution, conv-transposed is used instead of up-convolution and filters are resized.

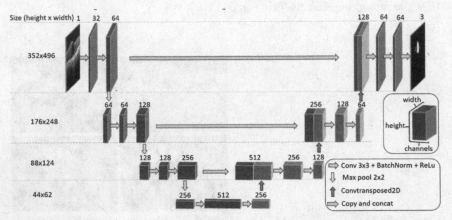

Fig. 2. Illustration of the auto encoder for segmentation based on u-net. Each blue block corresponds to a multi feature map. The model gets an OCT scan and the output is a mask. (Color online figure)

A common used metric for medical image segmentation is the Dice coefficient that compares the pixel wise agreement between a segmentation model prediction and their corresponding ground truth. The formula for Boolean data is defined as follow:

$$Dice = \frac{2TP}{2TP + FP + FN} \tag{1}$$

Where (TP) is True positive, (FP) False positive and (FN) False negative. The best segmentation is reached when dice $= 1$ while dice $= 0$ refers to a wrong segmentation. The dice loss function is defined as follow:

$$Loss_{dice} = 1 - \frac{1}{l} \sum_{j=1}^{l} \frac{\sum_{i=1}^{N} 2y_i^j \hat{y}_i^j + \varepsilon}{\sum_{i=1}^{N} y_i^j + \sum_{i=1}^{N} \hat{y}_i^j + \varepsilon} \tag{2}$$

Where y is the ground truth, $\hat{y}$ is the predicted segmentation, l is the total number of labels and N is the number of pixels. ε avoids the division by zero.

2.3 Comparison of Shallow Network Versus Deep Network

Following Alexnet architecture [19], researchers have mostly created deeper and more complex networks to increase performance [20–22]. These architectural expansions are beneficial for improving performance but make the network less efficient by increasing complexity and decreasing speed. Recently, studies have emphasized model efficiency by optimizing training methods and scaling strategies [8, 9, 23]. Here, a comparison of two segmentation networks differing by their depth is presented, where the objective is to determine if architectural differences can be overshadowed by data augmentation. The "deep network" refers to the segmentation network presented in Sect. 2.2 (Fig. 2) and consists in 22,807,617 parameters. To provide an objective comparison, the "shallow network" was constructed by removing the last level of the deep network (supplementary Table 1). As a result, the number of parameters for the shallow network drop by 35% to 14,940,737 parameters.

3 Evaluation

3.1 Dataset and Training Process

OCT scans were obtained from patients treated at the Retina service of the department of Ophthalmology, Rambam Health Care Campus, Haifa, Israel from 2016 to 2019. B-scans were extracted from the Heidelberg Spectralis device using a 49-line raster macula scan. The size of each OCT image used in this study consists of 352×496 pixels and no subsampling is applied.

OCT volume-scans of 120 subjects affected by DME were randomly extracted where only a single cross-section image of the macula was selected per each scan. Two of the most prevalent clinical features associated with DME, namely intraretinal fluid cysts (IRF) and intraretinal lipid (IRL) deposits, were manually segmented by a trained ophthalmologist and reviewed by a retinal expert. The data was randomly split into three sets: 60% for the training, 20% for the validation and 20% for the test set.

The network was trained with a batch size of 8 using Adam optimizer. Data augmentation was performed online at each epoch during the training session to remove memory constraints. The probability that an image undergoes a transformation is 0.5. We used pytorch library on a single NVIDIA Titan V GPU.

3.2 Evaluation of Data Augmentation Impact on Segmentation

To evaluate the impact of data augmentation on OCT segmentation, the dice score, sensitivity (Se) and specificity (Sp) metrics were calculated.

Table 2 summarizes results obtained for each transformation on the test set for the shallow and deep network. Specificity is close to one because there are many more background pixels than object pixels. Sensitivity is the true positive rate and measures the proportion of object pixels that are correctly identified. When each basic transformation (B-G) is applied separately, the dice score is only slightly improved compared to the baseline (A). However, when they are combined together (H) there is a significant increase over the baseline (A). Paradoxically, even applied alone, elastic deformation (I) performs as well as all basic transformations (H). Best performances are obtained with a combination of all transformations (J).

Table 2. Performance of the shallow and deep segmentation models on IRF and IRL

Augmentation			Shallow network			Deep network		
			Dsc (%)	Se (%)	Sp (%)	Dsc (%)	Se (%)	Sp (%)
A	No transformation	IRL	50.14	56.73	99.86	53.17	56.25	99.88
		IRF	70.2	73.46	99.58	75.2	79.13	99.62
B	Horizontal flip	IRL	57.32	**61.81**	99.88	58.1	57.45	**99.91**
		IRF	70.97	76.39	99.57	75.64	80.44	99.49
C	Rotation	IRL	56.18	57.86	99.88	57.36	59.43	99.89
		IRF	72.06	80.91	99.54	76.68	80.06	99.61
D	Shift	IRL	52.62	54.78	99.89	54.61	57.7	99.88
		IRF	72.51	71.07	**99.74**	75.22	79.51	99.54
E	Scale	IRL	56.57	58.76	98.87	57.57	59.86	99.88
		IRF	71.82	70.5	99.68	76.63	78.26	**99.69**
F	Brightness, contrast, saturation	IRL	50.28	59.74	99.82	54.6	56.23	99.9
		IRF	72.66	74.08	99.6	76.45	80.78	99.59
G	Noise	IRL	53.33	50.39	**99.92**	55.69	55.44	99.89
		IRF	70.43	78.73	99.54	75.7	79.66	99.62
H	Basic transformations	IRL	58.47	59.15	99.9	60.25	60.69	99.9
		IRF	76.02	**82.08**	99.51	78.05	81.8	99.63
I	Elastic deformation	IRL	58.69	57.74	**99.92**	60.2	59.17	**99.91**
		IRF	76.1	81.34	99.57	78.64	**82.75**	99.63
J	All transformations	IRL	**60.23**	61.06	99.9	**62.03**	**67.07**	99.87
		IRF	**77.25**	81.94	99.55	**79.36**	82.48	99.61

The chart presented in Fig. 3 compares our shallow and deep network for IRF and IRL. For both features and with the same transformations applied during the training, the deep network (in red) is always greater than or equal to the shallow network (in blue). But with all transformations (J) the shallow network succeeds to perform better than the deep network with each single basic transformation (A–G) and is comparable to elastic deformation and all basic transformations performance (H, I).

To get a quantitative sense of the effect of basic transformations (H), elastic deformation (I) and all transformations (J), the improvement in the test set accuracy was calculated in Table 3. Improvement over baseline is greater for shallow than deep network for IRF and IRL. Data augmentation has resulted by a reduction of 23.66% in the dice score error (IRF, shallow network). All transformations (J) reduced the dice score error by up to 3.9% compared to basic transformations and elastic deformation.

Figure 4 illustrates an example of segmentation outputs of the IRF and IRL features for the deep network with no augmentation (A) and with all transformations (J).

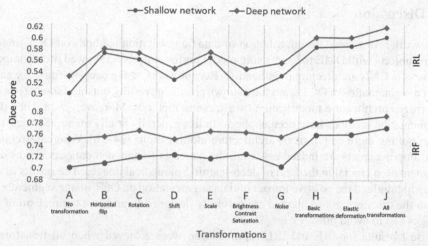

Fig. 3. Dice score values for distinct transformations on IRL and IRF. Each color represents a segmentation network: in blue the shallow and in red the deep. (Color figure online)

Table 3. Improvement when transformations are added. Difference of the dice score error (%).

Index	Augmentation	IRF Δ (%)		IRL Δ (%)	
		Shallow	Deep	Shallow	Deep
A	No transformation	0	0	0	0
H	Basic transformations	9.53	11,49	16 7	15.1
I	Elastic deformations	19.8	13.87	17.1	15
J	All transformations	23.66	16.77	20.2	18.9

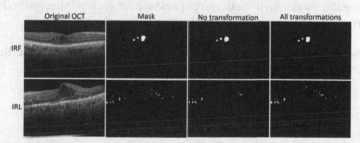

Fig. 4. Examples of IRF and IRL segmentation results with no transformation (A) and with all transformations (J) during the training for the deep network.

4 Discussion

This work investigated the contribution of data augmentation methods on OCT images from subjects with DME for improving model performance, and showed their competitiveness to CNN architecture modification. Recent works, using deep-learning for automated segmentation of OCT scans have shown promising results, but thus far most studies prioritized architecture modification over training methods. Moreover, even when data augmentation methods have been applied, studies generally briefly mention or describe them putting more emphasis on architecture modifications [24–26]. Whereas architectural improvements are indeed essential, the paucity of annotated datasets makes data augmentation crucial in the field of deep-learning of medical images. The results of our study highlighted the positive impact of data augmentation on OCT image segmentation when the transformations applied are carefully designed to preserve the realism of the images and to avoid bias.

Best results for IRF and IRL segmentation were achieved when all transformations were applied. Yet, sometimes transformations may add less value depending on the segmentation task. Moreover, as IRL features are smaller than IRF, manual and computational segmentation are less accurate, resulting in a lower dice score.

Each basic transformation applied separately improved much less performance than elastic deformation (I). Also, all basic transformations (H) applied together yielded similar results as elastic deformation (I). Its complexity compared to basic transformations has probably limited its application to OCT scans, but these results showed that they should be more commonly apply.

The comparison of two similar architectures differing by depth showed that architecture improvements can be overshadowed by data augmentation. Indeed, the shallow network using all transformations (J) for training outperformed the deep network without transformation (A) and with each basic transformation (B-G). Moreover, the performance was very tie for the shallow network using all transformations (J) and the deep network using all basic transformations (I).

Further studies will determine the proper balance between training methodology and architecture modification to reduce complexity and increase efficiency.

Acknowledgments. This work was supported by the Israeli Ministry of Health, Kopel Grant number 2028211.

References

1. Cheloni, R., Gandolfi, S.A., Signorelli, C., Odone, A.: Global prevalence of diabetic retinopathy: protocol for a systematic review and meta-analysis. BMJ Open **9**(3), e022188 (2019). https://doi.org/10.1136/bmjopen-2018-022188
2. Huang, D., et al.: Optical coherence tomography. Science **254**(5035), 1178–1181 (1991). https://doi.org/10.1126/science.1957169
3. Patel, P.J., Browning, A.C., Chen, F.K., da Cruz, L., Tufail, A.: Interobserver agreement for the detection of optical coherence tomography features of neovascular age-related macular degeneration. Investig. Ophthalmol. Vis. Sci. **50**(11), 5405–5410 (2009). https://doi.org/10.1167/iovs.09-3505

4. Lynch, C.J., Liston, C.: New machine-learning technologies for computer-aided diagnosis. Nat. Med. **24**(9), 1304–1305 (2018). https://doi.org/10.1038/s41591-018-0178-4
5. Stolte, S., Fang, R.: A survey on medical image analysis in diabetic retinopathy. Med. Image Anal. **64**, 101742 (2020). https://doi.org/10.1016/j.media.2020.101742
6. Yanagihara, R.T., Lee, C.S., Ting, D.S.W., Lee, A.Y.: Methodological challenges of deep learning in optical coherence tomography for retinal diseases: a review. Transl. Vis. Sci. Technol. **9**(2), 11 (2020). https://doi.org/10.1167/tvst.9.2.11
7. Tan, M., Le, Q.V.: EfficientNet: rethinking model scaling for convolutional neural networks. In: ICML 2019, pp. 10691–10700 (2019)
8. Bello, I., et al.: Revisiting ResNets: improved training and scaling strategies (2021). http://arxiv.org/abs/2103.07579. Accessed 02 June 2021
9. Zoph, B., Cubuk, E.D., Ghiasi, G., Lin, T.-Y., Shlens, J., Le, Q.V.: Learning data augmentation strategies for object detection. In: Vedaldi, A., Bischof, H., Brox, T., Frahm, J.-M. (eds.) ECCV 2020. LNCS, vol. 12372, pp. 566–583. Springer, Cham (2020). https://doi.org/10.1007/978-3-030-58583-9_34
10. Dvornik, N., Mairal, J., Schmid, C.: On the importance of visual context for data augmentation in scene understanding. IEEE Trans. Pattern Anal. Mach. Intell. **43**(6), 2014–2028 (2021). https://doi.org/10.1109/TPAMI.2019.2961896
11. Simard, P.Y., Steinkraus, D., Platt, J.C.: Best practices for convolutional neural networks applied to visual document analysis. In: Proceedings of the International Conference on Document Analysis and Recognition, ICDAR 2003, pp. 958–963 (2003). https://doi.org/10.1109/ICDAR.2003.1227801
12. Wang, M., Li, P.: A review of deformation models in medical image registration. J. Med. Biol. Eng. **39**(1), 1–17 (2018). https://doi.org/10.1007/s40846-018-0390-1
13. Devalla, S.K., et al.: DRUNET: a dilated-residual u-net deep learning network to digitally stain optic nerve head tissues in optical coherence tomography images. Biomed. Opt. Express **9**(7), 3244–3265 (2018). https://doi.org/10.1364/boe.9.003244
14. Bar-David, D., et al.: Elastic deformation of optical coherence tomography images of diabetic macular edema for deep-learning models training: how far to go? (2021). https://arxiv.org/abs/2107.03651v1
15. Ronneberger, O., Fischer, P., Brox, T.: U-Net: convolutional networks for biomedical image segmentation. In: Navab, N., Hornegger, J., Wells, W.M., Frangi, A.F. (eds.) MICCAI 2015. LNCS, vol. 9351, pp. 234–241. Springer, Cham (2015). https://doi.org/10.1007/978-3-319-24574-4_28
16. Venhuizen, F.G., et al.: Robust total retina thickness segmentation in optical coherence tomography images using convolutional neural networks. Biomed. Opt. Express **8**(7), 3292 (2017). https://doi.org/10.1364/BOE.8.003292
17. Tennakoon, R., Gostar, A.K., Hoseinnezhad, R., Bab-Hadiashar, A.: Retinal fluid segmentation in OCT images using adversarial loss based convolutional neural networks. In: Proceedings – International Symposium on Biomedical Imaging, pp. 1436–1440. May 2018. https://doi.org/10.1109/ISBI.2018.8363842
18. Asgari, R., Waldstein, S., Schlanitz, F., Baratsits, M, Schmidt-Erfurth, U., Bogunović, H.: U-Net with spatial pyramid pooling for Drusen segmentation in optical coherence tomography. In: Fu, H., Garvin, M.K., MacGillivray, T., Xu, Y., Zheng, Y. (eds.) OMIA 2019. LNCS, vol. 11855, pp. 77–85. Springer, Cham (2019). https://doi.org/10.1007/978-3-030-32956-3_10
19. Krizhevsky, A., Sutskever, I., Hinton, G.E.: ImageNet classification with deep convolutional neural networks. Adv. Neural Inf. Process. Syst., 1–9 (2012). https://doi.org/10.1016/j.protcy.2014.09.007
20. Szegedy, C., et al.: Going deeper with convolutions. In: 2015 IEEE Conference on Computer Vision and Pattern Recognition (CVPR), pp. 1–9. June 2015. https://doi.org/10.1109/CVPR.2015.7298594

21. He, K., Zhang, X., Ren, S., Sun, J.: Deep residual learning for image recognition. In: CVPR, pp. 770–778 (2016)
22. Huang, G., Liu, Z., Van Der Maaten, L., Weinberger, K.Q.: Densely connected convolutional networks. In: CVPR, pp. 4700–4708 (2017)
23. Cubuk, E.D., Zoph, B., Shlens, J., Le, Q.V.: Randaugment: practical automated data augmentation with a reduced search space. In: CVPR Workshops, pp. 702–703 (2020)
24. He, Y., et al.: Fully convolutional boundary regression for retina OCT segmentation. In: Shen, D., et al. (eds.) MICCAI 2019. LNCS, vol. 11764, pp. 120–128. Springer, Cham (2019). https://doi.org/10.1007/978-3-030-32239-7_14
25. Apostolopoulos, S., De Zanet, S., Ciller, C., Wolf, S., Sznitman, R.: Pathological OCT retinal layer segmentation using branch residual U-shape networks. In: Descoteaux, M., Maier-Hein, L., Franz, A., Jannin, P., Collins, D.L., Duchesne, S. (eds.) MICCAI 2017. LNCS, vol. 10435, pp. 294–301. Springer, Cham (2017). https://doi.org/10.1007/978-3-319-66179-7_34
26. Lu, D., et al.: Deep-learning based multiclass retinal fluid segmentation and detection in optical coherence tomography images using a fully convolutional neural network. Med. Image Anal. **54**, 100–110 (2019). https://doi.org/10.1016/j.media.2019.02.011

Representation and Reconstruction of Image-Based Structural Patterns of Glaucomatous Defects Using only Two Latent Variables from a Variational Autoencoder

Jui-Kai Wang[1,2,3], Randy H. Kardon[1,2], and Mona K. Garvin[1,3(✉)]

[1] The Iowa City VA Center for the Prevention and Treatment of Visual Loss,
Iowa City, IA, USA
[2] Department of Ophthalmology and Visual Sciences, The University of Iowa,
Iowa City, IA, USA
randy-kardon@uiowa.edu
[3] Department of Electrical and Computer Engineering, The University of Iowa,
Iowa City, IA, USA
{jui-kai-wang,mona-garvin}@uiowa.edu

Abstract. Glaucoma can result in both diffuse and regional patterns of retinal neuron loss due to damage to their axons at the optic nerve head. However, most quantitative estimates of glaucomatous progression use a global average and do not capture underlying spatial patterns. Motivated by the need for quantitative methods for describing and visualizing the spatial patterns of neuron loss in glaucoma, we evaluate the feasibility of spatial modeling of macular ganglion cell plus inner plexiform layer (mGCIPL) thickness maps using a deep learning variational autoencoder (VAE). More specifically, after training from optical coherence tomography based mGCIPL thickness maps of glaucoma and normal subjects, our VAE model was able to (1) succinctly represent the pattern of mGCIPL thickness maps with only two latent variables (using the encoder part of the VAE), and (2) reconstruct individual mGCIPL thickness maps given just two latent variable values. Based on evaluation of reconstruction errors on the mGCIPL thickness maps from an independent testing set of glaucoma and normal eyes, our results demonstrate the promise of the VAE model for a succinct representation of patterns of glaucomatous damage as well as use of the latent space for visualizing these patterns.

Keywords: Glaucoma · Optical coherence tomography (OCT) ·
Ganglion cell-inner plexiform layer (GCIPL) · Variational autoencoder
(VAE)

1 Introduction

Glaucoma is one of the leading causes of irreversible blindness related to optic nerve damage; it is further estimated that the number of glaucoma patients (aged

H. Fu et al. (Eds.): OMIA 2021, LNCS 12970, pp. 159–167, 2021.
https://doi.org/10.1007/978-3-030-87000-3_17

40–80) will increase to 111.8 million people worldwide by 2040 [1]. Although the exact causes of glaucoma are still unclear, elevated intraocular pressure (IOP), advancing age, family history, high myopia, nocturnal hypertension, and race are commonly recognized as main risk factors [2]. Optic nerve damage is currently considered non-reversible. Critical clinical decision-making focuses on whether glaucomatous damage is progressing, requiring advancement of treatment. The most valuable tests to detect glaucoma and its progression, besides IOP, are functional tests to map the visual field sensitivity (e.g., using standard automated perimetry, SAP) and structural tests to assess whether there is evidence for loss of nerves at the optic disc and the distribution of nerve loss in the corresponding areas of the retina. Monitoring progression can be observed and quantified by structural analysis of the retina and optic disc using optical coherence tomography (OCT) and by functional changes in sensitivity of the corresponding areas of the visual field (VF) [3–5].

Because glaucoma can result in both diffuse and focal loss of nerve axons (and corresponding loss of visual field sensitivity), there continues to be a need for approaches that enable quantitative tracking, visualization, and prediction of such changes over time. For example, both diffuse and focal nerve loss can be visualized (e.g., through use of inner retinal layer thickness maps and visual field maps) when following patients over time. Quantifying progression is primarily limited to the use of linear trends of global and/or regional parameters [e.g., measuring the slope of averaged peripapillary retinal nerve fiber layer or macular ganglion cell plus inner plexiform layer (mGCIPL) thickness from OCT over time]. However, there is a need for visualizing and quantifying the underlying spatial pattern of damage in order to detect progression at an earlier time when damage can be slowed or halted. More recent efforts have been directed at modeling patterns of damage using machine-learning approaches [6–8] for possible use in monitoring progression, but these have primarily been used for modeling visual field rather than structural maps from OCT.

In this work, we investigate the feasibility of using a deep-learning variational autoencoder (VAE) model [9] to allow for the succinct representation (in our case, using only two latent digits) and *reconstruction* of spatial structural thickness maps from OCT. The VAE involves two concatenated deep-learning networks: an encoder to allow representation of input structural image maps by two latent variables and a decoder to allow reconstruction of input image maps given only latent values. We specifically focus on modeling the mGCIPL thickness map, but our approach would easily extend to other structural maps as well. We first trained a VAE model to compute two latent variables that can span a latent space to cover the range of the spatial and global mGCIPL thinning patterns in the training set. Then, we evaluated the trained VAE model, in an independent testing dataset, to evaluate the correlation coefficients as well as signed/unsigned differences between sector thickness values computed from the input and reconstructed images.

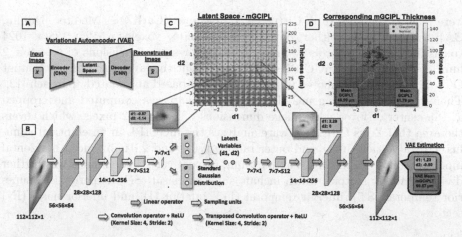

Fig. 1. Overview of a variational autoencoder (VAE) model for macular ganglion cell plus inner plexiform layer (mGCIPL) thickness maps as the input. (A) A basic VAE architecture. (B) Implementation of the proposed VAE model, with the encoder outputting two latent variables (d1, d2) and the decoder reconstructing the input mGCIPL thickness map from d1 and d2. (C) An illustration of the reconstructed mGCIPL thickness maps based on varying latent variables (d1, d2) from −4 to 4; which can be seen as the visualization of the VAE latent space. (D) The same arrangement as (C) but showing all the training data [red dots: 25 glaucoma subjects with 602 OCT scans; blue dots: 25 normal subjects with 899 OCT scans]. Note: the glaucoma eye whose d1 and d2 latent variable space lies within the normal subject data (cluster of red dots in the center of the cluster of blue dots) is from an eye with only peripheral loss. CNN· Convolutional neural network. (Color figure online)

2 Methods

2.1 Overview

Figure 1 shows an overall flowchart that describes the proposed VAE model in this study. We first introduce the preparation of the input images of the VAE (i.e., mGCIPL thickness map) in Sect. 2.2. Next, details of the VAE concept (Fig. 1A) and architecture (Fig. 1B) are provided in Sect. 2.3. Then, the created latent space (Fig. 1C), the training set case distribution (Fig. 1D) as well as network hyperparameters and the overall training/testing process are discussed in the Experimental Methods (Sect. 3).

2.2 Macular Ganglion Cell - Inner Plexiform Layer Thickness Map

Previous studies suggested that identification of defects using the mGCIPL thickness map may be easier than with use of standard automated perimetry (SAP) or with peripapillary retinal nerve fiber layer (pRNFL) thickness values in glaucomatous eyes [10,11]. In this study, we investigated spatial patterns of mGCIPL thinning in a 2D latent space using a trained VAE model. All the OCT images were macula-centered from Cirrus OCT machines (Carl Zeiss Meditec, Dublin, CA); the OCT image either contained $200 \times 200 \times$ voxels or $512 \times 128 \times 1024$ voxels, but both protocols covered the same physical dimensions of $6 \times 6 \times 2$ mm^3. To align all the mGCIPL thickness maps at the fovea location, each input OCT volume was segmented first using a graph-based automated approach [12]. Then, the corresponding mGCIPL thickness map was computed and cropped at the center of fovea with image dimensions of 162×162 pixels, which covers the area that Zeiss Cirrus software analyzes the mGCIPL in an elliptical annulus with a vertical inner and outer radius of 0.5 and 2.0 mm; and a horizontal inner and outer radius of 0.6 and 2.4 mm, respectively. The annulus was further divided into six sectors, which include superior nasal (SN), superior (S), superior temporal (ST), inferior temporal (IT), inferior (I), and inferior nasal (IN) sectors.

2.3   Variational Autoencoder

A VAE is commonly designed by concatenating two simultaneously trained convolutional neural networks (i.e., a encoder and decoder, shown in Fig. 1A) to provide a probabilistic model so that: 1) the encoder can learn how to effectively (and meaningfully from the decoder's perspective) decompose the input image into succinct digits, named latent variables, 2) the decoder can learn how to correctly (from the encoder's perspective) reconstruct the input image by only analyzing these succinct latent variables, which only contain two digits in this study [9]. In our design, the encoder and decoder have a symmetric structure of five concatenated convolutional layers with various channels followed by rectified linear units (ReLU); details are elaborated in Fig. 1B. To enforce that the latent space is smooth and easy to interpret, the sampling units introduced standard/normalized Gaussian distribution from the output of the encoder to constrain the distribution of the latent variables. In the training process, the loss function ($\mathcal{L}$) was designed to consist of two terms. The first term represents the reconstruction error ($\mathcal{L}_{Rec}$), which penalizes the difference between the input image (x) and the reconstructed image ($\hat{x}$). The second term uses Kullback-Leibler divergence ($\mathcal{L}_{KL}$) to constrain the learned latent variable distribution $q(z|x)$ to be as close as possible to the standard Gaussian distribution, $N(0, I)$. The overall loss function can be summarized as

$$\mathcal{L} = \mathcal{L}_{Rec}(x, \hat{x}) + \beta \times \mathcal{L}_{KL}(q(z|x), N(0, I)) \,, \tag{1}$$

where β is the Kullback-Leibler divergence coefficient.

3   Experimental Methods

This study included strictly separate training and testing datasets randomly sampled from an existing longitudinal clinical glaucoma dataset acquired at the University of Iowa [13]. For the training set of the proposed VAE model, 602 macula-centered OCT scans from 25 randomly selected glaucoma subjects and

899 macular-centered OCT scans from 25 randomly selected normal subjects were included (both eyes from multiple visits). Meanwhile, each eye at each visit had multiple repeated scans. Since two OCT protocols were involved in this dataset (i.e., $200 \times 200 \times 1024$ voxels or $512 \times 128 \times 1024$ voxels), all computed mGCIPL thickness maps were resized to 200×200 pixels before fovea alignment (details in Sect. 2.2) for consistency.

3.1 VAE Model - Training

For a more straightforward visualization and interpretation, two latent variables were used in our VAE model. However, it is worth noting that the same VAE concept can be directly apply to a higher-dimension latent space with very little modification. Meanwhile, other hyper-parameters included an epoch number of 100, batch size of 60 images, learning rate of 0.001, Kullback-Leibler divergence coefficient of 1.5, and Adam optimizer with weight decay of 10^{-5}.

As the results of training, Fig. 1C shows a montage of the reconstructed mGCIPL thickness map (i.e., each image tile) from the decoder that deciphers the latent variables (d1, d2) with a range between −4 to 4 and color bar units from 0 to 225 μm. By this arrangement, the latent space can be "visually" observed. Since the overall average mGCIPL thickness is one of the most common global measurements of glaucoma progression, Fig. 1D displays the latent space that is converted into the overall mGCIPL thickness domain (instead of the spatial pattern domain in Fig. 1C). In addition, Fig. 1D shows all of the training data with labels: the red dots represent glaucoma cases, and the blue dots represent the normal cases, respectively. Two examples, which are highlighted in separate tiles, with glaucomatous defects are also shown in Fig. 1.

3.2 VAE Model - Testing

An independent testing set in this study included another 25 randomly selected glaucoma subjects and five randomly selected normal subjects ($N = 30$) who were tested repeatedly on multiple visits. For the evaluation purpose, we chose the study eye (randomly decided) at the first visit for each subject. After segmentation and image quality control, 77 and 13 macular-centered OCT scans were left in the glaucoma and normal groups, respectively. Next, the mGCIPL thickness maps were computed. Then, the same processes of the image cropping and fovea alignment (Sect. 2.2) were applied. Assume that each subject at their first available visit had J repeated OCT scans of the study eye, each of these fovea-aligned cropped mGCIPL thickness map can be represented as x_{ij}, $i \in N$, $j \in J$.

Each of the testing images x_{ij} was sent to the VAE encoder, the corresponding latent variables $d_{i,j}^1$, $d_{i,j}^2$ were computed, and then the reconstructed image $\hat{x}_{ij}$ was generated by the VAE decoder. To evaluate the reconstruction ability of the VAE model, differences of the thickness at each sector in the mGCIPL grid (that is the same annulus setting as Zeiss software uses) between the original and reconstructed images were computed. To deal with the repeated scans for each eye, we first define the mean difference per eye as $\bar{x}_i = \frac{1}{J} \sum_{j=1}^{J} (x_{ij} - \hat{x_{ij}})$. Then the mean signed difference $(\frac{1}{N} \sum_{i=1}^{N} \bar{x}_i)$ and root-mean-square (RMS) difference $(\sqrt{\frac{1}{N} \sum_{i=1}^{N} \bar{x}_i^2})$ across subjects were computed for each mGCIPL grid sector.

4   Results

The corresponding latent variable pairs (d1 and d2) were computed by the VAE encoder for all the input testing mGCIPL thickness maps from randomly selected 25 glaucoma (77 scans) and five normal (13 scans) subjects (Sect. 3.2). Figure 2 shows the scatter plot of the mean d1 and d2 among the repeated scans of each test subject's study eye (i.e., $\frac{1}{J} \sum_{j=1}^{J} d_{i,j}^1$, $\frac{1}{J} \sum_{j=1}^{J} d_{i,j}^2$), where the red dots represent the 25 glaucoma eyes, and the blue triangles represent the five normal eyes. The background image is the same latent space tile montage as shown in Fig. 1C but with latent variable ranges of $-2 < d1 < 3$ and $-3 < d2 < 2$ for a better visualization. Next, all the 90 pairs of the latent variables were sent to the VAE decoder for reconstruction. Figure 3 demonstrates the ability of the VAE decoder to recreate the input thickness map and the sector thickness measurements in the mGCIPL grid. Furthermore, we computed the mean signed difference and RMS difference across the test eyes. Figure 4(a) shows that the proposed VAE model was slightly biased to overestimate the thinning (i.e., underestimate the thickness) of the retina in all six sectors (overall: 0.54 μm; the inferior sector had the highest bias of 1.66 μm). Figure 4(b) shows the mean RMS difference across all six sectors was 7.14 μm, with the smallest RMS differences in the superior and inferior sectors (approximately 5.5 μm) and the largest RMS differences in the temporal sectors (approximately 8.9 μm). Figure 5 illustrates (a) a scatterplot of the sectoral data points (each sector highlighted in a different color) with the correlation of all data points being 0.86 (p-value < 0.01; the shaded area represents 95% confidence interval for the regression), and (b) the correlation coefficients of 0.86, 0.90, 0.71, 0.81, 0.92, and 0.86 for the superior nasal, superior, superior temporal, inferior temporal, temporal, and inferior nasal sectors, respectively (all p-values < 0.01). The pattern in Fig. 4(b) and Fig. 5(b) are consistent.

5   Discussion and Conclusion

In this study, we investigated the VAE's ability to: 1) disentangle spatial features in the training dataset through the trained encoder and show a smooth 2D latent space for easy visualization by the trained decoder's reconstruction of the mGCIPL spatial pattern based on the two latent variables, 2) reconstruct the input image by evaluating the signed/unsigned differences between the original and reconstructed image by dividing the image into a commonly used mGCIPL sector grid. This is the first attempt to characterize the patterns of glaucomatous structural loss in the macula of individual eyes utilizing a latent space based on a VAE model. Our results showed that the latent space tile montage (Fig. 1C

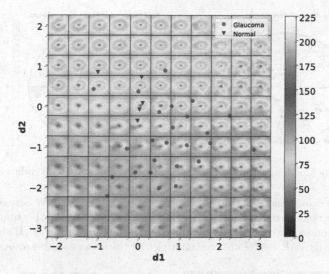

Fig. 2. Mean latent variable scatter plot of the testing dataset; 25 red dots represent glaucoma cases and five blue triangles represent the normal cases. (Color figure online)

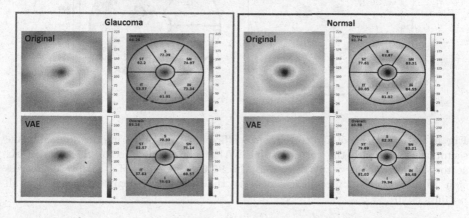

Fig. 3. VAE reconstruction of the thickness pattern from the original mGCIPL thickness map using only two latent variables. Shown are two examples of a glaucoma right eye and a normal right eye. The glaucoma eye shows a typical macular inferior arcuate pattern of loss. The thickness of each sector in micrometers is given along with the overall average thickness (upper left corner). SN: Superior Nasal, S: Superior, ST: Superior Temporal, IT: Inferior Temporal, I: Inferior, IN: Inferior Nasal, Overall: The mean thickness value in micrometers of all six sectors.

and Fig. 2) contains meaningful spatial patterns of glaucomatous defects corresponding to the known superior and inferior arcuate patterns of nerve loss due to nerve bundles being damaged at the optic nerve head. In both our training and testing set, the data with mGCIPL thinning were correctly described by the

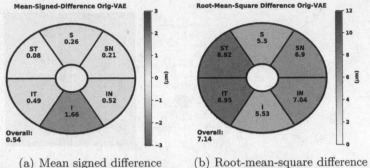

(a) Mean signed difference   (b) Root-mean-square difference

Fig. 4. Mean signed and unsigned (RMS) differences in micrometers between the input (original) and reconstructed images across all test images; Overall (bottom left corner) represents the mean value of all six sectors. In (a), the inferior sector (I) shows an 1.66 μm bias towards VAE model underestimating the thickness at this sector.

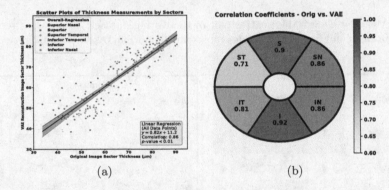

(a)   (b)

Fig. 5. Data scatter plot and correlation coefficients. (a) Comparing the original image sector thickness with the corresponding VAE reconstructed sector thickness at six sectors in micrometers; gray region is the 95% confidence interval for the regression. (b) The correlation coefficient between the two measurements at each sector; all p-values < 0.01.

VAE model, especially for these regional defects. The VAE model demonstrates a promising potential to be used for glaucoma/normal case classification and for monitoring of further glaucomatous progression in the clinic.

There also exist a few limitations in this study. First, in our current training dataset, we had used only 25 glaucoma and 25 normal subjects. Although 1501 OCT scans were used for training, adding more subjects with various levels of defects can further improve the robustness of the neural network and reduce the signed/unsigned differences. Second, the proposed encoder/decoder architecture can be replaced by more sophisticated designs to achieve better performance. Third, for the purpose of easy visualization/interpretation, only two latent variables were utilized in this study. Increasing the dimensionality of latent space can potentially extract more subtle changes in spatial patterns of glaucomatous defects.

Acknowledgments. We acknowledge Michael Wall (M.D.) for sharing the glaucoma OCT data, which were collected as part of the VA-sponsored Merit Grant on Improved Assessment of Visual Field Change (I01RX000140), and Young Kwon, (M.D., Ph.D) for the advice relevant to his expertise as a glaucoma specialist. This study was also supported, in part, by a National Institutes of Health (NIH) grant R01EY031544 and by the Iowa City VA Center for the Prevention and Treatment for Visual Loss, funded by the VA Rehabilitation Research and Development (RR&D) Division (I50RX003002).

References

1. Tham, Y.C., Li, X., Wong, T.Y., Quigley, H.A., Aung, T., Cheng, C.Y.: Global prevalence of glaucoma and projections of glaucoma burden through 2040: a systematic review and meta-analysis. Ophthalmology **121**(11), 2081–2090 (2014)
2. Worley, A., Grimmer-Somers, K.: Risk factors for glaucoma: What do they really mean? Aust. J. Prim. Health **17**(3), 233–239 (2011)
3. Bengtsson, B., Heijl, A.: A visual field index for calculation of glaucoma rate of progression. Am. J. Ophthalmol. **145**(2), 343–353 (2008)
4. Medeiros, F.A., Zangwill, L.M., Girkin, C.A., Liebmann, J.M., Weinreb, R.N.: Combining structural and functional measurements to improve estimates of rates of glaucomatous progression. Am. J. Ophthalmol. **153**(6), 1197–1205 (2012)
5. Bussel, I.I., Wollstein, G., Schuman, J.S.: OCT for glaucoma diagnosis, screening and detection of glaucoma progression. Br. J. Ophthalmol. **98**, 15–19 (2014)
6. Wang, M., et al.: An artificial intelligence approach to detect visual field progression in glaucoma based on spatial pattern analysis. Investig. Ophthalmol. Vis. Sci. **60**(1), 365–375 (2019)
7. Berchuck, S.I., Mukherjee, S., Medeiros, F.A.: Estimating rates of progression and predicting future visual fields in glaucoma using a deep variational autoencoder. Sci. Rep. **9**(1), 1–12 (2019)
8. Saeedi, O., et al.: Development and comparison of machine learning algorithms to determine visual field progression. Trans. Vis. Sci. Technol. **10**(7), 1–9 (2021)
9. Kingma, D.P., Welling, M.: An introduction to variational autoencoders. Found. Trends Mach. Learn. **12**(4), 307–392 (2019)
10. Shin, J.W., Sung, K.R., Park, S.W.: Patterns of progressive ganglion cell-inner plexiform layer thinning in glaucoma detected by OCT. Ophthalmology **125**(10), 1515–1525 (2018)
11. Shin, J.W., Sung, K.R., Song, M.K.: Ganglion cell-inner plexiform layer and retinal nerve fiber layer changes in glaucoma suspects enable prediction of glaucoma development. Am. J. Ophthalmol. **210**, 26–34 (2020)
12. Garvin, M.K., Abràmoff, M.D., Wu, X., Russell, S.R., Burns, T.L., Sonka, M.: Automated 3-D intraretinal layer segmentation of macular spectral-domain optical coherence tomography images. IEEE Trans. Med. Imag. **28**(9), 1436–1447 (2009)
13. Wall, M., Zamba, G.K., Artes, P.H.: The effective dynamic ranges for glaucomatous visual field progression with standard automated perimetry and stimulus sizes III and V. Investig. Ophthalmol. Vis. Sci. **59**(1), 439–445 (2018)

Stacking Ensemble Learning in Deep Domain Adaptation for Ophthalmic Image Classification

Yeganeh Madadi[1,2]([envelope]), Vahid Seydi[3], Jian Sun[2], Edward Chaum[4],
and Siamak Yousefi[2]

[1] University of Tehran, Tehran, Iran
madadi@ut.ac.ir
[2] University of Tennessee Health Science Center, Memphis, USA
[3] Bangor University, Bangor, UK
[4] Vanderbilt Eye Institute, Nashville, USA

Abstract. Domain adaptation is an attractive approach given the availability of a large amount of labeled data with similar properties but different domains. It is effective in image classification tasks where obtaining sufficient label data is challenging. We propose a novel method, named SELDA, for stacking ensemble learning via extending three domain adaptation methods for effectively solving real-world problems. The major assumption is that when base domain adaptation models are combined, we can obtain a more accurate and robust model by exploiting the ability of each of the base models. We extend Maximum Mean Discrepancy (MMD), Low-rank coding, and Correlation Alignment (CORAL) to compute the adaptation loss in three base models. Also, we utilize a two-fully connected layer network as a meta-model to stack the output predictions of these three well-performing domain adaptation models to obtain high accuracy in ophthalmic image classification tasks. The experimental results using Age-Related Eye Disease Study (AREDS) benchmark ophthalmic dataset demonstrate the effectiveness of the proposed model.

Keywords: Stacking ensemble learning · Domain adaptation ·
Ophthalmic image classification

1 Introduction

In real-world applications, it is typically challenging to obtain sufficient number of annotated training samples. To address this problem, domain adaptation (DA) [16] has been successfully developed to adapt the feature representations learned in the source domain with required label information to the target domain with fewer or even no label information.

There are two main categories for deep domain adaptation approaches: Domain-invariant features adaptation, and discriminators adaptation. The first tries to map source and target domains in the common subspace to learn the

© Springer Nature Switzerland AG 2021
H. Fu et al. (Eds.): OMIA 2021, LNCS 12970, pp. 168–178, 2021.
https://doi.org/10.1007/978-3-030-87000-3_18

shared features space approach by adding adaptation layers into deep neural networks [21,22]. The second approach attempts to adversarially recognize features in the variant domains by adding the domain discriminator [11].

Our proposed method is based on domain-invariant features adaptation. This category of methods is obtained through optimizing several measures of domain discrepancy, such as Maximum Mean Discrepancy (MMD) [6,10,22], Low-rank representation [7,15], and Correlation Alignment (CORAL) [3,4,19]. Furthermore, we propose a combination of deep DA methods through the stacking ensemble strategy. Stacking ensemble methods are an outstanding strategy in machine learning (win most Kaggle competitions) [17], and extending them with domain adaptation models makes the technique very useful for solving real-world problems. Ensemble learning methods integrate multiple machine learning models (base learners) that each model is trained to solve the similar problems and then the outcome of base models are combined for achieving better results. As the outcome is the majority voting (in the case of classification), the models could be both more accurate and more robust.

We proposed a novel model, Stacking Ensemble Learning in Domain Adaptation (SELDA), by introducing a deep domain adaptation method to acquire a cross-domain high-level feature representation and to reduce the cross-domain generalization error by the stacking learning method. In particular, we focus on the ophthalmic image classification task in an unsupervised scenario. Our model includes three base DA models and a meta-learner model. The model architecture for each of the three base DA models consists of domain-general and domain-specific representations across domains for unsupervised domain adaptation. For domain-specific parts, we apply a hybrid neural structure to extract multiple representations and extract more information from input images. Furthermore, to compute the adaptation loss and to decrease discrepancy between source and target domain distributions, MMD, Low-rank, and CORAL, are extended in base models. Our stacking DA model is illustrated in Fig. 1.

Our approach can be implemented via the most feed-forward methods and trained by using standard backpropagation. The contributions of this paper are summarized as follows:

- To the best of our knowledge, the proposed method (SELDA) is the first stacking model for deep domain adaptation in the ophthalmic image classification tasks.
- We propose the multi-representation deep domain adaptation networks as base models that are ensembled through a stacking strategy to reach high accuracy.
- The MMD, Low-rank, and CORAL are jointly extended to align the domain discrepancy in deep neural networks.
- Extensive experiments demonstrate that SELDA achieves state-of-the-art performance on Age-Related Eye Disease Study (AREDS) [20] benchmark ophthalmic dataset.

2   Proposed Model

Domain adaptation is effective in situations that efficient labeled data in the target domain does not exist or is scarce. We propose a DA framework to improve the accuracy of classification tasks using an innovative stacking ensemble learning approach on ophthalmic datasets.

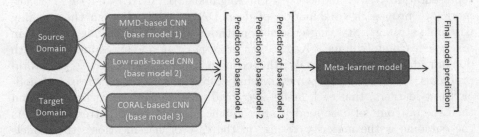

Fig. 1. Overview of the proposed model. Stacking combines multiple predictive models to generate a new combined model.

We are given a source domain $D_s = \{(\mathbf{x}_i^s, \mathbf{y}_i^s) \forall i \in [1 : n_s]\}$ where $(\mathbf{x}_i^s, \mathbf{y}_i^s)$ is tuple of source data and their labels, and n_s is the number of labeled source samples, and a target domain $D_t = \{(\mathbf{x}_j^t) \forall j \in [1 : n_t]\}$ where $\mathbf{x}_j^t$ is the target data, and n_t is the number of unlabeled target samples. The source and target domains have different probability distributions. The purpose is to align these distributions by designing deep DA models.

Almost all DA models apply the single-representation structure, which focuses on the partial information from the data, but multi-representation structures can extract more information on the data. So, we learn multiple domain-invariant representations to obtain better performance where a hybrid structure with multiple substructures is utilized to extract multiple representations from input images.

Furthermore, we apply MMD, Low-rank, and CORAL techniques to reduce the distributions discrepancy between the multiple representations extracted from the source and target domains on three CNN models. We obtain higher accuracy by proposing a stacking ensemble learning approach on them.

We introduce these MMD-based, Low-rank-based, and CORAL-based deep DA models as base learners and learn these models on the training data. For each of the three base learners, predictions are made for observations on the validation data. Then, we propose a meta-learner model and fit it on predictions that are made by the base learners as inputs. Finally, we test the meta-learner model on testing data.

2.1   Base Models

The structures of three base models are similar, but the domain adaptation methods used to train the parameters are different. The architecture of each

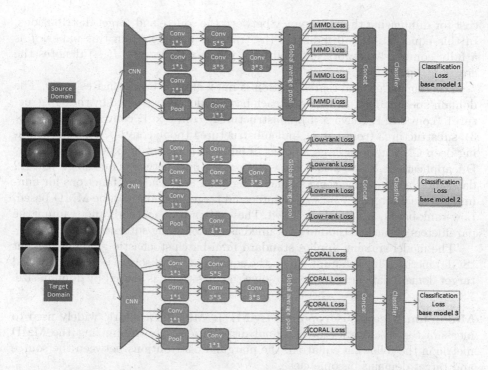

Fig. 2. The architecture of the base models in SELDA approach.

base model consists of three parts. The first part of each base model is the CNN, which is used to convert high-pixel images to low-pixel ones. The second part is the global average pooling for extracting representations from low-pixel images. Finally, the third part is the model prediction. The architecture of base models is illustrated in Fig. 2. We have four types of convolution-pooling layers to extract different representations of the data. In each base model, one of the DA methods is applied to all different representations.

The optimization problem of domain adaptation is weighted sum of two cost functions. The first cost is used to minimize the classification errors on the source set, and the second cost minimizes the discrepancy between the source and target data in each base model. Let $\mathbf{X}^s$ be a matrix containing all training data of the source domain, wherein ith row corresponds to ith datum $\mathbf{x}_i^s$. Similarly, $\mathbf{X}^t$ is a matrix containing all target domain data. Furthermore, assume g to be the general feature extractor, and $\{s_i\}_{i=1}^d$ be d different specific feature extractors. Then, the cost function can be defined as

$$\min_{f,g,\{s_i\}_{i=1}^d} \frac{1}{n_s} \sum_{i=1}^{n_s} J\big(f([s_1(g(\mathbf{x}_i^s)); ...; s_n(g(\mathbf{x}_i^s))]), y_i^s\big) + \lambda \sum_{i=1}^{n} D(s_i(g(\mathbf{X}^s)), s_i(g(\mathbf{X}^t))),$$

(1)

where $[s_1; ...; s_n]$ is the concatenated vector of different features, f is a function from stacked features to scores of different labels, J is the classification cost measuring the distance between label scores and true labels y, and D is the cost for minimizing the discrepancy between the source and target distributions. In this equation, $\lambda > 0$ indicates the trade-off parameter. In this paper, f is a fully connected network followed by a softmax layer, and $J(.,.)$ denotes the cross-entropy loss.

The domain-general representation is implemented based on ResNet50. The domain-special representations for each base model are extracted by the substructure1 (conv1 $\times$ 1, conv5 $\times$ 5), substructure2 (conv1 $\times$ 1, conv3 $\times$ 3, conv3 $\times$ 3), substructure3 (conv1 $\times$ 1), and substructure4 (pool, conv1 $\times$ 1). Since training deep CNN needs a large amount of labeled data that is expensive for many DA applications, so we utilize the CNN pre-training networks on ImageNet2012 data and then fine-tune them similar Long et al. [14]. The loss functions for minimizing the discrepancy between source and target domains can be MMD-based, Low-rank-based, and CORAL-based. These adaptation methods and training the parameters of each method are obtained as the following subsections.

The model training applies standard mini-batch stochastic gradient descent (SGD) method. In each mini-batch, the equal number of source domain data and target domain data are sampled to solve the bias which is caused by domain size.

Maximum Mean Discrepancy (MMD): MMD is a metric widely used to measure the discrepancy of marginal distributions. By minimizing the MMD metric in the following equation, the marginal distributions between the source and target domains become close:

$$D_{MMD}(\bar{\mathbf{X}}^s, \bar{\mathbf{X}}^t) = \left\| \frac{1}{n_s} \sum_{x_i \in \bar{\mathbf{X}}^s} \Phi(\mathbf{X}_i) - \frac{1}{n_t} \sum_{x_j \in \bar{\mathbf{X}}^t} \Phi(\mathbf{X}_j) \right\|_H^2, \qquad (2)$$

where Φ represents the kernel function, and $||.||_H$ is the norm in the Hilbert space.

Minimizing the difference between the conditional distributions of source and target domains is definitive for robust distribution adaptation. So we utilize conditional MMD (CMMD) instead of MMD to decrease domain discrepancy. We apply CMMD to the first base model for measuring the domains discrepancy D in Eq. (1) identical to [22]. Here we calculate the distance among the class conditional distributions $P(x_s|y_s = c)$ and $Q(x_t|y_t = c)$, which is called CMMD. Each class label in the source domain and each pseudo class label in the target domain is represented by $c \in \{1, ..., C\}$. The output of the deep NN, $\hat{y}_i^t = f(\mathbf{X}_i^t)$, could be utilized as the pseudo label for target data. We expect to iteratively improve the quality of pseudo labels of the target domain during the optimization.

$$D_{CMMD}(\bar{\mathbf{X}}^s, \bar{\mathbf{X}}^t) = \frac{1}{C} \sum_{c=1}^{C} \left\| \frac{1}{n_s^{(c)}} \sum_{x_i^{s(c)} \in \bar{\mathbf{X}}^s} \Phi(\mathbf{X}_i^{s(c)}) - \frac{1}{n_t^c} \sum_{x_j^{t(c)} \in \bar{\mathbf{X}}^t} \Phi(\mathbf{X}_j^{t(c)}) \right\|_H^2 \quad (3)$$

Low-Rank Coding: We apply Low-rank coding to the second base model for aligning source and target distributions and decreasing domains discrepancy in

Eq. (1). We can reach this aim by minimizing the Low-rank formulation, which is shown in Eq. (4).

$$D_{Low\_rank}(\bar{\mathbf{X}}^s, \bar{\mathbf{X}}^t) = \parallel \mathbf{Z} \parallel_* + \lambda \parallel \mathbf{E} \parallel_1 \quad s.t. \bar{\mathbf{X}}^t = \bar{\mathbf{X}}^s \mathbf{Z} + \mathbf{E}, \tag{4}$$

where $\parallel.\parallel_*$ is the nuclear norm of a matrix [13]. The reconstruction matrix $\mathbf{Z}$ and noise matrix $\mathbf{E}$ can be optimized by Augmented Lagrange Multiplier (ALM) method [12] through fixing one variable and optimizing the other one until it converges.

Correlation Alignment (CORAL): We apply CORrelation ALignment (CORAL) to the third base model for matching the second-order statistics (covariances) between the data distributions in Eq. (1). We can reach this aim by minimizing the CORAL formulation, which is shown in Eq. (5).

$$D_{CORAL}(\bar{\mathbf{X}}^s, \bar{\mathbf{X}}^t) = \frac{1}{4m^2} \left\| Cov^s - Cov^t \right\|_F^2, \tag{5}$$

where $\parallel.\parallel_F$ is the Frobenius norm. m is the dimensions of data. Cov^s and Cov^t are the covariance matrices for the source and target data, respectively.

2.2   Meta-learner Model

As we mentioned before, the goal of stacking models is to learn various base models and combine them via training a meta-learner model to obtain more accurate output predictions based on the multi predictions returned through these base models. In our classification problem, we choose a MMD based, a Low-rank based, and a Coral based classifiers as base learners, and decide to learn two fully connected layers neural network as a meta-learner model. The meta-learner comprises a fully connected layer of 64 units with ReLU activation and another fully connected layer with softmax activation function as the output layer. The meta-learner model will receive as inputs the outputs of our three base learner models and will learn for returning the final predictions. So we pursue the following steps:

Step 1: Choose three domain adaptation models as the base learners, and fit them to the training data.

Step 2: For each of these three base learners, make predictions for observations to the validation data.

Step 3: Fit the meta-learner model to the validation data by applying predictions that were made through the base learners as meta-learner inputs.

Step 4: Test the meta-learner model by testing data, and obtain the final predictions.

3   Experimental Results

We will evaluate our proposed model with retinal fundus images collected from patients with macular degeneration.

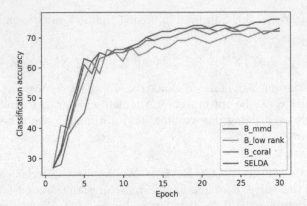

Fig. 3. Classification accuracy of the base models and ensemble approach versus epoch number based on the AREDS dataset.

3.1   Implementation Details

The algorithms were implemented in Python and Pytorch, and all convolutional and pooling layers were fine-tuned based on Pytorch-provided models of ResNet [9]. The optimization approach was mini-batch stochastic gradient descent (SGD) with momentum of 0.9 and learning rate $\eta_p = \frac{\eta_0}{(1+\alpha p)^\beta}$ where p was in range [0–1], $\eta_0 = 0.01$, $\alpha = 10$, and $\beta = 0.75$. The classifiers were trained based on back-propagation with a batch size 32 (minibatch) and the accuracy was obtained at epoch 30.

3.2   Benchmark Dataset

We evaluate our model on AREDS benchmark ophthalmic dataset.

AREDS [5] consists of fundus images from 4757 participants (55–80 years) who represented AMD during follow-up (1992–2005). AREDS dataset contains 14 different classes named, 0: Both-NV-AMD-and-GA, 1: Control, 2: Control-Questionable-1, 3: Control-Questionable-2, 4: Control-Questionable-3, 5: Control-Questionable-4, 6: GA, 7: Large-Drusen, 8: Large-Drusen-Questionable-1, 9: Large-Drusen-Questionable-2, 10: Large-Drusen-Questionable-3, 11: NV-AMD, 12: Other-non-control, 13: Questionable-AMD.

3.3   Results and Discussions

We applied our models on AREDS dataset. This dataset includes highly imbalanced classes with substantially greater number of samples in some classes (e.g., large drusen) and significantly small number of samples in other classes. Therefore, we randomly selected 4900 images with an equal number of samples from each class to train our models. We then split the selected images into two parts as AREDS_ source (80%) and AREDS_ target (20%). However, we tested the

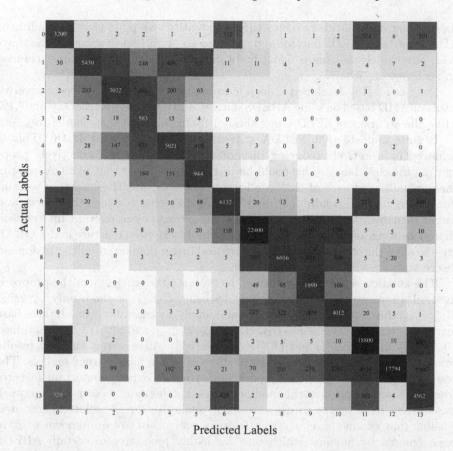

Fig. 4. The confusion matrix of the proposed model on AREDS dataset.

model to rest of data to assure generalizability. As some of the eyes included multiple fundus photographs, we assured samples from each eye and patient go to either training, testing, or validation to avoid bias. The classification accuracy of SELDA was obtained 77.85%. Figure 3 shows the accuracy versus epoch number and Fig. 4 shows the confusion matrix of the SELDA. SELDA achieved the highest accuracy compared to the base models and provided an accuracy of 77.85% for classifying fundus photographs to 14 AMD classes.

Burlina et al. [2] developed several deep learning models to detect four severity levels of AMD based on the AREDS dataset and obtained accuracy ranging from 83.2% to 91.6%. However, this model was able to detect only four severity levels while detecting AMD in finer levels has more clinical relevance. In a follow up study, the same team [1] developed a deep learning-based model to identify the detailed severity characterization of patients with AMD based on the AREDS dataset and obtained an accuracy level of 59.1% in identifying 9 different classes. Grassman et al. [8] developed a framwork based on an ensemble of six different deep learning architectures to identify 9-step (12 classes) grading of ADM based on AREDS dataset and achieved an overall accuracy of 63.3%. However, our model was able to identify 14 different classes of AMD and achieved an accuracy of 77.85%.

Peng et al. [18] developed a deep learning model to detect different severity levels of AMD based on same AREDS dataset and obtained an accuracy of 67.1% while the accuracy of SELDA was about 10% higher than their model too.

Results indicate that SELDA outperforms state-of-the-art [2,18]. This is achieved by iteratively reducing the domain discrepancy and effectively propagating the class labels. This could be justified by the fact that SELDA inherits the capabilities of each of the base learner methods; MMD guarantees to minimize marginal and conditional distributions difference between the source and target domains, the low-rank representation extracts more relevant information shared between domains by constructing the block-wise structure,and CORAL tries to align the covariances of the source and target domains to mitigate domain discrepancy.

The ablation study was performed to evaluate the efficiency of the proposed method. First, we run our model only by using B_{MMD}, second, only by using B_{Low_rank}, third, only by using B_{Coral}, and finally, by ensembling on all three base learners. The accuracies of B_{MMD}, B_{Low_rank}, B_{Coral}, and SELDA were obtained 73.33%, 72.61%, 72.35%, and 77.85%, respectively. As it is seen, the best results were obtained using SELDA, which utilizes all three base learner models. The results show that our proposed model has learned to extract important features from the macular region of the fundus images. Furthermore, because the network has learned the features which were most predictive for the related class, it is feasible that the model is utilizing features previously to be unknown or have been ignored by humans which may be highly predictive of certain AREDS classes, so it can be efficiently trained to detect specific disease-related changes on fundus images.

4   Conclusions

In this paper, we rethink domain adaptation problem and propose stacking ensemble learning by utilizing MMD-based CNN, low rank-based CNN, and CORAL-based CNN base DA learners and a meta-learner to address domain shift challenge in ophthalmology and diagnosis of eye diseases. We utilize a two-fully connected layer network as a meta-learner model to stack the output predictions of these three well-performing DA models to obtain high accuracy in ophthalmic image classification tasks. The proposed model jointly inherits the capabilities of each of the base learner models, efficiently. Extensive experimental results and analyses on AREDS visual benchmark dataset have illustrated the effectiveness of our model.

References

1. Burlina, P.M., Joshi, N., Pacheco, K.D., Freund, D.E., Kong, J., Bressler, N.M.: Use of deep learning for detailed severity characterization and estimation of 5-year risk among patients with age-related macular degeneration. JAMA ophthalmol. **136**(12), 1359–1366 (2018)
2. Burlina, P.M., Joshi, N., Pekala, M., Pacheco, K.D., Freund, D.E., Bressler, N.M.: Automated grading of age-related macular degeneration from color fundus images using deep convolutional neural networks. JAMA Ophthalmol. **135**(11), 1170–1176 (2017)
3. Chen, C., Chen, Z., Jiang, B., Jin, X.: Joint domain alignment and discriminative feature learning for unsupervised deep domain adaptation. In: Proceedings of the AAAI Conference on Artificial Intelligence, vol. 33, pp. 3296–3303 (2019)
4. Cheng, Z., Chen, C., Chen, Z., Fang, K., Jin, X.: Robust and high-order correlation alignment for unsupervised domain adaptation. Neural Comput. Appl. 1–13 (2021)
5. Davis, M.D., et al.: The age-related eye disease study severity scale for age-related macular degeneration: AREDS report no. 17. Arch. Ophthalmol. (Chicago, Ill.: 1960) **123**(11), 1484–1498 (2005)
6. Deng, W., Zheng, L., Sun, Y., Jiao, J.: Rethinking triplet loss for domain adaptation. IEEE Trans. Circuits Syst. Video Technol. **31**, 29–37 (2020)
7. Ding, Z., Fu, Y.: Deep transfer low-rank coding for cross-domain learning. IEEE Trans. Neural Netw. Learn. Syst. **30**(6), 1768–1779 (2018)
8. Grassmann, F., et al.: A deep learning algorithm for prediction of age-related eye disease study severity scale for age-related macular degeneration from color fundus photography. Ophthalmology **125**(9), 1410–1420 (2018)
9. He, K., Zhang, X., Ren, S., Sun, J.: Deep residual learning for image recognition. In: Proceedings of the IEEE Conference on Computer Vision and Pattern Recognition, pp. 770–778 (2016)
10. Kang, G., Jiang, L., Yang, Y., Hauptmann, A.G.: Contrastive adaptation network for unsupervised domain adaptation. In: Proceedings of the IEEE Conference on Computer Vision and Pattern Recognition, pp. 4893–4902 (2019)
11. Li, J., Li, Z., Lü, S.: Feature concatenation for adversarial domain adaptation. Expert Sys. Appl. **169**, 114490 (2021)
12. Lin, Z., Chen, M., Ma, Y.: The augmented lagrange multiplier method for exact recovery of corrupted low-rank matrices. arXiv preprint arXiv:1009.5055 (2010)
13. Liu, G., Lin, Z., Yan, S., Sun, J., Yu, Y., Ma, Y.: Robust recovery of subspace structures by low-rank representation. IEEE Trans. Pattern Anal. Mach. Intell. **35**(1), 171–184 (2012)
14. Long, M., Zhu, H., Wang, J., Jordan, M.I.: Deep transfer learning with joint adaptation networks. In: International Conference on Machine Learning, pp. 2208–2217 (2017)
15. Madadi, Y., Seydi, V., Hosseini, R.: Deep unsupervised domain adaptation for image classification via low rank representation learning. J. Adv. Comput. Res. **11**(1), 57–67 (2020)
16. Madadi, Y., Seydi, V., Nasrollahi, K., Hosseini, R., Moeslund, T.B.: Deep visual unsupervised domain adaptation for classification tasks: a survey. IET Image Process. (2020). https://doi.org/10.1049/iet-ipr.2020.0087
17. Pavlyshenko, B.: Using stacking approaches for machine learning models. In: 2018 IEEE Second International Conference on Data Stream Mining & Processing (DSMP), pp. 255–258. IEEE (2018)

18. Peng, Y., et al.: DeepSeeNet: a deep learning model for automated classification of patient-based age-related macular degeneration severity from color fundus photographs. Ophthalmology **126**(4), 565–575 (2019)
19. Rahman, M.M., Fookes, C., Baktashmotlagh, M., Sridharan, S.: On minimum discrepancy estimation for deep domain adaptation. In: Singh, R., Vatsa, M., Patel, V.M., Ratha, N. (eds.) Domain Adaptation for Visual Understanding, pp. 81–94. Springer, Cham (2020). https://doi.org/10.1007/978-3-030-30671-7_6
20. Study, T.A.R.E.D., et al.: The age-related eye disease study (AREDS): design implications AREDS report no. 1. Controlled Clin. Trials **20**(6), 573–600 (1999)
21. Zhu, Y., Zhuang, F., Wang, D.: Aligning domain-specific distribution and classifier for cross-domain classification from multiple sources. In: Proceedings of the AAAI Conference on Artificial Intelligence, vol. 33, 5989–5996 (2019)
22. Zhu, Y., et al.: Multi-representation adaptation network for cross-domain image classification. Neural Netw. **119**, 214–221 (2019)

Attention Guided Slit Lamp Image Quality Assessment

Mingchao Li[1], Yerui Chen[1], Kun Huang[1], Wen Fang[2], and Qiang Chen[1(✉)]

[1] School of Computer Science and Engineering, Nanjing University of Science and Technology, Nanjing 210094, China
Chen2qiang@njust.edu.cn
[2] Department of Ophthalmology, The First Affiliated Hospital with Nanjing Medical University, Nanjing 210094, China

Abstract. Learning human visual attention into a deep convolutional network contributes to classification performance improvement. In this paper, we propose a novel attention-guided architecture for image quality assessment (IQA) of slit lamp images. Its characteristics are threefold: First, we build a two-branch classification network, where the input of one branch uses masked images to learning regional prior. Second, we use a Forward Grad-CAM (FG-CAM) to represent the attention of each branch and generate the saliency maps. Third, we further design an Attention Decision Module (ADM) to decide which part of the gradient flow of both two branch saliency maps will be updated. The experiments on 23,197 slit lamp images show that the proposed method allows the network closer to human visual attention compared with other state-of-the-art methods. Our method achieves 97.41%, 84.79%, 92.71% on AUC, F1-score and accuracy, respectively. The code is open accessible: https://github.com/nhoddJ/CSRA-module.

Keywords: Slit lamp images · Image quality assessment · Forward Grad-CAM · Attention Decision Module

1 Introduction

Convolutional neural network has been widely used in image fusion, object detection and image classification and has achieved widespread success. In the field of medical image analysis, it also achieves performance close to human experts and beyond [1–4]. Recent research shows that learning human visual attention into a convolutional network can help improve classification effect [5]. This is because the introduction of clinical prior knowledge (e.g., the shape and size of the Lesion area) allows the network to learn more and becomes more robust.

Learning human visual attention into a deep convolutional network contributes to classification performance improvement [6–10]. Huang et al. [8] utilized masks between the internal limiting membrane (ILM) layer and the retinal pigment epithelium (RPE) layer to guide macular disease diagnose. Wang et al. [9] utilized iris region masks to assist image quality assessment (IQA) in the iris region. He et al. [11] proposed a multi scale

© Springer Nature Switzerland AG 2021
H. Fu et al. (Eds.): OMIA 2021, LNCS 12970, pp. 179–188, 2021.
https://doi.org/10.1007/978-3-030-87000-3_19

feature extractor to get deep features of fovea region masks to assist diabetic macular edema (DME) grading. These researches show that the clinical semantic region attention mechanisms often lead performance improvement of the classification task.

In this work, we focus on the task of slit lamp image quality assessment. Slit lamp images are mainly used to observe ocular surface diseases, which is one of the common clinical ophthalmology diseases. The common clinical manifestations include dry eye disease (DED), blepharitis, seasonal allergic conjunctivitis, etc. For DED, its ocular surface irritation and ocular surface damage have a significant impact on the visual acuity between blinks. In severe cases, it can cause ocular surface inflammation, lacrimal glands inflammation and vision loss. The latest epidemiological data survey shows that DED and new cases that occur with environmental changes account for about 20% of the population [11]. As an important tool to judge ocular surface inflammations and elevated intraocular pressure [12], bulbar conjunctiva hyperemia grading needs high-quality image to analyze morphological features of blood vessels. Lesions analysis and feature quantification also need high-quality images. Therefore, it is necessary to evaluate the image quality of the slit lamp images to screen high-quality images.

In this work, we propose a novel attention-guided architecture for image quality assessment of slit lamp images. Our key insight is to let the attention of the classification network focus on the region marked by human experts, so that the network learns human visual attention. To this end, we build a two-branch classification network, where the input of one branch uses masked images to learning regional prior. Second, we use a Forward Grad-CAM (FG-CAM) to represent the attention of each branch and generate the saliency maps. Third, we further design an Attention Decision Module (ADM) to decide which part of the gradient flow of both two branch saliency maps will be updated.

This paper makes contributions as follows:

(1) We propose a novel attention-guided architecture for image quality assessment of slit lamp images. Experimental results show that it achieves visual attention closer to human experts than state-of-the-art baselines.
(2) We design a Forward Grad-CAM and an attention decision module. The FG-CAM is used to represent the network attention and can participate in network training, while ADM is used to update the branch gradients.

2   Dataset

The dataset we use contains 47095 slit lamp images taken from clinical purposes among several hospitals between 18/3/2015 and 05/10/2019. The dataset contains a variety of diseases, e.g., pterygium, trichiasis, pinguecula, hemorrhage, edema and cases of different degrees of conjunctival hyperemia. Further, the dataset also contains a variety of lighting conditions, e.g., Retro-illumination and indirect illumination, while the cases with ocular fluorescein staining are excluded in this analysis.

We select 11831, 2000 and 9367 images as training set, validation set and test set, respectively. Note that, the training set and test set are patient-independent. All the images are resized to 224 × 224. To evaluate the image quality of the bulbar conjunctiva area in these images, 9 trained graduate students annotated three types of labels that illumination ('Good', 'Medium', 'Bad'), blur ('Slight', 'Medium', 'Sever') and image quality ('Accept' or 'Refuse') for the train and validation dataset, while only image quality ('Accept' or 'Refuse') for the test dataset. 2 experienced experts finally determine the category of image quality. To obtain the bulbar conjunctiva mask, the two experts performed pixel-level annotations on 1045 additional slit lamp images. A U-Net [13] model was trained to acquire bulbar conjunctival region masks for the above train, validation and test dataset. The final dataset, called SLIQA, contains slit lamp images, image quality labels, and bulbar conjunctival region masks.

3   Method

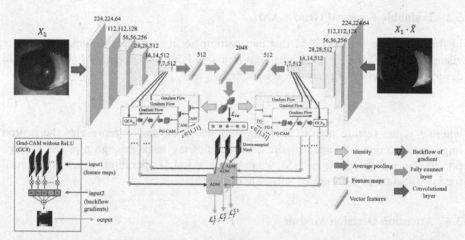

Fig. 1. The proposed attention-guided architecture for slit lamp image quality assessment.

Overview: Our proposed architecture as shown in Fig. 1 contains three parts: (1) Basic two-branch CNN. (2) Trainable Forward Grad-CAM. (3) Attention Decision Module. The two-branch CNN with different inputs is introduced in Sect. 3.1. The trainable Forward Grad-CAM (FG-CAM) used to obtain the saliency maps of two branches is introduced in Sect. 3.2. The Attention Decision Module (ADM) used to update the branch gradients is introduced in Sect. 3.3.

3.1   Multi-task Two-Branch Architecture

We denote the original slit lamp image as X and the bulbar conjunctiva region mask $\tilde{X}$. We firstly build a two-branch CNN, where the backbone we used is VGG [14], and the two branches are concatenated at the first length 512 fully connected layer. The inputs of two branches are X and $X \cdot \tilde{X}$ respectively, where $\cdot$ denotes pixel-wise multiplication. Then after two fully connected layers, the final fully connected layer output is length 11 category score vector relative to 4 classification tasks, including levels of illumination, blur, image quality and bulbar conjunctiva region area level.

The image quality classification is the main task while the others are auxiliary classification tasks. Level of the area L_{Area} is calculated as:

$$L_{Area} = \begin{cases} 0, A\left(\tilde{X}\right) < 0.15 \\ 1, 0.15 \leq A\left(\tilde{X}\right) < 0.3 \\ 2, 0.3 \leq A\left(\tilde{X}\right) \end{cases} \tag{1}$$

where $A(\bullet)$ indicates the area ratio of the bulbar conjunctiva area to the total area. This multi-tasking design is to extract more effective features while accelerating the convergence of the network.

3.2 Trainable Forward Grad-CAM

In this work, we seek a CAM that can participate in network training, not just for visualization. Inspired by [15], we use a trainable Forward Grad-CAM (FG-CAM) to describe the saliency of attention. It is expressed as:

$$A = conv(f, w) \tag{2}$$

where f is the feature map of the convolutional layer, and w represents the neuron importance weights obtained by the gradients flowing back through a global average pooling layer. Different from [15], we remove the ReLU operation, which is designed for visualization in the work of Selvaraju et al. [16].

3.3 Attention Decision Module

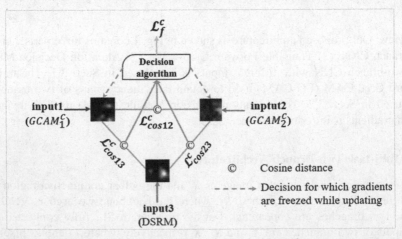

Fig. 2. Our proposed attention decision module. $GCAM_1^c$, $GCAM_2^c$ denote two outputs of FG-CAM modules in Fig. 1. DSRM denotes down-sampled semantic region mask. We compare the cosine distance of these three inputs one to one, and we make final decision which gradients flows will be frozen by Table 1.

We further propose an attention decision module (ADM) as shown in Fig. 2. For ADM with respect to class c, FG-CAM module outputs $GCAM_1^c$, $GCAM_2^c$ are obtained by Eq. (3) from two branch final convolutional layer features of our CNN respectively:

$$GCAM_i^c = \sum_k \frac{\partial y^c}{\partial A^k} A^k \tag{3}$$

where A^k denotes k^{th} feature map at the final convolutional layer, y^c denotes score of class c, $\frac{\partial y^c}{\partial A^k}$ denotes gradient matrix that contains derivative of function y^c with respect to A^k by forward propagation. The DSRM is calculated as:

$$DSRM = DownSample\left(\tilde{X}\right) - f\left(\tilde{X}\right) \tag{4}$$

where $DownSample(\bullet)$ denotes mean pooling module in this paper, and $f\left(\tilde{X}\right)$ is a scalar to adjust pixel value distribution of DSRM. Once three inputs are prepared, and then we calculate their cosine distances $\mathcal{L}_{cos13}^c$, $\mathcal{L}_{cos23}^c$, $\mathcal{L}_{cos12}^c$ with respect to the class c by:

$$\mathcal{L}_{cosij}^c = 1 - \frac{v_i \cdot v_j}{\|v_i\| \|v_j\|} \tag{5}$$

where v_i, v_j denote two vectors to be calculated cosine distance, $\mathcal{L}_{cosij}^c \in [0, 2]$, v_1, v_2, v_3 are flattened by $GCAM_1^c$, $GCAM_2^c$, DSRM respectively. After that we make a final decision of the output $\mathcal{L}_f^c$ by the following algorithm in Table 1:

Table 1. The decision algorithm of ADM with input1, input2, input3 in Fig. 2.

ADM Algorithm
1: Firstly, denote two thresholds $th_1 \in [0,1]$, $th_2 \in [0,1]$
2: If $\mathcal{L}_{cos12}^c > th_2$ and $\max\{\mathcal{L}_{cos13}^c, \mathcal{L}_{cos23}^c\} > th_1$:
$\quad \mathcal{L}_f^c = \mathcal{L}_{cos12}$
$\quad$ if $\mathcal{L}_{cos13}^c > \mathcal{L}_{cos23}^c$:
$\qquad$ freeze gradient flow of $GCAM_2^c$
$\quad$ else:
$\qquad$ freeze gradient flow of $GCAM_1^c$
$\quad$ end if
else:
$\quad \mathcal{L}_f^c = 0$
end if

th_1 is a threshold to describe the tolerability of disimilarity between $GCAM_i^c$ and DSRM. $\mathcal{L}_f^c$ will be set to 0 when $GCAM_i^c$ is similar to DSRM enough. $GCAM_i^c$ is expected to tend to be different from DSRM to some extend, because we believe that the weight distribution of the neural network attention region $GCAM_i^c$ is not necessarily similar to that of semantic region DSRM, and the specific extent is decided by the neural network itself. th_2 is a threshold to describe the tolerability of maximal angle between v_1 and v_2. $\mathcal{L}_f^c$ will be set t 0 when the angle is small enough. $GCAM_1^c$, $GCAM_2^c$ are expected to tend to focus on different regions, because we believe more information tends to mine when attention regions on the final convolutional layer features of two branches are different.

Combining Fig. 1, frozen the gradient flow of $GCAM_i^c$ denotes that in backpropagation the gradient backflow of $GCAM_i^c$ with respect to class c does not be optimized, which means the one that has a bigger difference with respect to down-sampled semantic region mask will learn to the other one but not learn with each other. Note that the last fully-connected layer parameters are shared between $GCAM_1^c$, $GCAM_2^c$, so the gradients of these parameters will not be frozen.

Overall, the total loss of our model is:

$$\mathcal{L}_{total} = \mathcal{L}_{CE} + \beta \cdot \frac{1}{l} \cdot \sum_c^l \mathcal{L}_f^c \tag{6}$$

where l denotes the number of classes, and β is a coefficient to adjust the contribution between cross entropy loss and the ADM loss.

4 Experiments

4.1 Implementation Details

All Experiments in this paper obey the following rules: The Adam optimizer is adopted with the learning rate of 0.0001 firstly. When the average training accuracy of the multi-task classification is above 85%, the learning rate is set to 0.00001. It will be early stopped when the training accuracy of task image quality is above 98%, which is judged to be overfitting. The mini-batch size is set to 8 and all the experiments run on an NVIDIA GTX 1080Ti GPU.

4.2 Parameter Influence

The th_1 and th_2 in Table 1 will affect the tolerability of dissimilarity among Grad-CAM maps and the semantic region mask, and the β in Eq. (6) will affect the balance between cross-entropy loss and ADM loss. As shown in Table 2, we can see different th_1 and th_2 have little effect on AUC, F1, Accuracy, which shows our proposed method has good robustness. When β is set to 0.03, it will have an obvious performance deduction on the metrics. The reason is that our ADM loss accounts too small proportion to guide neural network attention to the goal region.

4.3 Comparison with Other Methods

Our method is compared with other similar methods as shown in Table 3. All the inputs of the compared methods are the original images. The AFN [1] and LACNN [5] are designed for lesion region mask attention, so there are not any improvement on our task compared with baseline [14]. AFN has long train time because extra structure is added on fully connected layer. The GAIN proposed by Li et al. [15] first utilized forward

Table 2. Parameter influence. Each experiment is repeated three times. The basic combination of the parameters is $th_1 = 0.8$, $th_2 = 0.4$, $\beta = 0.1$. We change one of these parameters, and the other two parameters remain unchanged for one experiment.

Parameter	AUC (%)	F1-score (%)	Accuracy (%)
$th_1 = 0.7$	97.30 ± 0.10	84.29 ± 0.39	92.67 ± 0.09
$th_1 = 0.8$	97.42 ± 0.09	84.81 ± 0.55	92.65 ± 0.16
$th_1 = 0.9$	97.32 ± 0.04	84.34 ± 0.55	92.36 ± 0.33
$th_2 = 0.3$	97.37 ± 0.07	84.60 ± 0.61	92.65 ± 0.17
$th_2 = 0.5$	97.29 ± 0.08	84.44 ± 0.79	92.76 ± 0.16
$\beta = 0.03$	97.18 ± 0.09	83.75 ± 0.77	92.20 ± 0.48
$\beta = 0.3$	97.37 ± 0.08	84.41 ± 0.28	92.52 ± 0.06

Grad-CAM to guide CNN's attention, and it has slightly improvement on AUC and F1-score compared with baseline, but its serial repeat feature extractors take big cost of time. The DFS proposed by Wang et al. [9] is designed for semantic region mask attention, and it has a little improvement compared with baseline, but its added segmentation head attention takes long time. Our proposed method has obvious improvement on AUC, F1-score and accuracy, and also takes short training time because our architecture has not any extra structures or serial repeat parts.

Table 3. Comparison with other similar methods, where each experiment is repeated six times. We denote the train time of the baseline as one unit time.

Method	AUC (%)	F1-score (%)	Accuracy (%)	Train time
Baseline [14]	96.99 ± 0.13	83.31 ± 0.41	92.10 ± 0.28	1
AFN [1]	96.97 ± 0.15	83.07 ± 0.48	91.87 ± 0.26	3.115
GAIN [15]	97.07 ± 0.20	83.46 ± 0.77	91.96 ± 0.33	3.067
LACNN [5]	96.99 ± 0.18	83.21 ± 0.52	91.92 ± 0.33	1.308
DFS [9]	97.16 ± 0.13	83.58 ± 0.48	92.00 ± 0.17	3.719
Ours	$\mathbf{97.41 \pm 0.14}$	$\mathbf{84.79 \pm 0.42}$	$\mathbf{92.71 \pm 0.28}$	1.966

The FG-CAM visualization results of each method is shown in Fig. 3. For column A, AFN has a deviation while other methods focus on the overexposure region. For column B, AFN and our proposed method focus on the left underexposure region in column B2 while baseline and LACNN focus on the error region of the cornea in column B1. For column C, all the methods focus on the overexposure region in column C2, but the semantic region masked image has many black holes in the overexposure region which will impede semantic comprehension. Only baseline and our proposed method focus on the whole overexposure region in column C1. For column D, baseline, LACNN and our proposed method focus on the pterygium region in D1, and our proposed method pays more attention to the bulbar conjunctiva region, while baseline and LACNN pay more attention to the angulus oculi medialis region which is out of the bulbar conjunctiva region. Overall, our proposed method not only focuses on the bulbar conjunctiva region, but also notices the specific abnormality regions. Moreover, our method also notices the whole abnormality region on the original image branch, while the semantic region masked image has obvious black holes that have a big influence on semantic comprehension.

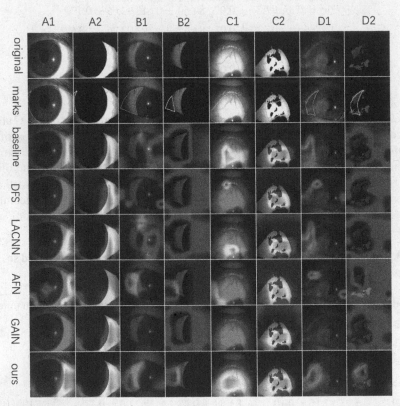

Fig. 3. Grad-CAM visualization results of each method. Column A1, B1, C1, D1 are four examples with different original inputs respectively. A2, B2, C2, D2 are bulbar conjunctiva regions masked image with respect to A1, B1, C1, D1 respectively. The first row contains the original images of four pairs of examples. The second row contains eight marked images, where yellow marks in the odd column show reference bulbar conjunctiva regions while green marks in even column show reference abnormality regions. The third row to the eighth row are the visualization of each method. (Color figure online)

5 Conclusion

We proposed an attention-guided architecture with two-branch CNN for the slit lamp image quality assessment. Experimental results show that it achieves visual attention close to human experts and thus improves classification performance. Compared with the-state-of-art methods, our proposed method has a better performance on AUC, F1-score, Accuracy metrics. Moreover, our method has the potential to migrate to other attention-dependent tasks.

References

1. Lin, Z., et al.: A framework for identifying diabetic retinopathy based on anti-noise detection and attention-based fusion. In: Frangi, A.F., Schnabel, J.A., Davatzikos, C., Alberola-López, C., Fichtinger, G. (eds.) MICCAI 2018. LNCS, vol. 11071, pp. 74–82. Springer, Cham (2018). https://doi.org/10.1007/978-3-030-00934-2_9
2. Yang, Y., Li, T., Li, W., Wu, H., Fan, W., Zhang, W.: Lesion detection and grading of diabetic retinopathy via two-stages deep convolutional neural networks. In: Descoteaux, M., Maier-Hein, L., Franz, A., Jannin, P., Collins, D.L., Duchesne, S. (eds.) MICCAI 2017. LNCS, vol. 10435, pp. 533–540. Springer, Cham (2017). https://doi.org/10.1007/978-3-319-66179-7_61
3. Zhou, Y., et al.: Collaborative learning of semi-supervised segmentation and classification for medical images. In: CVPR, pp. 2074–2083 (2019)
4. Kermany, D.S., et al.: Identifying medical diagnoses and treatable diseases by image-based deep learning. In: Cell, pp. 1122–1131 (2018)
5. Fang, L., Wang, C., Li, S., et al.: Attention to lesion: lesion-aware convolutional neural network for retinal optical coherence tomography image classification. IEEE TMI 38(8), 1959–1970 (2019)
6. Rasti, R., et al.: Macular OCT classification using a multi-scale convolutional neural network ensemble. IEEE TMI 37(4), 1024–1034 (2019)
7. Chen, Q., et al.: Automated drusen segmentation and quantification in SD-OCT images. Med. Image Anal. 17(8), 1058–1072 (2013)
8. Huang, L., et al.: Automatic classification of retinal optical coherence tomography images with layer guided convolutional neural network. IEEE Signal Process. Lett. 26(7), 1026–1030 (2019)
9. Wang, L., Zhang, K., Ren, M., et al.: Recognition oriented iris image quality assessment in the feature space. In: 2020 IEEE International Joint Conference on Biometrics (IJCB), pp. 1–9 (2020)
10. Wang, X., Ju, L., Zhao, X., Ge, Z.: Retinal abnormalities recognition using regional multitask learning. In: Shen, D., et al. (eds.) MICCAI 2019. LNCS, vol. 11764, pp. 30–38. Springer, Cham (2019). https://doi.org/10.1007/978-3-030-32239-7_4
11. He, X., Zhou, Y., Wang, B., Cui, S., Shao, L.: DME-Net: diabetic macular edema grading by auxiliary task learning. In: Shen, D., et al. (eds.) MICCAI 2019. LNCS, vol. 11764, pp. 788–796. Springer, Cham (2019). https://doi.org/10.1007/978-3-030-32239-7_87
12. Masumoto, H., et al.: Severity classification of conjunctival hyperaemia by deep neural network ensembles. J. Ophthalmol. 2019, 1–10 (2019)
13. Ronneberger, O., Fischer, P., Brox, T.: U-Net: convolutional networks for biomedical image segmentation. In: Navab, N., Hornegger, J., Wells, W.M., Frangi, A.F. (eds.) MICCAI 2015. LNCS, vol. 9351, pp. 234–241. Springer, Cham (2015). https://doi.org/10.1007/978-3-319-24574-4_28

14. Simonyan, K., Zisserman, A.: Very Deep Convolutional Networks for Large-Scale Image Recognition. arXiv preprint arXiv:1409.1556 (2014)
15. Li, K., et al.: Tell me where to look: guided attention inference network. In: CVPR, pp. 9215–9223 (2018)
16. Selvaraju, R.R., Cogswell, M., Das, A., et al.: Grad-CAM: visual explanations from deep networks via gradient-based localization. In: ICCV, pp. 618–626 (2017)

Robust Retinal Vessel Segmentation from a Data Augmentation Perspective

Xu Sun, Huihui Fang, Yehui Yang, Dongwei Zhu, Lei Wang, Junwei Liu, and Yanwu Xu[✉]

Intelligent Healthcare Unit, Baidu Inc., Beijing, China
ywxu@ieee.org

Abstract. Retinal vessel segmentation is a fundamental step in screening, diagnosis, and treatment of various cardiovascular and ophthalmic diseases. Robustness is one of the most critical requirements for practical utilization, since the test images may be captured using different fundus cameras, or be affected by various pathological changes. We investigate this problem from a data augmentation perspective, with the merits of no additional training data or inference time. In this paper, we propose two new data augmentation modules, namely, channel-wise random Gamma correction and channel-wise random vessel augmentation. Given a training color fundus image, the former applies random gamma correction on each color channel of the entire image, while the latter intentionally enhances or decreases only the fine-grained blood vessel regions using morphological transformations. With the additional training samples generated by applying these two modules sequentially, a model could learn more invariant and discriminating features against both global and local disturbances. Experimental results on both realworld and synthetic datasets demonstrate that our method can improve the performance and robustness of a classic convolutional neural network architecture. The source code is available at https://github.com/PaddlePaddle/Research/tree/master/CV/robust_vessel_segmentation.

Keywords: Roust retinal vessel segmentation · Gamma correction · Vessel augmentation · Color distortion · Pathological changes

1 Introduction

Retinal vessel segmentation plays a crucial role in computer-aided screening, diagnosis, and treatment of various cardiovascular and ophthalmic diseases such as stroke, diabetics, hypertension and retinopathy of prematurity [9]. A substantial amount of work has been reported in the last two decades for automated detecting blood vessels in retinal fundus images. These algorithms can mainly be categorized into two groups: the unsupervised and supervised methods. The unsupervised methods rely on strong but intuitive priors of the blood vessel

---

X. Sun and H. Fang—Contributed equally to this work.

© Springer Nature Switzerland AG 2021
H. Fu et al. (Eds.): OMIA 2021, LNCS 12970, pp. 189–198, 2021.
https://doi.org/10.1007/978-3-030-87000-3_20

appearance [2,3], while the supervised methods utilize labelled datasets based on given features [4,14]. Among these algorithms, supervised segmentation of blood vessels based on deep learning has reached new performance levels [1,5,18].

Despite architectural advances based on deep learning have led to enormous progress at segmenting vessels in curated datasets, their ability to generalize to new situations is rarely studied. In contrast, the generalization ability, which refers to robustness, is an important factor for algorithms performance. To improve robustness, there exist two issues which need special attention. First, in the real world context of retinal fundus image analysis, the input images may come from different kinds of digital fundus camera systems. Since the tonal quality of a fundus image is affected by the characteristics of these systems [16], models fitting well to datasets collected from a specific class of fundus camera might fail to generalize to those captured from other types of machines. Second, for retinal vessel segmentation models to be adopted in practice, they also need to be robust on pathological changes, especially on those not included during the training stage.

These issues can be alleviated by different strategies. Image pre-processing techniques like contrast limited adaptive histogram equalization try to shrink the difference among samples by redistributing their pixel values, However, they only lead to limited improvement yet require additional inference time. Domain adaptation, on the other hand, learns to adapt models between domains. But more data from the target domain are needed to retrain the models when encountering a new circumstance. In contrast, data augmentation methods, which includes input transforms that the model should be invariant against, show great merits of without requiring any extra training data or inference time. Motivated by that, in this paper we investigate the robust retinal vessel segmentation problem from a data augmentation perspective.

Our method consists of two novel data augmentation modules, *i.e.*, channel-wise random gamma correction and channel-wise random vessel augmentation, for training robust retinal vessel segmentation models. The former aims at varying the tonal quality of the whole image, while the latter only focuses on augmenting the visual appearance of retinal vessels. By doing so, the models are able to learn more representative features regardless of both global and local variations. The experimental results on three real world datasets suggest that the proposed method significantly increases the robustness on samples that are captured by different camera systems and/or affected by diverse pathological changes. Furthermore, we also conduct a thorough set of synthetic datasets to demonstrate that our augmentation scheme achieves reduced sensitivity to the variations of image brightness, contrast and saturation.

2 Methodology

In this section, we present a novel scheme to improve the robustness of retinal vessel segmentation, which comprises two data augmentation modules that increase the global and local invariance, respectively. Figure 1 illustrates the process of virtual sample generation through the proposed data augmentation method.

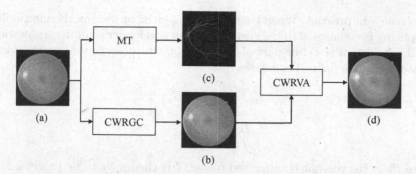

Fig. 1. Illustration of the proposed data augmentation scheme. (a) Original image from the DRIVE [15] training set. (b) Sample image augmented via channel-wise random gamma correction (CWRGC). (c) A rough vessel map generated by morphological transformation (MT). (d) Sample image augmented via channel-wise random vessel augmentation (CWRVA).

2.1   Channel-Wise Random Gamma Correction (CWRGC)

Gamma correction is a nonlinear operation used to encode and decode luminance or tristimulus values, and has been widely used as a image preprocessing step in automated vessel segmentation systems. Unlike current approaches which employ gamma correction in the HSV (Hue, Saturation, value) color space [11,19], we suggest to apply it directly in the RGB (Red, Green, Blue) color space. And, different from the preprocessing method to make the spatial distribution of training test samples more consistent, we use the data augmentation method to increase the diversity of sample distribution, so that the model learning can overcome the interference of task-independent features and learn more effective features. In particular, a simple yet effective data augmentation technique, termed channel-wise random gamma correction, is developed. This method is formulated as

$$\widehat{V}_i = V_i^{\gamma_i} \tag{1}$$

where $\widehat{V}_i$ and $V_i^{\gamma_i}$ represent the intensity of the image before and after transformation, respectively. $\gamma_i > 0$ is the correction value, and subscript $i \in \{R, G, B\}$ denotes the corresponding red, green, or blue channel. By varying γ_i randomly, virtual examples covering a wide range of tonal quality can be created at the training stage. Figure 1(b) shows one of the generated images.

2.2   Channel-Wise Random Vessel Augmentation (CWRVA)

Different from the first method that transforms the whole fundus images, our second method only focuses on blood vessel regions. This can be achieved by taking advantages of existing unsupervised methods, as they are able to provide the rough vessel maps without requiring annotations. To be specific, morphological transformation [10] is used here due to its simplicity of implementation and effectiveness in practice. When the structuring element used in the morphological opening is orthogonal to the vessel direction and longer than the vessel width, it will eradicate a vessel or part of it. Based on this observation, morphological transformation is defined as follows

$$I_{\text{th}}^{\theta} = I - (I \circ S_e^{\theta}), \tag{2}$$

$$I_{S_{\text{th}}} = \sum_{\theta \in A} I_{\text{th}}^{\theta} \tag{3}$$

where I_{th}^{θ} is the top-hat transformed image, I is the image to be processed, $\circ$ is the opening operation, S_e ia the structuring element, and $\theta \in A$ is the angular rotation equally distributed in $[0, \pi)$.

Given the top-hat transformed image, the blood vessel attention map for each color channel of the fundus image can then be obtained by

$$M_i = \mathbb{N}(I_{S_{\text{th}}}) \cdot \lambda_i \tag{4}$$

where $\mathbb{N}(\mathbf{x})$ is a normalization function which scales and shifts the input array $\mathbf{x}$ so that the minimum and maximum value of $\mathbf{x}$ are 0 and 1, respectively, and $\lambda_i \in [0, 1]$ is a random decay coefficient with $i \in \{R, G, B\}$.

The proposed channel-wise random vessel augmentation is formulated as

$$\widetilde{V}_i = V_i \cdot (1 - M_i) + M_i \cdot 255 \tag{5}$$

where $\widetilde{V}_i$ and V_i denote the intensity values of the image before and after vessel augmentation, respectively. Virtual images with various visual effect can be generated through changing λ_i in Eq. (4). A typical example is shown in Fig. 1(c).

3   Experiments

To evaluate the effectiveness of our method, a thorough set of ablation study experiments are conducted. The first experiment is performed on three real world datasets to show how our method impacts robustness on testing images collected by a different fundus camera and/or affected by different pathological changes. Furthermore, we also utilize synthetic datasets to investigate the sensitivity of different models to the variations of image brightness, contrast and saturation.

3.1   Experiments Setup

We adopt the U-Net architecture [13] in our experiments due to its popularity in medical image analysis community and formation of the basis for most of the recent architectural advances at segmenting retinal vessels [6,17]. In particular, we replace its feature encoder module with the pretrained ResNet-50, remaining the first five feature extraction blocks without the global averaging pooling layer and the fully connected layers.

We employ random horizontal flip and random vertical flip with a probability of 50% as the basic data augmentation strategy (BS). In addition, two commonly used randomized data augmentation methods in literature are also implemented for comparison:

- RGN: Disturb the intensity of the red, green and blue channels by adding Gaussian noise with mean of 0 and standard deviation of 20.
- SVGC: Gamma correction of Saturation and Value (of the HSV color space) by raising pixels to a power in [0.25, 4].

In our experiments, γ_i in Eq. (1) for the channel-wise random gamma correction (CWRGC) is randomly selected from [0.33, 3], and λ_i in Eq. (4) for the channel-wise random vessel augmentation (CWRVA) is randomly picked in [0, 1]. All the models are trained on the DRIVE [15] training set using a publicly available library[1]. We use the "step-scaling" method provided in the library to resize the input images to 640 × 640, setting the scaling factor range from 0.75 to 1.25 with a step of 0.25. We use adam as the optimizer. The learning rate is initially set to be 0.005 and then decays following the "poly" policy with a power of 0.9. Instead of training all parameters from scratch, we fine-tune the network end-to-end from an ImageNet pre-trained model. We integrate both dice loss and binary cross entropy loss to train all models for 3000 epoches.

Following previous work, the retinal vessel segmentation results are evaluated quantitatively by the area under the receiver operation characteristic curve (AUC), accuracy (ACC), specificity (SP), sensitivity (SE), and F1-score (F1). However, we mainly focus on AUC and F1 when comparing the performance of different methods as they are more reliable for evaluating binary classifiers (say, to classify if a pixel belongs to vessels or not) [8]. In particular, when we conclude that one method outperforms another, we mean that it achieves both the higher AUC and F1 if without stating which metrics are used.

3.2   Generalization Across Different Datasets

To validate how our augmentations impact robustness in a realistic setting, models trained on the DRIVE training set are applied to three datasets:

- **Testing set of DRIVE** [15]: the fundus images are captured from the same digital fundus camera system.
- **Full set of STARE** [7]: the provided images come by a different type of fundus camera, and contain more kinds of pathological changes
- **Full set of CHASE-DB1** [12]: the images are captured by another type of fundus machine which has a smaller field of view.

From the evaluation results shown in Table 1, we can observe that: 1) BS+CWR-GC+CWRVA achieves the best results in all datasets; 2) BS+CWRGC and BS+CWRVA outperform BS, BS+RGN and BS+SVGC in all datasets. 3) BS

---

[1] https://github.com/PaddlePaddle/PaddleSeg.

Table 1. Performance comparison on three Datasets.

	Method	AUC	ACC	SP	SE	F1
DRIVE	BS	0.9755	0.9531	0.9750	0.8055	0.8126
	BS + RGN	0.9769	0.9531	0.9746	0.8088	0.8131
	BS + SVGC	0.9772	0.9540	**0.9752**	0.8108	0.8167
	BS + CWRGC	0.9777	0.9539	0.9744	0.8150	0.8174
	BS + CWRVA	0.9783	**0.9545**	0.9741	0.8225	0.8205
	BS + CWRGC + CWRVA	**0.9788**	**0.9545**	0.9741	**0.8227**	**0.8209**
STARE	BS	0.9287	0.9334	0.9512	0.7103	0.6699
	BS + RGN	0.9147	0.9556	0.9812	0.6157	0.6273
	BS + SVGC	0.9288	0.9602	**0.9837**	0.6500	0.6769
	BS + CWRGC	0.9892	0.9676	0.9738	0.8902	0.8056
	BS + CWRVA	0.9771	0.9665	0.9816	0.7711	0.7652
	BS + CWRGC + CWRVA	**0.9893**	**0.9683**	0.9745	**0.8908**	**0.8082**
CHASE-DB1	BS	0.8794	0.9344	0.9825	0.2989	0.3768
	BS + RGN	0.9165	0.9394	0.9715	0.5159	0.5279
	BS + SVGC	0.9258	0.9465	**0.9893**	0.3848	0.4841
	BS + CWRGC	0.9812	**0.9623**	0.9702	0.8565	0.7563
	BS + CWRVA	0.9555	0.9522	0.9772	0.6230	0.6385
	BS + CWRGC + CWRVA	**0.9838**	0.9612	0.9673	**0.8818**	**0.7565**

performs worst on DRIVE, DRIVE-GRAY and CHASE-DB1, but outperforms BS+RGN in STARE; 4) the performance of BS+RGN and BS+SVGC degenerates significantly on STARE and CHASE-DB1; 5) although CWRVA works slightly better than CWRGC in the DRIVE testing set, such superiority fails to generalize to other datasets; 6) SVGC achieves the highest SP in all testing set, at the expense of getting a much lower SE when comparing to BS+CWRGC, BS+CWRVA, and BS+CWRGC+CWRVA; 7) CWRGC outperform SVGC in all datasets in terms of AUC and F1. This experiment shows that in RGB space is indeed significantly better than in HSV space due that directly applied to RGB space can be targeted to optimize the hue change problem. Figure 2 shows some visual examples of the segmentation results. The results on real world datasets suggest that the proposed method possess the significant generalization improvement to samples captured by different camera systems and/or affected by diverse pathological changes. This is due to the different camera systems resulting in the various image hues, while gamma correction is good at generating augmentation images with multiple different hues to improve the robustness of the model. In addition, pathological changes are mainly reflected in the local changes of fundus image texture and vascular region, and random vessel augmentation could increase the variation diversity of vascular region, thus improving the robustness of the model in the region with pathological changes.

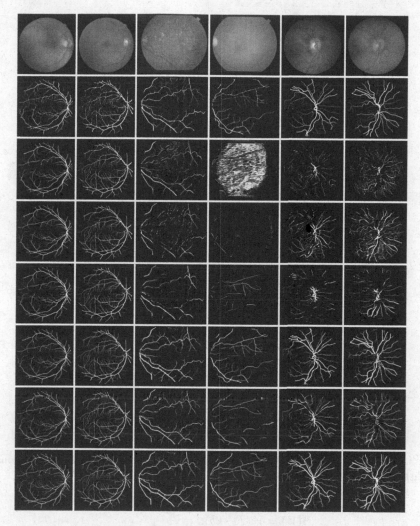

Fig. 2. Sample results on three different datasets. From up to bottom: input image, ground truth and predictive results of BS, BS+RGN, BS+SVGC, BS+CWRGC, BS+CWRVA, and BS+CWRGC+CWRVA. From left to right: sample images from DRIVE, DRIVE, STARE, STARE, CHASE-DB1, CHASE-DB1.

3.3   Robustness to Brightness, Contrast and Saturation

In order to investigate a model's robustness on the more complex situation, the virtual dataset are employed. Thus, three image processing functions are respectively introduced to adjust the brightness, contrast and saturation of a color fundus image. Let V be the input image in RGB space, $\mathbb{G}(V)$ be the function to convert the input image from RGB space to gray space, and $\mathbb{M}(V)$ be the mean function, the brightness jitter, contrast jitter and saturation jitter can then be defined, respectively, as

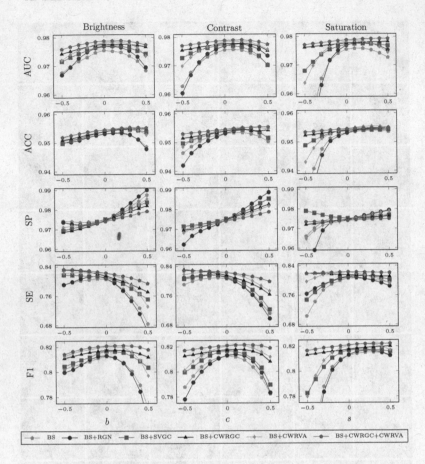

Fig. 3. Evaluation results to illustrate robustness of different methods to variations of brightness, contrast and saturation

$$\mathbb{B}(V) = V \cdot (1 - b), \tag{6}$$
$$\mathbb{C}(V) = V \cdot (1 - c) + \mathbb{M}(\mathbb{G}(V)) \cdot c, \tag{7}$$
$$\mathbb{S}(V) = V \cdot (1 - s) + \mathbb{G}(V) \cdot s \tag{8}$$

where $b \in [-1, 1]$ is brightness jitter ratio, $c \in [-1, 1]$ is the contrast jitter ratio, and $s \in [-1, 1]$ is saturation jitter ratio. The output values of these functions are all limited to $[0, 255]$.

By respectively varying b, c and s from −0.5 to 0.5 with a step of 0.1, we construct 30 more datasets with different degree of brightness, contrast and saturation based on the testing set of DRIVE. The evaluation results of different data augmentation strategies on these datasets are shown in Fig. 3. It can be obviously seen that : 1) models trained with the proposed methods are less sensitive to the variations of image brightness, contrast and saturation than BS and BS+RGN in terms of all the five evaluation metrics; 2) BS+CWRGC+CWRVA method consistently achieves the best results for all sorts of settings. These results indicates the proposed algorithms lead to reduced sensitivity to these naturally occurring variations.

4 Conclusion

This paper investigates the practicability and robustness of retinal vessel segmentation from a data augmentation perspective, with the advantages of not requiring extra training data or inference time. Our method comprises two new data augmentation modules to increase the performance and robustness of models learned. The channel-wise random gamma correction module aims at covering a wide range of tonal quality of the global image, while the channel-wise random vessel augmentation module focuses on diversifying the local visual appearance of the retinal vessels only. The proposed methods achieve excellent results on both real-world and virtual datasets. Experimental results on various real-world public datasets show that the proposed method could consistently stabalize the segmentation performance on samples captured by different cameras or affected by various pathological changes. Moreover, by conducting synthetic databases, we also observe that the proposed method is less sensitive to the variations of image brightness, contrast, and saturation. In the future, we plan to explore more general techniques for robust automated image analyzing systems.

References

1. Araújo, R.J., Cardoso, J.S., Oliveira, H.P.: A deep learning design for improving topology coherence in blood vessel segmentation. In: Shen, D., et al. (eds.) MICCAI 2019. LNCS, vol. 11764, pp. 93–101. Springer, Cham (2019). https://doi.org/10.1007/978-3-030-32239-7_11
2. Bankhead, P., Scholfield, C.N., McGeown, J.G., Curtis, T.M.: Fast retinal vessel detection and measurement using wavelets and edge location refinement. PLoS ONE **7**(3) (2012)
3. Fan, Z., et al.: A hierarchical image matting model for blood vessel segmentation in fundus images. IEEE Trans. Image Process. **28**(5), 2367–2377 (2018)
4. Fraz, M.M., et al.: An ensemble classification-based approach applied to retinal blood vessel segmentation. IEEE Trans. Biomed. Eng. **59**(9), 2538–2548 (2012)
5. Fu, H., Xu, Y., Lin, S., Koo Wong, D.W., Liu, J.: DeepVessel: retinal vessel segmentation via deep learning and conditional random field. In: Ourselin, S., Joskowicz, L., Sabuncu, M.R., Unal, G., Wells, W. (eds.) MICCAI 2016. LNCS, vol. 9901, pp. 132–139. Springer, Cham (2016). https://doi.org/10.1007/978-3-319-46723-8_16
6. Gu, Z., et al.: Ce-net: context encoder network for 2d medical image segmentation. IEEE Trans. Med. Imaging **38**(10), 2281–2292 (2019)
7. Hoover, A., Kouznetsova, V., Goldbaum, M.: Locating blood vessels in retinal images by piecewise threshold probing of a matched filter response. IEEE Trans. Med. Imaging **19**(3), 203–210 (2000)
8. Japkowicz, N., Shah, M.: Evaluating Learning Algorithms: A Classification Perspective. Cambridge University Press, Cambridge (2011)

 9. Kanski, J.J., Bowling, B.: Clinical Ophthalmology: A Systematic Approach. Elsevier Health Sciences, Philadelphia (2011)
10. Leandro, J.J., Cesar, J., Jelinek, H.F.: Blood vessels segmentation in retina: preliminary assessment of the mathematical morphology and of the wavelet transform techniques. In: Proceedings XIV Brazilian Symposium on Computer Graphics and Image Processing, pp. 84–90. IEEE (2001)
11. Liskowski, P., Krawiec, K.: Segmenting retinal blood vessels with deep neural networks. IEEE Trans. Med. Imaging **35**(11), 2369–2380 (2016)
12. Owen, C.G., et al.: Measuring retinal vessel tortuosity in 10-year-old children: validation of the computer-assisted image analysis of the retina (caiar) program. Investig. Ophthalmol. Vis. Sci. **50**(5), 2004–2010 (2009)
13. Ronneberger, O., Fischer, P., Brox, T.: U-Net: convolutional networks for biomedical image segmentation. In: Navab, N., Hornegger, J., Wells, W.M., Frangi, A.F. (eds.) MICCAI 2015. LNCS, vol. 9351, pp. 234–241. Springer, Cham (2015). https://doi.org/10.1007/978-3-319-24574-4_28
14. Soares, J.V., Leandro, J.J., Cesar, R.M., Jelinek, H.F., Cree, M.J.: Retinal vessel segmentation using the 2-D gabor wavelet and supervised classification. IEEE Trans. Med. Imaging **25**(9), 1214–1222 (2006)
15. Staal, J., Abràmoff, M.D., Niemeijer, M., Viergever, M.A., Van Ginneken, B.: Ridge-based vessel segmentation in color images of the retina. IEEE Trans. Med. imaging **23**(4), 501–509 (2004)
16. Tyler, M.E., Hubbard, L., Boydston, K., Pugliese, A.: Characteristics of digital fundus camera systems affecting tonal resolution in color retinal images. J. Ophthal. Photo. **31**(1), 1–9 (2009)
17. Wang, B., Qiu, S., He, H.: Dual encoding U-Net for retinal vessel segmentation. In: Shen, D., et al. (eds.) MICCAI 2019. LNCS, vol. 11764, pp. 84–92. Springer, Cham (2019). https://doi.org/10.1007/978-3-030-32239-7_10
18. Zhang, S., et al.: Attention network guided for retinal image segmentation. In: Shen, D., et al. (eds.) MICCAI 2019. LNCS, vol. 11764, pp. 797–805. Springer, Cham (2019). https://doi.org/10.1007/978-3-030-32239-7_88
19. Zhou, M., Jin, K., Wang, S., Ye, J., Qian, D.: Color retinal image enhancement based on luminosity and contrast adjustment. IEEE Trans. Biomed. Eng. **65**(3), 521–527 (2017)

Correction to: Impact of Data Augmentation on Retinal OCT Image Segmentation for Diabetic Macular Edema Analysis

Daniel Bar-David, Laura Bar-David, Shiri Soudry, and Anath Fischer

Correction to:
Chapter "Impact of Data Augmentation on Retinal OCT Image Segmentation for Diabetic Macular Edema Analysis"
in: H. Fu et al. (Eds.): *Ophthalmic Medical Image Analysis*, LNCS 12970, https://doi.org/10.1007/978-3-030-87000-3_16

The original version of this chapter was revised. The last name of an author was incorrect. The author's last name has been corrected to "Soudry".

The updated version of this chapter can be found at
https://doi.org/10.1007/978-3-030-87000-3_16

© Springer Nature Switzerland AG 2021
H. Fu et al. (Eds.): OMIA 2021, LNCS 12970, p. C1, 2021.
https://doi.org/10.1007/978-3-030-87000-3_21

Author Index